A LEADER BORN

A LEADER BORN

*The Life of
Admiral John Sidney McCain,
Pacific Carrier Commander*

ALTON KEITH GILBERT

CASEMATE
Philadelphia

Published by
CASEMATE

© 2006 Alton Keith Gilbert

All rights reserved.
For further information please contact
Casemate Publishers, 1016 Warrior Road, Drexel Hill, PA 19026.

ISBN 1-932033-50-5

Cataloging-in-publication data is available from the
Library of Congress.

10 9 8 7 6 5 4 3 2 1

CONTENTS

Maps

FOREWORD

By Senator John S. McCain, III

I was not quite nine years old when my grandfather died. My memories of him are few but vivid. He rolled his cigarettes with one hand. He knew the skill fascinated me and he would always make a show of performing it when he visited. When he used the last of his tobacco, he would make a present to me of the empty bag of Bull Durham, which I dutifully treasured.

During the war years, I became aware that my grandfather had become an important person, famous enough to grace the cover of magazines, making his company all the more appreciated. But his visits then were few and far between, which, my mother explained to me, was the normal course of things for the McCains in wartime. War, after all, had been my family's business for many generations, and its demands took precedence over the comforts of family life.

The memories I have of him from that time are of quick visits, often late in the evening, that he made as he traveled either back from or back to the Pacific Theater. My mother would rouse us from our beds and hurry us downstairs for a few stolen moments and a quick snapshot with our busy grandfather. He would greet us as effusively as ever, tease our grogginess away with his high spirits, joke and kid with us for a few minutes, tell us not to be any trouble to our mother, and then, as he gave us a few quick pats on the head, he would make for the door and the waiting car outside that would carry him back to a world at war. After I returned to bed, unable to sleep, I would imagine our next meeting when I might be able to coax a few war stories out of the old man.

He was slightly built, short and rail-thin, with a surprisingly deep voice that ran up an octave when he was laughing, as he often was. He smoked constantly, cussed a blue streak, drank bourbon and branch water and gambled whenever he could. He wore a crushed cap, which the wife of one of his aviators had given him, and which he was quite superstitious about. He was as irregular in his appearance as it was possible to be in the United States Navy. When my grandmother tried to share with him an article about a new treatment for ulcers (which he suffered from), he slapped the magazine he was reading against his leg and shouted "Not one dime of my money for doctors. I'm spending it all on riotous living!" He was unself-conscious, fun-loving, completely devoted to his service, and brave. He was, despite his long absences, the central figure of my family's life. My grandmother protected him. My mother adored him. He was my father's ideal, and, after my father, he was mine as well.

His first duty was aboard a gunship, commanded by Ensign Chester Nimitz, cruising the Philippine Islands in the early years of the 20th century. He served aboard the flagship of Teddy Roosevelt's Great White Fleet. He was fifty-two years old when he earned his naval aviator's wings. He commanded all land-based aircraft in the South Pacific during the Solomon Islands campaign. He spent a couple of years in Washington as the Chief of Naval Aviation. And then, for the last year of the war, commanded Bull Halsey's fast carrier task force, his last command and the one he most distinguished himself in.

When I think of him as a wartime commander, I conjure up an image of him, shared with me by someone who served with him, as if I had seen him there myself. Leaning on the railing of his flagship, *Shangri-La*, cigarette hanging from the corner of his mouth, watching unperturbed as a kamikaze prepared to dive toward him, and calmly counseling a comrade not to worry: "Those five-inchers will get him."

He stood in the front row of officers aboard the U.S.S. *Missouri* as the Second World War ended. Later that day, he spent a few minutes alone with my father aboard a submarine tender in Tokyo Bay. Then he flew home to Coronado, where my grandmother had arranged a party to welcome him home. He fell ill and died that night. He was sixty-one years old, though he looked much older, worn down to an early death by the terrible strains of the war, and the riotous living he had so enjoyed. According to Admiral Halsey's Chief of Staff, Admiral Bob Carney, he had suffered an earlier heart attack at sea and managed to keep it hidden. "He knew his number was up," Carney observed, "but he wouldn't lie down and die until he got home."

My father could not get home in time for the funeral and burial in Arlington National Cemetery. Just as well, he told my mother, because "it would have killed me." I don't think my father ever knew a single day, through the many trials and accomplishments of his own life, when he didn't mourn the loss of his father. Their love for one another was complete. While the demands of their shared profession often kept them apart, their deep respect for each other, and for their shared sense of honor, made the bond between them as strong as any I have ever observed. My father would become the first son of a four star admiral to reach the same rank. He credited the accomplishment to his father's example.

My father spoke of him to me often, as an example of what kind of man I should aspire to be. But much of what I know of my grandfather's experiences as a senior commander in the war I learned from officers who led the Cold War Navy but came of age in World War II, who recorded their oral histories for a Naval Institute project. Many of them had served under or knew and admired my grandfather, and mentioned him respectfully. Histories of the naval war in the Pacific usually include a few lines or paragraphs about him. But no one has ever authored a full scale biography of this colorful, courageous and dedicated war fighter until now.

Keith Gilbert's *A Leader Born* provides a detailed and compelling look at a fascinating character and his remarkable career. By so doing, he has, of course, the gratitude of his subject's family. But much more importantly he has offered an honest portrait of a man whose contributions to our country have not always been accorded the attention they deserve, with revealing insights into the character of the man whose honorable, eventful and richly enjoyed life will, I am confident, prove as inspiring to the reader as it has inspired those of us who were very fortunate to have known him while he lived.

JOHN MCCAIN

PREFACE

The seed for this effort was planted when the Naval ROTC "Hollo-way" program offered this San Francisco schoolboy a chance for a college education at the University of Mississippi. On October 7, 1947, I and the other midshipmen who would eventually become the graduating class of 1951 were in formation to witness the dedication of McCain Hall by Mrs. John S. McCain, honoring her late husband. Fleet Admiral William F. Halsey, Jr., gave the principal speech.

A large part of the 88-year-old observatory building had been turned over to the Navy as McCain Hall, which became the site for naval science classes, mustering for drill, a few parties, and commis-sioning ceremonies. Noteworthy were the Navy sedan and station wagon conveniently left unlocked by the chief petty officers so that penniless midshipmen could entertain their dates.

The observatory building was restored to near-original state in 1990—92 and renamed Barnard Observatory in honor of Frederick Barnard, the first person to hold the title of University Chancellor. During alumni reunions several of the "Navy Boys" (the Navy ROTC alumni) became curious about the fate of the original 1947 dedication plaque. This eventually led to a campaign for a new McCain Hall on the campus. This campaign bore partial fruit in April 2003, when the McCain Quarterdeck was dedicated as the ceremonial entrance to the new Naval ROTC spaces at Ole Miss.

Curiosity about Admiral McCain prompted me undertake a bit of research into his life and times. An obvious starting point was the book *Faith of My Fathers* by Senator John McCain and Mark Salter.

The first chapters are about the Senator's grandfather, "Slew" McCain. Also, Elizabeth Spencer had written lovingly of her Uncle Sidney in her memoir *Landscapes of the Heart*.

The trail soon led to 625 A Avenue in Coronado, California. It was there that Admiral McCain died on September 6, 1945. Residing in the home today is Margaret La Grange, the admiral's granddaughter, along with a treasure trove of swords, insignia, awards, medals, photographs, and personal papers. The opportunity was too good to pass up.

The first step was to inventory the material in Coronado. In 1982 many of Admiral McCain's files from World War II were sent to the archives of the Hoover Institution at Stanford University. Most of the Hoover material covers the war years, although a sizable batch of letters covered the period from 1934 through 1941. This filled some important vacancies in the Coronado files.

Two scrapbooks from the Coronado collection were golden, full of personal data. One provided the few surviving handwritten letters. The other, once loaned to Samuel Eliot Morison for use in preparing his fifteen-volume history of the Navy in World War II, contained newspaper details about 1944 and 1945.

But all in all, when compared to many other biographical studies, not a lot of original material has been unearthed about John McCain. The correspondence, orders, and fitness reports are wonderful sources; but, as his granddaughter commented, he seems to have been a spare man. He just didn't have personal diaries or a lot of other memorabilia. It's fascinating to think what a wonderful treasure would have been left to us if John McCain had survived long enough to pass down his memories or produce an oral history. If sufficient time had passed since the events of the war, I don't think he would have held back on any issue or personality; I think he would have given us some very salty comments.

Finally, as I plowed through this challenging effort, I came to realize that something else was afoot. I realized that John Sidney McCain had grown to be a personal hero to me, and I was beginning to think of him as if he was *my* grandfather. Further, I came to think of this work as a bit of payback to the Navy. The Navy gave me a university education, led me to the girl who would become my wife of nearly 55 years, and gave me the irreplaceable gift of life-long friends. Maybe this book will count toward some of that debt.

KEITH GILBERT
San Diego, California
March 2006

INTRODUCTION

Vice Admiral John Sidney "Slew" McCain, Sr., was a rare bird. He has been described variously as fearless, modest, extroverted, human, immensely positive, and a pleasant companion. But also as aggressive, profane, impulsive, volatile, and occasionally hotheaded.[1]

One historian described him as "A tough, wizened aviator, who wrote an indecipherable scrawl, rolled his own cigarettes and left a trail of tobacco bits wherever he went, and was ready to fight like a demon."[2] He was famous for his combat-area headgear, which Bill Halsey affectionately called "The most disreputable one I ever saw on an officer."[3]

McCain was energetic—he couldn't sit still for long. He had a powerful handclasp and a wonderful smile. He could light up any room he entered. He was hospitable and friendly, and he was dearly loved by his men.

E.B. Potter, in his 1985 work *Bull Halsey*, wrote, "There were few wiser or more competent officers in the Navy than Slew McCain, but whenever his name came up, somebody had a ridiculous story to tell about him—and many of the stories were true. Possibly his reputation for comical adventures had something to do with his appearance. With bony frame, hooked nose, and sunken cheeks, he looked at least ten years older than his age. Junior officers and enlisted men often referred to him as Popeye the Sailor Man, whom he superficially resembled."[4]

McCain was not a large man, but he was tough and wiry. He was five feet, seven and a half inches tall, and weighed 140 to 150 pounds. He wore full dentures, and had to correct the vision in his left eye

1

although he was able to retain flight status. His official Navy fitness ratings were tops, of course, with the few lower marks usually in the areas of "Military Bearing" and "Neatness of Personal Dress."

Without question he loved the Navy. He once told his son Jack (the future four-star admiral): "Any naval duty is good duty and any naval duty is excellent duty if the officer concerned makes it so. . ."

Admiral McCain is probably best known for his service as the commander of a fast carrier task force in World War II. Operating under William F. "Bull" Halsey, he led raids against the Japanese in 1944 and 1945 that destroyed thousands of enemy aircraft and hundreds of enemy ships. Halsey was widely quoted about what he thought of his carrier commander, "Not much more than my right arm."

McCain's command style has been described across the range from being a nice old man but not a dynamic leader, to: "A legend . . . a giant of a guy." War correspondent Dick O'Malley described McCain as one of the finest, most effective leaders in the Pacific. "When he gave an order in his soft, clear voice, there was never any doubt there was command in it."[5]

Earlier in the war, in the South Pacific in 1942, Slew McCain distinguished himself as commander of all land-based aircraft in the theater. He was particularly renowned for his aggressive support of the Marines on Guadalcanal. At the end of the war, McCain was in the front row of admirals and generals who witnessed the signing of the surrender documents on September 2, 1945, aboard the USS *Missouri*.

John Sidney McCain died of heart failure or just plain fatigue in his Coronado, California, home, just four days after the surrender ceremony.

John McCain was not only a successful fighter *against* the Japanese enemy, but he was a successful fighter *for* the Navy. He was not fond of Washington duty, but he was a key figure in the Navy Department during the buildup of carrier aviation from 1942 to 1944. Earlier in his career he had developed a lion's share of the legislation affecting officer personnel.

John Sidney McCain was born in 1884 to a prominent Mississippi family. He attended the University of Mississippi and graduated from the U.S. Naval Academy. His brother and an uncle were Army generals. McCain had a well-rounded early career in ships ranging from a gunboat to battleships, along with shore duty in Washington. When the Navy needed senior officers qualified in aviation, Captain John McCain won his wings—at age 52. He commanded the aircraft carrier USS *Ranger.* By December 7th he had attained flag rank and was running the Navy's patrol planes on the West Coast and in Hawaii.

McCain won three Distinguished Service Medals, and was awarded the Navy Cross for saving two cruisers in his task group after they had been severely damaged by the Japanese. The government of Peru gave him two medals before the war, and he was appointed Honorary Knight Commander in the Order of the British Empire after the war.

McCain's fourth star was awarded to him posthumously. McCain Hall at Ole Miss; McCain Field in Meridian, Mississippi; and the USS *John S. McCain* carried on his name. Admiral McCain is buried in Arlington National Cemetery along with other family members.

John McCain was, above all, a commander. To take on command is to take on risks—risks of success and failure, and risks of praise and criticism. McCain experienced a bit of each. But in his thirty-nine year naval career, John Sidney McCain reached the top echelon of Navy leadership. He was truly a leader born, and an American hero of World War II who gave his life for his country.

1

FROM TEOC TO TOOL ROOM

In 1941, John Sidney McCain wrote: "I was born on a plantation at Teoc, Mississippi, August 9th, 1884, the son of John S. and Elisabeth Young McCain. Both parents are now dead. My brother, Mr. Joseph P. McCain, still runs the plantation. Living with him is my spinster sister, Katie Lou McCain. Another married sister, Mrs. Luther Spencer, lives in the nearby metropolis of Carrollton, Mississippi. A brother, Harry Hart McCain, died in Wisconsin four years ago—no children. My remaining brother is Brigadier General William A. McCain, in command of the Quartermaster depot in Philadelphia. My only other surviving close relative is Major General Henry P. McCain, Retired, Washington, D.C. I visit the plantation every year or two, as does my Army brother, and it looks to me more peaceful and pleasant every time I see it. My father was a grand old gentleman, completely unselfconscious—that is he would talk as readily to the President as he would to a field hand. He wandered by mistake one day into the office of Admiral Charles F. Hughes, then the chief of naval operations, which was the beginning of a beautiful friendship. My father had access to the Admiral's office at all times. When my father died the entire county and half the state attended the funeral. That, of course is an exaggeration."

McCain's older brother, Brigadier General William Alexander McCain, was born in 1878, attended Ole Miss, and then graduated from West Point in 1902. He received Distinguished Service medals in both world wars. By 1948 he was retired and living in Doylestown, Pennsylvania. McCain's uncle, Henry Pinckney McCain, graduated

5

from West Point in 1885, attained the rank of major general, and was Adjutant General of the Army in World War I.

The brother, William Alexander, was quite a character (as was John Sidney himself). As a cavalryman, Bill McCain helped "Black-jack" Pershing chase Pancho Villa through the Mexican foothills. He was a poker-playing polo player who earned the nickname "Wild Bill" for his daring riding of his polo ponies. In fact, injuries from polo forced him to give up the cavalry and transfer to the quartermaster corps. He retired before World War II as a colonel, but he was recalled and promoted to brigadier general.

Camp McCain, an army post near Grenada, Mississippi, was named "In honor of a famous family of military men from neighboring Carroll County, including Carroll county native Major General Henry P. McCain."

The McCains of Teoc

Author Elizabeth Spencer, Admiral McCain's niece, wrote of McCain's father. He was also named John Sidney McCain, but was not called "senior" or "1st." She knew him in his later years, and he was the only grandparent she knew.

She described him as tall, with a white mustache and blue eyes. Year-round he wore dark suits and a black bow tie. He owned and used a variety of walking sticks, and distrusted motor cars. As a youth he tried to join the Confederate cause, but was turned away as too young—he was only fourteen. In his elder years he could often be found in an armchair by the fireplace or on the porch.

The elder McCain, called "Mister Johnny," was devoted to Teoc and his family. He instilled in John Sidney and his siblings the traditional McCain family values of honesty, loyalty, integrity, and a thirst for education.

Elizabeth Spencer recorded of her fond memories of Teoc:

The original family home, overlooking the flat expanse of Delta land, stood on a hill and was once described to me by my uncle Bill, the eldest son, as "impressive . . . in the old Southern style." By that I could imagine a mansion if I chose, but I now think it was probably a traditional two-story plantation home. It burned down the year of my mother's birth.

My mother was born soon after the fire, in the only shelter the family had to go, one of the Negro houses on the place.

These houses, as I recall them, having been constantly in and out of so many when I visited Teoc, were simple but comfortable and roomy.

The house, expanded and embellished, became a real home place, plain at first, but tended charmingly, with verandas added. The oaks planted around it grew and flourished, forming a shady grove.[1]

There were churches and schools on the farm to serve the large population living there and working the land. Today, of course, the land is nearly empty, farmed from afar and by machinery.

Teoc Today

To visit Teoc today, you drive about five miles north from Greenwood, Mississippi, on Highway 7. A small green highway sign with an arrow and "Teoc" points to the east. A sharp right turn leads onto a paved road that soon traverses the McCain fields "that Uncle Sidney plowed as a boy."[2]

About three and a half miles east on that road, crossing Teoc Creek, brings you to Teoc itself. Bill McCain, John Sidney's nephew, said the family had queried the Smithsonian about the name "Teoc" and were told that it is a Choctaw word for "tall pines." Bill's ancestor, William Alexander McCain, bought the land from Mr. Vick (the namesake of Vicksburg of hallowed rebel memory) in 1851.

A long northwest—southeast bluff line runs through Mississippi, separating the hill country to the east from the flat delta lands to the west. Teoc sits at the foot of that bluff. A dirt road leads off to the north from the paved road to the old house. Close by the intersection, on the north side of the paved road, is the old McCain-Spencer general store. When the dirt road extended to the south (as it did in olden days) it crossed an antique iron bridge, called the "iron bridge." That was the original entrance to Teoc.

Today the store still stands pretty solid, with a large main hall plus two small rooms at the back. On one side of the main hall is a swing-up door to a port for weighing cotton. The old scales are still in place, built right into the wall. Bill McCain relates that in the old days they had a one-cylinder cotton gin during the picking season.

Outside over the front door is a faded sign "US GOVERNMENT MOTOR GASOLINE." Around the corner to the side of the store is where Sidney used to pitch pennies, a favorite pastime of the brothers.

As you drive north along the graveled road, on the right is an African-American cemetery. Then on the left the old house appears. To reach the building, you crawl through some brambles and cross a meadow. On the north side of the meadow is an old flower bed and a "potato house." Further back is the old orchard site. To the west are the flat 1,800 acres planted in soy beans and cotton. Off to the north is Sharkey's Bayou. The bayou is locally called the "slew," which provides one family theory about the origin of John Sidney's nickname.

The house is truly a derelict; the porches have nearly all fallen off, but the tin roof seems okay. Trees, weeds, and vines have grown up all around the outside. Inside, the floors and walls are reasonably solid. Wallpaper is peeling from the walls, but the wooden paneling on the walls looks pretty good; it could be salvaged. There are two fireplaces, one older than the other. There are bookshelves on the wall beside the older fireplace. Nephew Bill McCain remembers that the house was always full of books.

Both John Sidney and brother Bill visited when they could. John Sidney probably was there for the last time in February 1945, while on his way back to the Pacific to relieve Marc "Pete" Mitscher as commander of the fast carrier task force. When he was home, John Sidney sometimes paced the porches, waiting for the official start of the cocktail hour. He frequented Lusco's in Greenwood, a restaurant with a long-standing reputation for good dinners (and bootleg liquor).

The number of people on the farm has dropped from dozens to virtually none. The houses and outbuildings are gone. The store is closed. But you can still get the lay of the land and imagine what it must have been like to get up in the morning, walk out on the porch, sniff the air, and greet the day.

Carrollton

McCain's father, in addition to running the farm, held county offices.

Carrollton, the county seat of Carroll County, is a beautiful town, with lots of shade trees, lovely old homes, a small square, and a courthouse in the Southern tradition. There is one family tale about John Sidney, as a youth in Carrollton, taking on the responsibility of protecting his sisters. When he saw and heard movement outside one night, he let go with shotgun blasts. The next day it was found he had thoroughly destroyed a nearby tree.

Sidney attended school in Carrollton even though there were school houses out at Teoc. William Thomas was the superintendent of schools in Carroll County, and recounted to his family that his greatest accomplishment was retaining his job for nine years as a Baptist with a school board of Methodists, and that Admiral John McCain was his star pupil.[3]

Elizabeth Spencer recalled in a letter that, for a time, her Uncle Sidney was the telephone operator for all of Carrollton. Once, during a severe thunderstorm, he rang his father to ask if he should close up until it was over. The advice came back "Stick to your post, son!"

On his last visit to Carrollton in 1945, when he was ready to go back to the war, John Sidney (nominally a Presbyterian) asked his sister "Jimmy" (Mary James, who married Luther Spencer) to "have all the Episcopalians pray for me."

Ole Miss

Sidney attended the University of Mississippi for the 1901—02 academic year. His name appears as number 238 on the President's Register of Students, and he is listed in the 1900—1903 catalogue as a Bachelor of Science freshman. It's not clear exactly which aspects of science he studied in his year at Ole Miss, but he did attend Greek or Latin classes taught by Katherine Vaulx of Arkansas, a lady who was to figure prominently in his life. He also joined the Phi Delta Theta fraternity.

Annapolis

In his book, Senator John McCain described the McCains of Teoc as "clannish, devoted to one another and to their traditions." One of these traditions was an Army career starting at West Point. In a switch of direction that was to set a tradition for at least three more generations, Sydney obtained a senatorial appointment to Annapolis on

September 25, 1902. He took the Naval Academy exams only as practice for the future West Point tests, but he scored so well that he opted
for Annapolis.[4]

His appointment by Senator A. J. McLauren was one of the first
by a U.S. senator. Prior to that, all appointments had been made by
representatives only. Also, McCain and his classmates were the first to
hold the title of midshipman. Up to 1902, Academy entrants were
known as naval cadets.[5]

This was a propitious time to enter the Naval Academy and the
United States Navy. The Spanish-American war in 1898 had left the
United States, like it or not, as a colonial power with global responsibilities. President Theodore Roosevelt, previously an assistant secretary of the Navy, and looked upon the fleet as the "big stick" he carried while "walking softly." Congress (and the public) agreed and
authorized a steady stream of new battleships. Six new battleships
were commissioned in 1906, McCain's graduation year, followed by
four in 1907. Soon the United States Navy was second in the world
only to the Royal Navy.[6]

In 1899 reconstruction of the entire Naval Academy began. By
1903 the new Macdonough and Dahlgren halls were opened to house
academic departments. The first wing of a new dormitory, Bancroft
Hall, opened in 1904. Not all of the Class of 1906 was allowed to
taste its luxuries, but some enjoyed their first class (senior) year in the
more spacious new surroundings.[7] The class of 1906 history, published in 1954, commented that the majority of the class lived for the
larger part of the academic year in two-story frame barracks called
annexes. The annexes were described as having few of the comforts of
home and "lacked the benefit of the modern plumbing installed in the
marble halls then building." The class history went on to say, "The
isolation of the annexes was not conducive to strict discipline and the
result was rough-housing at all hours and the performance of innu-
merable pranks conceivable only in the fertile minds of youth."[8]

In 1903 the student body expanded from four companies to eight.
The brigade marched in President Roosevelt's inaugural parade in
1905, a year that also saw the remains of John Paul Jones returned
from France and laid to rest at the Naval Academy.

Other than studies, drills, and sports (and youthful escapades), the

Academy offered little diversion. The only extracurricular activities were the choir and the YMCA.[9]

Senator McCain noted regarding his grandfather: "He was a popular midshipman but less than a serious student, graduating in the bottom quarter of his class."[10] He was ranked 80th of 116. In 1937 McCain, then a captain, commented about his grades: "As for myself, my classmates Towers and Noise [future Admiral John H. Towers and future Vice Admiral Leigh Noyes] can have the *Saratoga* the *Lexington*, fame, prestige and all. I myself much prefer the *Ranger* and if those two goats can beat me it will be the first time they ever beat me at anything except getting marks at the Navy School."

Midshipman McCain's dormitory room (his "den") was a regular hangout for McCain cohorts, who considered him quite a character. He was identified as "the skeleton in the family closet of 1906."[11] Could this have been a foreshadowing of his sometimes unorthodox approach to issues?

McCain's assignments for his summer training cruises (and his early duty assignments) are set down in beautiful clerical handwriting in his "Record of Officers, U.S. Navy," part of his permanent service record. On his first summer, 1903, he spent about one month each in *Chesapeake* (a three-masted bark), *Indiana* (a battleship veteran of the Spanish-American War), and *Hartford* (a pre-Civil War sloop). In 1904 McCain was back in *Hartford* as well as battleship *Massachusetts* (also a Spanish-American War veteran). His final cruise, in 1905, was split between *Florida* (a new monitor) and *Terror* (an older monitor that also fought the Spanish).

Notable classmates included future flag officers William Calhoun (future Commander, Service Force, Pacific Fleet), Milo Draemel (future Commander, Amphibious Force, Pacific Fleet), Aubrey "Jake" Fitch (future Deputy CNO), Frank Jack Fletcher (future carrier task force commander at Coral Sea and Midway), Robert "Hook" Ghormley (future Commander, South Pacific Area), Isaac Kidd (posthumous award of the Medal of Honor, was on the *Arizona* at Pearl Harbor), Leigh Noyes (future Commander, Air Force, Pacific Fleet), John Towers (future organizer of the "NC" trans-Atlantic flight in 1919, and later Commander-in-Chief, Pacific Fleet) and Russell Willson (future Deputy Commander-in-Chief, U.S. Fleet).[12]

Due to the need for junior officers in the growing fleet, Annapolis classes of the day were graduated in the middle of their last year.[13] Thus John Sidney McCain graduated from the Naval Academy on February 12, 1906, and was sent to the Asiatic Station with the rank of "Passed Midshipman." On March 10 he took passage from Seattle to the first of many assignments in the Far East.

Asiatic Station

As a Passed Midshipman, McCain served in the Asiatic Fleet in the USS *Ohio* (Battleship No. 12), USS *Baltimore* (Cruiser No. 3), and the gunboat *Panay*.

A classmate recalled a story about John Sidney while they were shipmates in the *Ohio*. A recurring problem was the unauthorized practice of the crew during hot weather to hang their hammocks from the boat davits in the cooler air above decks. McCain provided a solution. The ship was assigned to carry the casket of a deceased admiral from China to Japan, and the casket was placed on the boat deck. Midshipman McCain got a black cat from the fore hold and, on the stroke of midnight, twisted its tail and tossed it on the casket. The resulting screech and the implication of bad luck was enough to clear the boat deck of sleeping sailors.[14]

McCain's next assignment was in the *Panay* [the namesake of the larger and newer gunboat *Panay,* which was "accidentally" sunk by the Japanese on December 12, 1937 on the Yangtze River]. McCain's *Panay* had been launched in 1885 and was later purchased from Spain by the U.S. Army. She was transferred to the Navy in 1899. She was a twin-engine shallow-draft vessel originally designed for river patrol. *Panay* served during the Philippine Insurrection as one of the group of gunboats that supported Army garrisons and intercepted enemy supply boats.[15]

The *Panay* was decommissioned in 1902 and then re-commissioned in January 1907, under the command of Ensign Chester Nimitz. With a crew of two officers (Nimitz and McCain) and about thirty men, she cruised the southern islands of the Philippines under a roving commission, which meant her captain could pick and choose the ports he wanted to visit.[16]

Panay's job was to show the flag, and it turned out to be high adventure. In 1940 McCain wrote of this trip:

> On the gunboat *Panay*, cruised in the southern Philippines not so very long after the so-called days of the empire. In those days a red flag flown at the masthead meant for the head man to report aboard with chickens, vegetables, and other eatables. Took part in one midnight raid on a Moro stronghold which was abortive, the Moros having received information through a supposed fifth columnist.
>
> Was frequently boarded by Army officers in those days who drank up everything aboard. Inexpensive, however,—Old Tom gin being forty-five cents a quart and White Horse sixty-five cents a bottle.
>
> With two double-barreled discharges of a 12-guage shotgun killed 98 ducks. Admiral Nimitz, chief of navigation, manned the other gun. Story never believed by anyone.
>
> Entertained for a brief period on *Panay* the present King of England, then a subaltern RN [Royal Navy] touring the world.

McCain's next assignment was as chief engineer in the USS *Chauncey* (Destroyer No. 3) and as assistant to the captain of the Cavite Navy Yard. During this period, and after two years of satisfactory service and success in the examination for promotion, McCain was promoted to ensign on March 18, 1908.

McCain finished his tour with the Asiatic Fleet in 1908 and returned to the United States via the Suez Canal in the USS *Connecticut* (Battleship No. 18). The *Connecticut* was the flagship of the Great White Fleet that was then completing the final legs of its famous round-the-world cruise. *Connecticut* stopped briefly in Manila in late October, then visited Japan, and then returned to Manila in early November for the annual competitive gunnery exercises. McCain joined her in Manila in late November, after the exercises had been completed. Before starting on the homeward run, the Great White Fleet (actually the Atlantic Fleet) exchanged a large number of officers and men with the Pacific Fleet on Asiatic station, and McCain was in the group.

The *Connecticut* left Manila in December 1908 and arrived in Hampton Roads, Virginia, in February 1909 after stops at Colombo, Naples, and Gibraltar. *Connecticut* also made a brief stop in Messina to help with earthquake relief. The arrival in Virginia was a grand parade of ships reviewed by President Roosevelt and featured an unending cascade of twenty-one gun salutes.[17]

Shortly after *Connecticut* returned home, McCain did the same; he took thirty days leave. At the end of that period he received orders to the USS *Pennsylvania* (Armored Cruiser No. 4) on the Pacific coast. He reported in and promptly extended his leave for another twenty days.

The Big Step

The reason for all this leave activity on the part of a very junior officer was soon apparent. With another ten days of leave in his pocket, on August 9, 1909, in Colorado Springs, Colorado, Ensign John Sidney McCain, USN, wed Katherine Davey Vaulx of Fayetteville and Hot Springs, Arkansas. The ceremony was performed by the bride's father, clergyman James Junius Vaulx. This was the start of a solid thirty-six year marriage.

Katherine (1876–1959) was born in Fayetteville and attended the University of Arkansas. Their children were John Sidney, Jr. (1911–1981), James Gordon (1913–1985), and Catherine Vaulx McCain (1915–2000). John Sidney, Jr.—"Jack"—was the future four-star admiral and father of Senator John S. McCain, III.

Senator McCain said this about his grandmother: "My paternal grandmother was a well-educated woman of gifted intellect and refined manner. She had been an instructor of Latin and Greek at the University of Mississippi, where she taught my grandfather. Bookish and eight years his senior, she won the devotion of the much coarser but widely read naval officer. Throughout their union, they indulged together their shared love of literature, reading aloud to each other whenever time allowed."[18]

One has to wonder a bit about their courtship. Although they were on the same campus at Ole Miss for a year, John Sidney was soon off to Annapolis for four years, then to the Philippines for two, and then aboard ship for the next year. With that much separation, he must have been a persistent and persuasive long-distance suitor.

Watch and Division Officer

As mentioned, McCain had served as watch and division officer in the *Connecticut* during transit back to the United States, a typical assignment for a young officer. Then he was assigned to the USS *Pennsylvania* in the Pacific Fleet until December 1909.

McCain's next assignment was in the USS *Washington* (Armored Cruiser No. 11) from December 1909 to December 1911. The *Washington* served in the Pacific initially and then circled South America to duty on the East Coast.[19] Although *Washington* was at the pier for maintenance in mid-1910 and early 1911, such sea duty cannot be considered an optimum way to start married life. But knowing John Sidney's love of the Navy and Katherine's resolute nature, they undoubtedly were prepared for the separations and relocations of Navy life.

Some insight into McCain from this period can be seen in the following excerpt from a letter written to an ex-shipmate in 1935. It concerns a time when McCain was arrested for breaking the speed limit: "I was peremptorily escorted to the police station by a couple of policemen and was duly charged. I thought, in fact I knew, that I had seen the sergeant behind the desk someplace before. I noted, too, that his eye was on me once or twice. Finally he said 'What are you doing here, Mr. McCain?' and I replied 'I am under arrest for speeding.' He said 'Hell no, you aren't under arrest. Don't do it again.' He then introduced himself as a former boatswain's mate on the old cruiser *Washington*. He came around to see me afterwards and drank up some of my liquor."

On February 2, 1911, McCain appeared before an examining board consisting of a rear admiral and three captains to be questioned about seamanship, navigation, gunnery, and steam engineering. On March 3, 1911 he was certified as qualified for promotion to lieutenant (junior grade), and he was promoted on March 10th.

The Tool Room

From February 1912 to April 1914, McCain served as officer-in-charge of the Machinists' Mate School at the Navy Yard in Charleston, South Carolina. Although McCain's fitness grades up to this time were good, he was consistently marked as "excellent" during this duty assignment. It is likely that he further developed and fine-tuned his leadership skills at the school.

McCain appeared before an examining board at the Washington Navy Yard on July 8, 1912, and was examined and found qualified for promotion to lieutenant. The step upward occurred on August 5th, with a date of rank of July 1, 1912.

Before leaving the school in April 1914, McCain was cited by letter for the "clean, neat and orderly appearance of the Machinist's Mate School."

2

THE GREAT WAR

While the cruise of the Great White Fleet had demonstrated that the United States was indeed a world naval power, its very success in transiting the globe allowed Congress to withhold support for a two-ocean fleet. Although President Taft attempted to continue Teddy Roosevelt's naval policies, the building program began to lag. By 1909 the United States had ceded second place among the world's fleets to Germany. (Britannia, of course, was number one.) The United States remained reasonably strong in terms of battleships, but—as World War I would demonstrate—more cruisers and destroyers were needed.

USS *Colorado*

It was back to sea for McCain in May 1914, just after World War I broke out in Europe. He was assigned to the USS *Colorado* (Armored Cruiser No. 7) as engineering officer. The *Colorado* was in reduced commission until February 1915, when she was restored to full commission and became the flagship of the Pacific Fleet.[1]

A letter of commendation appears in McCain's files dated March 3, 1915: "From a material standpoint the condition of the *Colorado* is excellent and the Commander-in-Chief attributes this condition of the ship as due, in a large measure, to the thorough and efficient administration and supervision of Lieutenant John S. McCain, U.S. Navy, engineer officer on the *Colorado*, who for about ten months just prior to the inspection acted as commanding officer of the ship." That was a nice feather in Lieutenant McCain's cap.

One of *Colorado's* duties during her period of full commission was patrolling Mexican waters during the ongoing Mexican revolution. In that war, Pancho Villa suffered a major defeat against General Alvaro Obregón at Celaya in April 1915. After that loss, Villa turned his attention back to where his strength lay in northern Mexico. Eventually this led to his incursion and raid on Columbus, New Mexico. That in turn led to General John J. Pershing's expedition and brought Sidney's brother, Bill, into the fray. By that time, of course, Sidney and the *Colorado* were long gone.

USS *San Diego*

McCain was transferred from the *Colorado* to the USS *San Diego* (Armored Cruiser No. 6) in September 1915. This was a fortunate move because it kept McCain in cruisers that would be needed so desperately for escort duty after the United States entered the World War I. He kept up his good record and was commended on August 5, 1916: "The Engineer Officer, Lieutenant J. S. McCain, U.S. Navy, the Supply Officer, Paymaster C. S. Baker, U.S. Navy, and the Torpedo Officer, Lieutenant (JG) H. J. Carstarphen, U.S. Navy, are deserving of commendation for the excellent condition of their departments."

McCain's fitness reports also contained laudatory remarks:

This ship conducted a full power trial during this period with complete success due to the thoroughness of preparation and condition of personnel and engineering material—the credit for this success is Lt. McCain's.

Has splendid organization, men well trained in their special duties and in general drills. Excellent cooperation with other departments of the ship. Upkeep and general condition of his department excellent. The state of discipline he maintains in his department leaves little to be desired.

I consider Lieutenant McCain a most excellent officer and difficult to replace.

The early years of World War I were a time of strict neutrality by the United States. But submarine attacks on unarmed passenger vessels and eventually Germany's declaration of unrestricted submarine warfare brought the United States into the war in April 1917. *San*

Diego served as flagship for the Commander-in-Chief of the Pacific Fleet until she went into reserve status on February 12, 1917. *San Diego* was returned to full commission on April 7th, the day after America's declaration of war against Germany. On this tour she served as flagship for the commander of patrol forces in the Pacific Fleet.

Although the Naval Act of 1916 proposed construction of ten battleships, sixteen cruisers, fifty destroyers, and sixty-seven submarines over the next three years, there was no role for such a great battle fleet in the Great War. The German fleet was blockaded in port and thus not a threat. But the submarine threat was huge. Germany was close to victory in early 1917 because of allied shipping losses. Escorted convoys were the answer.

World War I was a logistics war for the United States Navy. Two million U.S. troops were transported to Europe, half by the United States. To support this effort, the original 1916 building program was set aside and a program for the construction of two hundred additional destroyers was undertaken to provide urgently needed escorts.

San Diego was a part of that magnificent effort. Initially she served at the Mare Island Navy Yard as a base for recruiting and mobilization of the naval militia. That task finished, *San Diego* then escorted an interned German ship under tow from Honolulu to Port Townsend, Washington. Then she sailed for San Diego, and left that port on July 18, 1917, to become part of the Atlantic Fleet. Upon arrival in Hampton Roads in August, she coaled and then moved onward to New York to report to the commander of the Cruiser Force, Atlantic Fleet. *San Diego* was assigned a conventional role for an armored cruiser, that of escort duty. Although her first assignment was to transport midshipmen to Annapolis, *San Diego* soon embarked on her primary mission of protecting convoys on the first leg of their dangerous journey through the stormy and sub-infested Atlantic. Based in Tomkinsville, New York, and Halifax, Nova Scotia, she made a half-dozen escort runs to the mid-Atlantic and amassed a perfect record—no ship losses.[2]

San Diego's longest voyage during this period was in November and December, 1917, when she escorted a troop convoy from New York to Le Croisic and Brest, France. On the return trip, *San Diego* was cited for a dash from Brest, France, to New York at 18 to 20 knots: "The Chief of Naval Operations congratulates the *San Diego* on her splendid run, particularly the fire room force as the small amount of smoke given off and the ability to make this long run at high speed indicates marked efficiency in the fire and engine room."

McCain's good work continued. He received a high commendation in October 1917: "I have inspected the Engineering Department of the *San Diego* and find it to be in excellent condition as regards cleanliness and preservation. I am of the opinion that in respect to the Engineering Department, the ship is entitled to be called a 'smart ship' and that credit attaches to Lieutenant J. S. McCain, U.S. Navy, Engineer Officer."

It is interesting to note this high praise for organization and upkeep for an officer whose lowest scores on his fitness reports were for "Military Appearance and Manner" and "Neatness of Person and Dress"! But this was not the last time that McCain's vessels were to be termed "smart ships."

Also in early October 1917, McCain was sent to the Washington Navy Yard for examination for promotion to lieutenant commander. Promotion followed quickly on October 18, 1917, back-dated to August 31st.

By 1918 McCain had picked up an additional duty as navigation officer in the *San Diego*. That conjures up visions of hustling up and down the ladders between the bilges and the bridge.

All of this is the "official" McCain. Officers like McCain, who were seen by their superiors as destined for the higher ranks, were written-up using the "walk on water" style, i.e., top grades whenever possible. Some insight into the more human McCain can be seen in the following excerpt from a letter written to an ex-shipmate in 1935:

I have nothing but affection in my memory for the members of the old *San Diego* crew. They shot craps in the drum rooms, and had liquor in the corners, but if there was anything to do they always did it. A Hell and High Water crew as I remember. Sometimes I think the Navy is getting a little bit soft-handed and collegiate. At any rate I am sure that I would feel more at home among an H. A. (sic) crew than among our present high school boys.

Do you remember when the bird in charge of the ice machine left a bottle of Old Taylor for me? I inspected the bottom under the ice machine and found a full case of Old Taylor and a broken case with nine bottles in it. I went away to get the Executive and the Master-at-Arms and when I returned, the case had disappeared and only one bottle was left of the nine. This [sailor] whose name was Miller told me years afterwards that he knew the Executive turned over confiscated liquor to the officers making week-end fishing trips, of which I was a permanent member, so he left the bottle for me.

Then there was a log room messenger on the *San Diego*. Do you remember the skinny little devil? Grown enormously fat, he approached me one day at the Bowie race track and gave me a few winners and many losers; all with the excellent intention of making me rich.

McCain left the *San Diego* in May 1918. Two months later, on July 19, 1918, she was sunk off the Fire Island lighthouse by a mine laid by the German submarine *U-156*. It was her first trip out after McCain left.[3] The *San Diego* was the only major ship lost by the U.S. Navy in World War I. The hulk remains there today and is a favorite recreational dive site.

McCain was ordered to the Bureau of Navigation in Washington, D.C., in May 1918 as an "appointment officer." Even in just the few months until the end of the war the Bureau expressed its appreciation for "valuable work accomplished by you and the personnel under your command, in training officers and men."

Upon his assignment to shore duty in Washington, McCain was promoted to the rank of commander.

3

SHORE DUTY

Between the world wars, McCain served four tours of duty in Washington, D.C. at the Bureau of Navigation (later the Bureau of Naval Personnel). His first two tours, from 1918 to 1921 and from 1923 to 1926, were as an appointment officer. The third, from 1929 to 1931, was in recruiting and procurement; and from 1933 to 1935 McCain's assignment was as officer-in-charge of the Planning Division.

McCain offered his own assessment of his efforts ashore: "The most constructive work of which I claim to credit has to do with Navy personnel. Existing laws governing officers are to a considerable extent my own work."

His fitness reports were right at the top during these tours; but unfortunately, they did not cover what he really accomplished. Some typical comments were: "Has charge of officers' records and preparing details for use of selection boards and data for information of Congress"(1919); "Commander McCain has an unusually keen mind and great ability to quickly come to correct decisions"(1920); "He is thoroughly informed in the intricate problem of officers' personnel legislation." (1924); and "Well fitted for informing Members of Congress regarding naval personnel matters"(1930).

McCain later claimed to detest duty in Washington, but it was a very large part of his career between World War I and his entry into naval aviation. Between 1918 and 1935 he spent 124 months at the Bureau of Navigation as contrasted to 66 months at sea.

The years between the wars were tough on the Navy, even though, as McCain wrote, "Never before has the Navy been so widely known as now." This was because of the highly visible convoy efforts during the war.[1] But that acclaim did not generate dollars. In 1919 the Navy proposed to complete and expand on the 1916 building program, but Congress refused to approve. Then, as a result of the First International Conference on Limitation of Naval Armaments—the so-called Washington Conference of 1921 and 1922—the United States agreed to a capital ship ratio of 10:10:6 with Great Britain and Japan; agreed to scrap fifteen active battleships and cancel eleven of the fifteen battleships under construction; agreed not to build new capital ships for ten years; and agreed not to establish fortified bases west of Hawaii.

As a policy, the United States had its eye on solving world problems through diplomacy rather than armed conflict. Beyond that, the nation was soon hammered with an economic depression. As a result of these pressures, even the treaty ship parity levels with other nations were not reached.

Demobilization

McCain's first tour in Washington, 1918 to 1921, involved what he later considered to be some of the most arduous work he had ever done. This period was one of momentous change for the Navy. At the end of World War I the Navy had more than 32,000 officers, nearly 500,000 enlisted men, and 1,362 ships in service. By January 1922 the totals were down to slightly more than 6,000 officers, 100,000 enlisted men, and 900 ships. More reductions were in the offing as a result of the armament limitation treaties.[2] McCain and his staff were responsible for preparing legislation to implement the transition from the Navy's war-time footing to a peace-time force.

McCain's boss, Admiral Richard H. Leigh, was highly complimentary about McCain's work. He cited McCain's enthusiasm, cheerfulness, and willingness to put in long working hours. He also mentioned McCain's competence when working with the naval committees of Congress.

Carl Vinson had the second longest tenure in U.S. history in the House of Representatives, serving from 1914 to 1965. He was "Mr. Navy" all the way. Vinson was a member of the House Naval Affairs

Committee from 1917 to 1947, overlapping all of McCain's shore duty periods. He described his long-term relationship with McCain: "Johnny was one of my most intimate friends. I owe much to him for we grew up together in the Navy, Johnny on the uniformed side and I on the congressional side. He did much to steer me through my early days on the Naval Affairs committee."

Legislation

From June 1923 to June 1926, one of McCain's major efforts was the Staff Equalization Bill. This legislation dealt with the numbers and promotions of staff officers. The Navy officer corps includes both unrestricted line officers on the path to command at sea and staff officers with specialties such as supply, engineering, and medicine. The Equalization Bill assigned a line officer "running mate" to each staff officer, so that when the line running mate became eligible for promotion, the companion staff officer did too.[3] McCain felt that some old timers were dissatisfied with the outcome of the legislation and laid the blame on him.

Another piece of legislation under McCain's wing was the Britten Bill, which dealt with inequalities in the numbers of officers in various grades. This proposal set forth a system to help ensure equal consideration for promotion for all who had spent time in grade. This bill became law in 1931.

McCain felt that the entire Navy personnel system from 1918 to 1935 was the result of his work.

Proceedings

Several articles written for the periodical *U.S. Naval Institute Proceedings* by Commander McCain provide insight into the complex analysis behind the legislative proposals. In "A Personnel Survey," which appeared in the January 1923 issue of *Proceedings*, McCain delved into the promotion potential for the higher officer ranks. Based on his analysis of the Personnel Law of 1916, he presented tables for rear admiral, captain, commander, and lieutenant commander in which he showed vacancies expected to occur in each rank between 1924 and 1934 due to the size of the Navy, retirements for age, promotions, and "casualties"—death, retirements for other than age, and so forth. He concluded that there would be, for example, 72 rear admiral vacancies to be filled from among 157 captains. Commanders were going to have an easier time of it with 268 captain vacancies for 267 commanders. He then explored several ideas to solve the captains' predicament.

An interesting point made in McCain's article is that a 1:1 officer parity should be achieved with England, along with a 5:3 ratio with Japan. This, of course, is in line with the capital ship ratios of 5:5:3 incorporated in the Washington Naval Treaty of 1922.[4]

Perhaps the most significant thing to be found in this rather arcane analysis is McCain's support for the six-year old selection board process of officer promotion, a position he maintained and espoused even after being passed over for flag rank.

Finally, in the May 1925 issue of *Proceedings,* McCain presented a fascinating data set under the title "Service Since Graduation *vs.* Age In Grade Retirement." This was written to compare the two methods of retirement in terms of the number of officers likely to be promoted and the number likely to be retired under each system. Taking into consideration a normal course of events and avoiding extreme assumptions, McCain predicted little difference between the two approaches.

The centerpiece of this analysis was a data set showing all 4,776 line officers of the Navy arrayed by age and by years of service. This array included 54 rear admirals, 211 captains, 373 commanders, 644 lieutenant commanders, 1,357 lieutenants, 1,017 lieutenants (junior grade), and 1,120 ensigns. The range was from two 65-year old rear admirals with 44 years of service in the upper left corner of the table, down to the lower right-hand corner with 409 ensigns from the class of 1924 at age 20 with zero service. It was an amazing presentation that, while it must have required an enormous amount of hand tallying, summarized the scope of the Navy's leadership.[5]

The Morrow Board

In 1925, while McCain was a commander on duty with the Bureau of Navigation, President Calvin Coolidge appointed the Morrow Board, a presidential commission of qualified citizens to study the problem of aircraft in national defense. Recommendations of the commission led to the creation of the office of the Assistant Secretary of the Navy for Air and the requirement that commanding officers of aircraft carriers and naval air stations be qualified aviators.

One aspect investigated by the Morrow Board was the establishment of a separate flying corps, along with the creation of special schools for the study of strategy and tactics for officers of the flying corps. McCain opposed the idea. He was reported as outspoken and bitter in his opposition. He had recently finished working for the passage of his staff officer bill (the Equalization Bill) and undoubtedly saw serious problems with the establishment of yet another separate officer corps on top of existing staff corps for medical, supply, engineering, and other specialties. He perceived the separation of aviators purely and simply as a scheme to ensure promotions; and he feared that such separation would lead to an attitude of mutual neglect on the part of both the sea-going line officers and the aviators. He was right. Without a separate corps, naval aviators were encouraged to think of themselves as naval line officers to the great benefit of all.[6]

His opinions—and forceful way of delivering them—may have created grudges that lasted all the way through World War II. Although aviator Pat Bellinger was a strong advocate for the proposed flying corps, he and John McCain seemed to have reconciled (if that was necessary) and held mutual respect and friendship for each other when they were running patrol planes in the Pacific during 1941 and 1942. But maybe this was not true for others. Some aviation advocates may have let their opinions about John McCain become permanently colored by the disagreements (or what they heard about McCain's ideas), even though McCain later became one of the service's most outspoken advocates for naval aviation.

The Naval War College

In June 1928 McCain concluded a stint at sea as executive officer aboard the USS *New Mexico* with his assignment to the Naval War College at Newport, Rhode Island. He was part of the class of 1929. At the War College McCain completed a thesis entitled "The Foreign Policies of the United States." A reader's note at the bottom of the last page judged: "A complete, concise, and very interesting paper. Subject is well-thought-out, and well-covered. Excellent."

This must have been a pleasant respite for the family. By this time son Jack was at the Naval Academy, but son Gordon and daughter Catherine were still at home.

Rebuilding the Navy

McCain's last two tours with the Bureau of Navigation were in recruiting and procurement (1929 to 1931) and as officer-in-charge of the Planning Division (1933 to 1935). His recruiting duties called for a great deal of travel. He made trips to New York City, Memphis, Chicago, San Diego, San Francisco, and Newport.

During his recruiting tour of duty, in September 1930, John Sidney came down with a perforated duodenal ulcer. He was sent to the Naval Hospital in Washington, and from there for a one-month recuperative sick leave. He was certified as physically fit in October. McCain suffered from ulcers and drank sodas all day long. Once Kate told him about a cure, but he pounded the table and roared that he wouldn't spend cash on medical care.

Things turned around for the Navy during McCain's last tour at the Bureau of Navigation. From the depths of the Great Depression, when the Navy reduced allowances for quarters and required officers to take leave without pay, President Roosevelt's National Recovery Act of 1933 authorized new construction, including the carriers *Yorktown* and *Wasp*. This was followed by the Vinson-Trammell Act in 1934 to bring the Navy up to treaty limits. Annual appropriations began to climb. The need for national economic relief, plus the growing threat from Japan, provided the impetus. Japan announced in 1934 that it would no longer adhere to treaty limits on shipbuilding.

Issues for the Planning Division under McCain included development of a Force Operating Plan covering the years ahead through 1942. Other issues included recruitment and training, budgets, the length of tours of sea duty, and expansion of naval aviation. McCain hoped that enlisted complements would reach 85 percent on the larger vessels by 1936.

The Force Operating Plan laid out the Navy's future. McCain was jubilant. In a letter to a friend and colleague he reported: "We now have a Navy for every year up until 1942." By this time, Carl Vinson was chair of the Naval Affairs Committee and noted about McCain:

"I increasingly looked to him for advice and direction."

During this last tour of duty in Washington, there was a spate of family correspondence. In March 1934 John Sidney had concerns about son Jack's health. He pulled strings with his buddies to keep track of the case. As it turned out, Jack (then a newly married submarine officer at Pearl Harbor) and wife Roberta were busy being newlyweds and not watching out for their nutrition and health. In August they presented Sidney and Kate with their first grandchild, Alexandra.

His son Gordon was nearby in law school at George Washington University, working by day and going to school at night. John Sidney had thoughts about Gordon going back to Mississippi to practice there and possibly take over the farm. Daughter Catherine was in business school, also at George Washington, and was described as "full of energy" by her dad.

In November 1934 McCain, ever the gambling enthusiast, sent a letter to the *Washington Post* to urge that gambling laws be amended to be less restrictive. He pointed out that "People will gamble. They always have gambled. They always will. They will wager honestly and lawfully in the light of day, or with cheats in dark places."

McCain's own gambling, other than once in a while on the ponies, centered on cards at the Army-Navy Club. He later related, "Walked into the club yesterday. There were three birds playing 10-cent coon can. I affably suggested 5-cent coon can and was spurned. So that being the only game there was, I went into it. I won $13.50 on the very first hand and continued. Loud squawks from all sides."

McCain kept up with his brother Harry, and gratefully accepted a gift of Wisconsin cheese. He inquired about the prospects in Marshfield, Wisconsin, for a future lawyer: his son, Gordon. During this last tour, in July 1934, Mrs. McCain suffered a broken leg, recovering fully by October.

Such domestic concerns would soon become less of a priority for McCain as events accelerated, both internationally and in his naval career.

4

SEA DUTY

After World War I, McCain alternated sea duty with his assignments on shore. His shore duty, as discussed, was mostly at the Bureau of Navigation in Washington. As was typical for the time, he spent about three years ashore for every two years at sea. There simply weren't enough sea-going billets to go around, so officers had to spend the majority of their time ashore.

USS *Maryland*

McCain's first tour of sea duty in this period of his life was from June 1921 to May 1923 as navigator on the battleship USS *Maryland* (BB-46). The Maryland was commissioned in July 1921 in Newport News, Virginia, with McCain aboard as a plank-owner. She had a new type of seaplane catapult and the first 16-inch guns mounted on a U.S. ship. She was the pride of the Navy. *Maryland* participated in many special ceremonies at home, such as graduation at the Naval Academy and the anniversary of the battle of Bunker Hill. In August and September 1922, *Maryland* transported the secretary of state to Brazil for that nation's centennial exposition.[1]

In his performance during this period McCain was termed an "Excellent navigator . . ."

First Command

The next sea duty is significant, though short-lived. McCain left the Bureau of Navigation in July 1926 to take command of the freighter USS *Sirius* (AK-15), which was assigned to the Naval Transportation

Service to carry cargo and passengers.[2] He took command of *Sirius* at the Mare Island Navy Yard after traveling from Washington with a stop in Carrollton. Although this assignment was to last only a month and a half and was a temporary measure, it is always a good career step for a senior naval officer to become the skipper of a U.S. Navy ship and have that on his record.

Executive Officer

McCain next moved upward in size but backward in position. In September 1926 McCain was ordered to the battleship USS *New Mexico* (BB-40) as executive officer. He left the *Sirius* in the Brooklyn Navy Yard and crossed the country again to join the *New Mexico* at the Puget Sound Navy Yard at Bremerton, Washington.

Even though this was not a command assignment, the responsibility of the day-by-day operations of a battleship added another important chapter to McCain's record. His evaluations included: "Commander McCain is gifted with unusual ability to handle men. . . Due largely to Commander McCain's efforts the *New Mexico* has moved to first place in gunnery, engineering, and communications; and been complimented by the Commander-in-Chief for smartness, cleanliness, and material condition."

While aboard the *New Mexico* McCain used his connections to keep track of his son Jack's progress getting into the Naval Academy. Also he was able to have Jack spend two weeks aboard *New Mexico* while the ship was undergoing overhaul at the Bremerton, Washington, shipyard.

Captain McCain

From the *New Mexico* McCain was assigned to the Naval War College, and then again to the Bureau of Navigation. In June 1931, he received orders to report to the ammunition ship USS *Nitro* (AE-2) as commanding officer. He joined the ship on June 9, 1931, in Hingham Bay, Hull, Massachusetts. *Nitro* was specially built and refrigerated to carry explosives and ammunition for the battle fleet. She made an average of three cruises each year from the East Coast to the West Coast as she carried out her mission of moving explosives among various depots and supplying the fleet with target ammunition. *Nitro* was also configured to accommodate 10 officer and 250 enlisted passengers in addition to her cargo of explosives. She usually carried a full load on each trip.[3]

In mid-September 1931, while the *Nitro* was in the navy yard at Norfolk, Virginia, Commander John McCain was ordered to report to the Board of Medical Examiners for his promotion physical and to the Supervisory Examining Board for a professional examination. He passed both, and on December 29, 1931, he was promoted to captain, backdated to June 30, 1931.

Son Jack, now commissioned and aboard the *Oklahoma,* married Roberta Wright on January 21, 1933. They eloped and were wed at Caesar's Bar in Tijuana. John Sidney and the *Nitro* were in San Diego at the time so he was able to join them to stand at Jack's side.

After a year and a half in command of the *Nitro*, Captain McCain was ordered back to the Bureau of Navigation. In March 1933, he left the *Nitro* at the Naval Ammunition Deport at the Mare Island Navy Yard in Vallejo, California, and traveled back to Washington by rail. This trip took him via Council Bluffs, Iowa, where Kate's sister lived and where son Jack had been born in 1911. It wouldn't be a bad guess that he and Kate spent some leave time there. In the transition, he took one month's advance pay—$483.35.

During these alternating tours of sea and shore duty, McCain's periods of leave allowed him to return from time to time to his beloved Mississippi home. He spoke of his affection for Teoc, and Carrollton was listed as his home of record on many fitness reports. Elizabeth Spencer provides a glimpse into his visits to Teoc:

> As a child, I was in great awe of my two older uncles. Uncle Sidney came home more often than Uncle Bill, and I prized the affectionate attention he fixed on me, ready to praise whatever good he could observe. He criticized as well, but it was a kind of teasing. "When you pout, you're the Duchess. Now smile and be the Princess." His wife, Aunt Kate, an authoritative lady with rich brown hair, had been his teacher, eight years his senior, admirable for her high intelligence, which he, with his love of a keen mind, must have been drawn to.
>
> Once when he visited us alone, I remember, on a warm

evening, my father being absent, he, my mother, and I sat in
our wide hallway, and he said that I must have some children's
books by George MacDonald. My mother named the many
books I loved, which she was always reading from aloud.

"Those are fine," he said, "but these MacDonald books
are not like anything I ever read before. She must have them."

They arrived soon after—*The Princess and the Goblin* and
The Princess and Curdie. They were, as he said, a real feast.[4]

McCain the Author

An unexpected side to McCain's life during the inter-war years are his
literary efforts. McCain's scope of interests was wide. Short articles
range from a mystery story to commentary about social and economic issues. Military pieces range from a board game to essays about
global strategy. His most ambitious work was a fifteen-chapter,
40,000-word adventure novel.

The McCain works are difficult to date. About the only way,
unless a note or letter accompanied the piece, is to use a return address
and his Navy rank at the time.

McCain was not what one could call a successful author. Only the
three articles mentioned in the last chapter seem to have ever seen the
light of day. As mentioned, they were published in *U.S. Naval Institute
Proceedings*. At least one other article was submitted to that forum.
That piece, titled "Selection a la Race-Track Method," compared the
naval officer promotion selection process (done under wraps by a
board of officers) to racehorse handicapping. He starts the article
with, "Well, demmit, why not?"

Although not published, his literary efforts leave an amazing lega-
cy to his family and others eager to know more about the personality
of this complex and accomplished man. In retrospect, Margaret La
Grange, the Admiral's granddaughter, commented that all McCains
thought they were writers, but only Elizabeth Spencer really made it.
Of course, Senator John Sidney McCain III authored with Mark Salter
the bestseller *Faith of My Fathers*. Another motivation for McCain's
literary efforts in the 1920s and 1930s might have been to augment his
meager Navy salary.

Writings by Commander McCain, beyond those submitted to *Naval Institute Proceedings*, include:

- "The Perfect Crime," a 5,000-word submission to be published under the authorship of "Casper Clubfoot." This piece is a mystery story involving a retired police detective, mistaken identities, forged checks, and a scheme to cheat a bank of $100,000.
- "Alcohol a Necessity?" in which McCain suggests that beer and wine should be in wide distribution and easily available to the public.
- "Prohibition," in which he discusses some of the background and reasoning for alcohol prohibition, and suggests that the 18th Amendment was approved only when the high-minded electorate voted dry for the "other fellow."
- In "Barons of the Past and Future," McCain defines feudal "Barons of the Sword," financial "Barons of Gold," and the working man's "Barons of Lab," and calls for a fight against the "Barons of Ruin" who would seek to destroy it all.
- "The Hellcat and the Wolfhound" was a flowery Casper Clubfoot tale about a hero from a Georgia plantation who works with the federal police to combat evil in New York City.
- The "War Game" may fit into this era. It is played on a board like checkers or chess, but is won by tossing dice and moving troops.

A very interesting, 1,550-word article, written by McCain while he was on the USS *Maryland* sometime between 1921 and 1923, is "Reflections on the Ku Klux Klan." A clarifying hand-written notation "By a Non-member" appears beneath the title. In the article he lays out two poignant memories of childhood:

Terrors came up with memory. The first was when as a small boy in town of a Saturday visiting a kinsman, I was hurried from the yard into the house. Escaping surveillance, I flattened my nose against a window pane and saw the Ku Klux gallop into town, their regalia a dazzling white in the sunlight, their guns glittering. I heard the shooting at the Court-House and saw Negroes running—one lay down and died in front of the house. I was very sorry for them. All those I knew were badly frightened for a long time, and for days spoke only in whispers.

We lived on a plantation surrounded by Negroes, to me lovable and likable folk. We were far from any white neighbors. Sometimes it was necessary for my father to be away for the night. Then it was that terror sat by the open fire or stalked from room to room. The shades were always closely drawn, the windows barred and jammed, the doors locked and chairs placed under the knobs. My mother, a delicate and beautiful woman, moved carefully and lightly and often told the children to "hush." She always placed a small table by her bedside with a pearl handled revolver on it. Many times I have seen her, by the flickering firelight, rise up in bed to listen intently.

McCain seems to sum up his feelings about the Klan by labeling it as an "unbelievable anachronism." But he did give some consideration to the possibility that social degradation in the United States might lead to creation of a secret society using the same name.

Another interesting piece is *The Rout of the Red Mayor*. This short novel was also written by McCain when he was a commander on duty at the Bureau of Navigation, and it might be considered as having its roots in the Ku Klux Klan article mentioned above. A copyright transfer certificate exists, dated December 30, 1929, wherein *Talking Picture Magazine* assigned its rights to McCain. Thus this work must have been completed in 1928 or 1929, although the actual effort could have started as early as 1923. This fifteen-chapter novel was also to be published under the authorship of Casper Clubfoot.

The "Rout" reads as though it was intended as an adventure novel for young boys. The text is wordy and the characters are somewhat overblown—too heroic and too evil. His plot has New York City under the control of Bolsheviks and gangsters.

The heroes of the plot are, of all things, the Ku Klux Klan. In this case McCain casts the Klan as an honorable army from the South and West that converges on the city and restores honest government. This certainly has to represent an entirely different Klan from what McCain knew as a child, particularly inasmuch as McCain was known to be opposed to the Old South version.

The Bolshevik threat stayed on McCain's mind. In 1935 he addressed the Fleet Reserve Association and suggested that it could use its widespread organization to monitor communist activities throughout the United States.

McCain's promotion to captain in 1931 didn't slow his production, but he focused on military subjects and his writing became less flowery and easier to read. "The Spirit of John Paul Jones" lauds Commander F. R. King, who went down with his ship while clearing mines in the North Sea. "Bombs Revolutionize Existence" contains sweeping predictions about changes in the world due to airpower. McCain notes that "Airpower is the breath of destruction . . . On the sea, destruction is itself decisive."

"Force—Or the Lack of It," although rejected for publication by the Naval Institute in 1933, showed McCain's grasp of world social and economic forces. He points out how armed force—or the lack of it—has changed the course of history. A strong U.S. Navy and U.S. Army might have constrained England and Germany in 1914. Further, he pinpoints Japan's lack of iron and oil, and her need to expand. He laments the lack of support in the United States for strong armed forces and comments that "The day will surely come when the craft and engines of battle will be worth their weight in gold." How sadly true.

In a subsequent article "What Might Have Been," possibly written in Coco Solo around 1939, McCain again points out that we had no effective forces in 1914 and that the Naval Building Bill in 1916 came too late. He calculated that for an expenditure of $4 or $5 billion we could have avoided war entirely and would not have had to waste a much larger number of billions nor lose 100,000 young men.

McCain continued to write throughout his career. During the war he authored several newspaper and magazine articles, although these appear to be collaborative efforts.

5

AVIATION

Up to this point, Admiral John Sidney McCain, Sr., USN, has been referred to as "McCain" or "John Sidney" or just "Sidney," as the family called him. There is a Southern tradition of using middle names within the family and among friends. Thus the admiral was "Sidney" in his private life, just as his son James Gordon McCain was "Gordon." The exception was son John Jr. who was called "Jack." (He didn't want to be known as "Junior.")

Henceforth the nickname "Slew" will be introduced. Nobody admits to knowing when or where this nickname was born, but one must suspect it came from McCain's days at the Naval Academy, as did so many officers' nicknames. "Slew" appears in many anecdotes about McCain and as a salutation on a few letters. There is even one letter where the salutation is "Slue." In another reference, McCain was called "Slutsie," which probably would have been a little too "cutsie" for him if he heard about it. A few called him "Mac" and "Jock" or "Jocko" as well. But most correspondents simply called him "John."

Going Flying

In an interview later in his career, Slew McCain claimed an intense interest in aeronautics right from his graduation from the Naval Academy.[1] This certainly squared with his keen and inquiring mind. Several articles in the press set the year as 1926 when McCain became air-minded. Either way, he seems to have recognized the potential of naval airpower early in his career.

In February 1935, he mentioned in a letter, "I have definitely decided to go flying. My approved request is now in the files, and strange to say, I passed the physical 100%. While Katie does not altogether approve, she is at any rate acquiescent."

The door to McCain's entry into naval aviation was opened when the Navy recognized that it had plenty of naval officers trained as pilots, but few pilots trained for command at sea. The Navy Department decided to look for experienced commanders who might be willing to go to the naval flight program at Pensacola. The golden wings of an aviator or aviation observer were needed by those seeking command of an aircraft carrier or a naval air station. Legislation arising in the 1920s from the Morrow Board's recommendations levied this requirement. And such a command was on the path to flag rank.

During this era there were some fifty-four major ship command billets.[2] Competition for these assignments on battleships, carriers, and cruisers was fierce among the more ambitious officers in the senior ranks. John McCain had been executive officer of the battleship *New Mexico*, but his only significant ship command to date was not a major combatant ship. Rather, it was command of the *Nitro*, an ammunition hauler. Thus his decision to take the aviation route was a wise career move. It opened the door to a carrier command.

McCain wrote to a friend in January 1935: "I am thinking about applying for aviation this summer . . . not as an observer but as a pilot, and if I can not make pilot, I will not take observer. As a professional move, what do you think of the idea? I would not do it unless it was my own opinion that it would enhance my future success." The ever-aggressive Slew McCain wanted to be a pilot, not an observer. It was all or nothing with him on this issue.

Pensacola

So at age fifty, John McCain, with the rank of captain, took his place among the flight cadets.

In a 1941 letter Slew admitted, "I went into aviation in 1936, finishing the course at Pensacola with extreme difficulty." He also later commented to the press, "I never would have tried it if I'd known it was so hard to teach an old dog new tricks."[3]

The admiral's grandson, Joe McCain, relates the following anecdote, and he has no doubt that something very much like this actually happened:

> When he approached a young instructor for his first orientation flight, Captain McCain advised him in a fatherly tone, "Just treat me like any other student." The instructor came to formal attention, saluted and replied, "Aye, aye, sir!"
>
> They climbed aboard, took off, and the instructor went into a series of violent maneuvers that terrified Captain McCain. He said later that as far as he knew, the pilot had fainted, jumped out, or just plain died.
>
> Finally, the plane pulled out of the spins and loops, leveled off, and made a soft, perfect landing. According to many thoroughly amused witnesses, a completely disoriented Captain McCain fumbled with the harness, pulled himself out of the cockpit, and stumbled off the wing to the tarmac. When McCain regained his senses, the young pilot came to attention again, saluted properly, and asked, "Did I do as ordered, sir? Not worry about you being a captain?"
>
> McCain, with all the blood drained from his face, nevertheless saluted back and said, "You did just fine, Lieutenant. Thank you."
>
> And then, according to witnesses, McCain went behind a building and discharged his last few meals. When he returned, white-faced, he commented wryly to one of his fellow captains, "You know, you're never too damned old to get a lesson in leadership."

This period of McCain's career probably was not considered a highlight by the future admiral, although he appears to be the sort of person who took tough times philosophically. His record of aviation training shows marks of 3.49 to 3.84 in ground school. The Navy uses a 4.00 grading system, so these are at the 90 percent level. But the grades for flight school were from 2.80 to 3.15 (the higher in fighting planes), a grade level of 70 percent. His final mark was 3.22 (the 80 percent level), and his record shows him qualified as a catapult pilot.

Reportedly he was an eager student but somewhat mechanical. It seems that the aviation cadets at the time liked to buzz the family housing area with a dive and a blip of the throttle. But, if a plane flew by conservatively at a constant altitude and speed, that was Slew McCain. Once a landing three pastures away from the runway produced a torrent of profanity directed at the Stearman trainer and its instruments.[4]

Before graduation, McCain was sent on temporary duty as an observer aboard several aircraft carriers. He left Pensacola on April 18, 1936, and arrived in San Diego on April 21st. After checking in with the Commander of Aircraft, Battle Force, aboard the USS *Saratoga*, he reported aboard the USS *Lexington* where he was greeted by Captain Aubrey Fitch, a classmate and friend of McCain's who had earned his wings in 1930 at age 46. Their paths were destined to cross many times. Then McCain spent nearly two weeks aboard the USS *Ranger*, and returned to Pensacola on June 10th.

Even though his performance in flight school might not have been pleasant for an achiever like McCain, he persevered and was awarded the wings of a naval aviator. He was certified as Naval Aviator number 4280 in August 1936—at age 52!

Bill Halsey had faced the same challenges a year earlier. He had been offered command of the carrier *Saratoga*, but in order to command the carrier, Halsey had to successfully complete aviation observer training at Pensacola. During his training he finagled a change in designation from student observer to student pilot, thinking that he gained a better appreciation of a pilot's problems as a pilot himself.[5] Bill Halsey was "winged" on May 15, 1935 at the age of 52 and a half. Both Halsey and McCain are recognized as among the oldest persons to have received wings. Halsey nosed out McCain on the list by six months. Neither were proficient pilots, but they became skilled wielders of naval air power.

This program of flight training for senior surface officers did not solve all the problems. Resentments, sometimes intense, developed on the part of the old-time aviators directed at the newcomers. All through World War II, pilots contended that naval aviators were not getting their fair share of commands. Theodore Taylor comments in his biography of Marc Mitscher about "synthetic aviators." Mitscher was a "pilot," Halsey and McCain were "flyers." But it is interesting to note that near the end of his book Taylor classifies McCain as one of "three big names in naval tactics."[6]

Clearly their late entry into naval aviation did nothing to diminish the ability of Halsey and McCain to achieve stunning victories over the Japanese.

Coco Solo

Captain McCain's first aviation duty after winning his wings was in the Panama Canal Zone. He left Pensacola on September 17, 1936, for New Orleans, and he most likely detoured to Carrollton and Teoc for a few days leave. On October 10th he and the family took passage from New Orleans on the United Fruit Line's steamship SS *Sixaola*. He reported in to the Fleet Air Base at Coco Solo on October 19th and relieved Commander Sam Ginder as Commander Aircraft Squadrons and Attending Craft, as well as commanding officer of the Fleet Air Base.

A warm welcome awaited the McCains. Ginder sent a message: "The house is ready for immediate occupancy. In fact I will arrange for the serving of breakfast in your quarters on Friday, 16 October."

For a brief period, John Sidney's command at Coco Solo and son Jack's duty in the Canal Zone overlapped. Grandpa McCain was able to get acquainted with his first grandson, John Sidney McCain III. His daughter-in-law, Roberta, observed that Sidney was able to create harmony and better working relationships between the flyers and submariners in the Canal Zone, undoubtedly due to having a foot in both camps. He wouldn't allow any one-upmanships from either bunch.

Senator McCain includes a comment in his book about his grandfather's flying proficiency at Coco Solo: "The base prayed for his safe return each time he flew."[7] But flying was not the principal purpose of McCain's assignment; his time in Panama appears to have been somewhat of a holding pattern while the carrier command situation was sorted out. His first aviation duty after Pensacola was penciled in to be commanding officer of the USS *Yorktown* (CV-5), but the *Yorktown* was delayed in commissioning until September 1937. So Slew marked time at Coco Solo, all the while chomping at the bit for a sea command.

By December 1936 the pot was merrily boiling about the next

duty station. In a letter he commented: "Halsey may be detached from the *Saratoga*, if selected for admiral, which he has been, and myself ordered to her in January." In February 1937 Slew wrote to a friend: "I lost out on the *Saratoga*. Billy Halsey is staying until July."

In the meantime the main task on McCain's plate was preparation for extended flight exercises. Admiral Ernest J. King, then Commander, Aircraft, Base Force, and a key man in Slew's future, arrived at Coco Solo in February 1937 aboard the USS *Wright*. King was McCain's boss at this time, and King's chief of staff at this point was Commander Charles A. Pownall. McCain offered King and Pownall the hospitality of his home while they were in port.

The exercises ran from late February through mid-March. McCain was pleased that "Admiral King has inspected the station and has expressed himself in rather enthusiastic terms with respect to conditions, appearance, etc. If we operate well in the forthcoming maneuvers, I will have made a powerful and enduring friend. We have some nice problems for the exercise which, on paper, we have solved to our satisfaction. It remains to be seen how the practice will work out."

It looks like McCain's plans worked out just fine. His fitness report included the following: "His participation in extended flight exercises in the Caribbean in February–March 1937 was marked by keen appreciation of the problems involved and by eminently satisfactory conduct of operations assigned to his control."

John Sidney commented to his brother Joe in March 1937:

I received your letter at the end of extensive war maneuvers on the Caribbean. . . . We flew over nine thousand miles and fought many bloody engagements all around the fringe of the Caribbean and Leeward Islands, where the French, English, and Spanish fought so many battles.

I am detached from here in May, ordered to the command of the *Lexington*. Though I have not seen the wording of my orders, it seems likely that I may come by New Orleans and get to see you all for a day or two.

About this time, April 1937, McCain took time out to write to son Jack with some advice about getting along with a new commanding officer and about Navy service in general. This letter, even with a few errors and unclear references, opens the door just a little bit more on John McCain's character and ideals:

> I received your letter of recent date and have read it very carefully. I don't think that you need worry about your new commanding officer ruining your submarine record. Most young officers lack the assurance or the confidence in their own judgment to give a junior an excellent report based on short experience. Your report was a very good report and was nothing whatever to be ashamed of.
>
> Also Son, any Naval duty is good duty and any Naval duty is excellent duty if the officer concerned makes it so; so quit worrying, buckle down and make your training boat the best training boat that ever was.
>
> If he wants snappy salutes and pressed uniforms, let him have them; it is his privilege to want those things and your duty to deliver them. Your attitude toward enlisted men I know to be absolutely correct. In this regard, change your manner, but not your heart. In other words, in those things which you received comparatively low marks, make sure that they are raised in the next report and by so doing you can make no more favorable impression on the reviewing authorities . . .
>
> You are probably a little too proud about the way you do your job so that you have a tendency to resent advice and criticism from a superior, particularly a new superior. Your superior has the same right that you have over your inferiors, that is, he wants a job done in a certain way just as you do. It is your business to do it his way just as you make it the business of the people under you to do theirs your way. Permit such small matters to run off of you like water off a duck's back. You can be too sensitive in the Navy; fight against it.
>
> Study his criticisms and take those to heart which you know to be sound. As for the others, do the job to suit him . . . but reserve your own independent judgment. For instance, smart clothes and a military manner are very desirable attributes.

When you go under a new superior you should handle yourself with reserve, study him and do not, in the beginning, try to force your ideas or ways of doing things on him; figure him out just as you do the men under you.

All these things can be done without sacrificing your self respect or deviating from your principles. So I don't think you have anything to worry about in reality.

How are your drinking habits? I have not had a drink in two months and two days.

I expect to leave here on 8 May, go by Mississippi and take command of the *Ranger* in 1 June. We will live in Coronado. I much prefer the *Ranger* to the *Lexington*.

How are John Sidney, 3rd, Sandra and Roberta??

McCain was also looking out after son Gordon in Washington, where he had arranged for Gordon to have privileges at the Army-Navy Club. He wrote Gordon about bills from the club and Gordon's share of the debt. He reassured Gordon, "I believe your mother beat me to this piece of mail, so I guess she saw your chits; however, don't lose any sleep over it."

USS *Ranger*

As he mentioned in his letter to his son Jack, Captain McCain got the USS *Ranger* (CV-4) instead of *Lexington*. Although he puzzled about the change from *Lexington* to *Ranger*, he preferred the assignment he received. He commented, "It has not the sky line nor the prestige, but it is a better boat for the purpose."

So after just seven months at Coco Solo, the McCains pulled up stakes and headed for San Diego. John Sidney wrote to his brother Bill that he would be arriving in New Orleans aboard the SS *Sixaola* and planned to "motor across the continent, stopping in San Diego to plant Kate and Catherine." McCain and family were able to spend a few days of leave with Luther Spencer in Carrollton and with his brother Joe at Teoc.

On June 5, 1937, while the *Ranger* was moored in San Diego, Captain John S. McCain relieved Captain Patrick N.L. Bellinger as commanding officer. A simple flight-deck ceremony was held. Pat

Bellinger and John McCain were to work together again in the future as flag officers.[8] McCain's boss, once again, was Vice Admiral Ernest J. King as Commander, Aircraft, Battle Force. McCain's executive officer on *Ranger* was Commander Alfred E. Montgomery, who later served with the fast carriers in the Pacific war.

The pre-war Navy was really a very small club. The same names kept popping up as senior officers moved through commands. Montgomery, Fitch, Bellinger, Towers, Nimitz, and Halsey are all examples. All would serve with or around one another in World War II.

The *Ranger* was the first vessel in the United States Navy designed and built from scratch as an aircraft carrier. Earlier carriers—*Langley*, *Lexington,* and *Saratoga*—were converted from other ship types. One of the direct benefits of the 1922 Washington Naval Treaty, with its ten-year ban on construction of capital ships, was the conversion of two 33,000-ton battle cruiser hulls into the aircraft carriers *Lexington* and *Saratoga*. These two large, fast carriers were the precursors of the fast carriers that so dominated the Pacific in World War II.

The *Ranger* was laid down in 1931 and commissioned on June 4, 1934, in Newport News, Virginia. Her 14,500-ton displacement was less than half that of *Lexington* and *Saratoga*. Further, *Ranger* was slower; she was too small for four propeller shafts, and her twin-shaft configuration delivered only 29.5 knots. Also, cost considerations had restricted elevator capacity, ammunition storage, and the number of deck catapults. On the other hand, she had efficient arresting gear and carried a full complement of planes. *Ranger's* flight deck was rectangular—not curved to match the curve of the hull. Thus she had additional flight deck area as compared to her big sisters. This feature was carried over to all new carriers for the next twenty years.[9]

Ranger, like *Lexington* and *Saratoga,* was an offspring of the Washington Naval Treaty. Carrier tonnage was allocated in the same manner as the battleships, in a 5:5:3 ratio. That gave the U.S. and Britain 135,000 tons each, with 81,000 tons for Japan. *Lexington* and *Saratoga* ate up 66,000 tons, so the Naval Planning Board opted to use the balance for five smaller carriers. But the Great Depression took center stage and only one small carrier, *Ranger,* was built. Thus *Ranger* was not a direct predecessor of the light carriers and escort carriers of World War II. She turned out to be more of a one-time test bed of carrier features.[10] She gave skipper John McCain a lot of food for thought.

Good Will Tour

For the first three months after Captain McCain took over, *Ranger* operated in the San Diego area, conducting training and carrier qualifications for the airmen. In early July, three of her squadrons were reassigned to *Lexington* to take part in the search for aviators Amelia Earhart and Fred Noonan, who had gone missing in the central Pacific.

On September 4 *Ranger* departed San Diego for a good will trip to South America. She crossed the equator on September 12, 1937. Captain McCain officially welcomed Neptunus Rex aboard for the initiation of the "Pollywogs"—those who had not crossed the equator before. The rite involved a lot of electrical devices and cold water. McCain, a pollywog, was certified as a "shellback" that day. One wonders how the skipper was handled during the ceremonies.

Ranger arrived in Callao, Peru, on September 15. The time there was filled with the expected rounds of receptions and parties. *Ranger's* planes flew over Lima on the 17th in an impressive display of naval air power.

On the visit to Peru, McCain was awarded the "Cruz Peruana de Aviacion" on September 16, 1937, and the "El Sol de Peru" on September 21st. Although both were presented to Captain McCain by the president of Peru in Lima, he could not "officially" accept them until he received a go-ahead from Congress in 1940.

Home Again, Briefly

Captain McCain brought *Ranger* back to San Diego on October 5th. Then it was off to Bremerton on the 27th for overhaul at the Puget Sound Naval Shipyard. She returned to San Diego on January 31, 1938, for local operations and training until March 15th, when she departed for Fleet Problem XIX.[11]

Fleet exercises under or simulated against Ernest King were always important events. King remained a demon at exercises; he was constantly determined to win. McCain had already worked under King in the Caribbean exercises and now, under carrier commander Vice

Admiral King, participated in the 1938 West Coast drills.

Early on in the exercise, *Ranger's* planes (as part of the White fleet) "attacked" and damaged *Lexington* (in the Black fleet) off the West Coast. Later, off Hawaii, as part of the Blue fleet, *Ranger* covered troop landings on French Frigate Shoals. Next she provided air coverage for the troop landings at Lahaina, Maui. Then *Ranger* "suffered" serious damage from a patrol plane bombing attack. In the last phase of the exercise, *Ranger* (now in the Green fleet) was fatally torpedoed by Purple destroyers, but she struck back and put all four out of action before "sinking."[12]

Ranger was back in San Diego by the end of April. She was involved in West Coast operations for the rest of the year including a fourth of July visit to Monterey with Admiral King aboard. Assignments also included the first test-firing of antiaircraft guns against a radio-controlled drone target aircraft. There also was a presidential review in San Francisco, and a brief dry-dock stay at Hunter's Point.

Ranger departed San Diego in January 1939 for winter fleet operations in the Caribbean. There she took part in Fleet Problem XX. As part of the Black Fleet, McCain ran close-in antisubmarine and long-range scouting patrols. Unlike Fleet Problem XIX, when the carriers were given some leeway for independent operations, during Problem XX the flattops were more closely linked to the main battle force. On February 25, *Ranger's* aircraft "sunk" *Enterprise* and a destroyer with the "loss" of fifteen planes. She later "lost" seven bombers in an attack on three battleships of the White main body. On the 27th *Ranger* was attacked by *Yorktown* planes and suffered no damage, but McCain was moved to comment about the vulnerability of carriers operating close to the main body.[13]

When the exercise was completed in mid-March, *Ranger* plied the Caribbean for a few weeks and then sailed to her new home port in Norfolk, where she arrived on April 12. She visited New York as part of the World's Fair celebration in May, and then returned to Norfolk for a scheduled overhaul.[14]

Captain McCain was relieved as commanding officer by Captain-selectee Ralph Wood on June 3, 1939. The McCain record as commanding officer of the USS *Ranger* seems top-notch. In 1939 his fitness report included these remarks: "A keen, capable officer of high personal and military character. His leadership and enthusiastic devotion to his command has been reflected in the excellent performance of *Ranger* (decidedly a smart ship) and her squadrons during the present cruise."

Carrier Tactics (I)

John McCain has never been given a lot of credit for his innovative thinking about carriers and carrier tactics. Although he undoubtedly started to think early in his aviation career about how carriers should be designed and utilized, it was as skipper of the *Ranger* that he was able to effectively enter the debates.

The series of fleet exercises in the 1930s yielded many lessons, such as the need for both large carriers for major operations and small carriers for escort duty and minor operations. The small carrier role was not dissimilar to that which evolved in World War II for the CVE escort carriers.[15]

A main question in the late 1930s was whether or not the carriers should remain with the surface battle force or operate independently. Tying the carriers to the main body prevented them from using their superior speed for evasive action. Further, the unarmored carriers in the battle line could be subjected to direct bombardment from the enemy fleet. But traditional thinking held that the carriers were a vital part of the main body for submarine protection and scouting.

On the other hand, carriers operating independently could engage enemy carriers and win control of the air. Without control of the air, there could be no security for the battle line.[16] Beyond that, Rear Admiral Joseph Mason Reeves had demonstrated the deadly potential of air attacks from free-ranging carriers against shore facilities (in this case, the Panama Canal locks) during Fleet Problem IX in 1929.[17]

This was an issue of the *defensive* use of carriers (in the battle line) versus the *offensive* use of carriers (acting independently). These very terms would arise again about the use of carriers in World War II, with McCain firmly espousing the *offensive* role.

But in 1938, McCain's thinking was still evolving. He specifically suggested that small carriers could operate in the battle line of battleships and cruisers, moving quickly out of the battle line to launch planes and then moving quickly back to gain the protection of the big guns before the enemy could strike back.[18]

He also suggested that the baby flattops have armored decks, a topic that he pursued in his dogged way for many years.

North Island

Following his departure from *Ranger* on June 3, McCain reported on July 1, 1939 as commanding officer of the Naval Air Station, San Diego, better known as North Island. One month's pay advance was now up to $500.

The Naval Air Station, San Diego, was a major command. In fact, it was the only naval air station on the West Coast until Alameda was opened in November 1940. When McCain took over, the station was manned by 50 officers, 998 enlisted men, and 1,107 civilians. The command also encompassed fourteen outlying fields and two islands, San Clemente and San Nicholas.

A new radio-equipped air operations tower went into service under McCain; and the Assembly and Repair Department, the Supply Department, the paved landing areas, and the airplane taxi lanes were all expanded.

North Island was home to the Pacific carrier fleet as well. The *Enterprise, Saratoga, Lexington, Yorktown,* and *Ranger* all were in and out as operations demanded, often shuttling back and forth to Hawaii. The loading of aircraft onto the carriers was an amazing sight. The squadrons taxied down the street leading to the dock in a long single file to wait for the flight-deck crane to hoist them aboard.[19]

Slew's tenure as commanding officer of North Island was full of civic and social events, as expected of the commander of a principal naval facility in a navy town. He was active with the San Diego Chamber of Commerce and addressed the Junior Chamber several times. There were luncheons at the Cuyamaca Club for various dignitaries, and he was given a season pass to the Del Mar Turf Club.

On the Navy side, McCain dealt with the problems of construction and maintenance of facilities as well as personnel training, aircraft repair, ferry service between San Diego and North Island, and getting scheduled aircraft overhauls done on time. The scope of problems ranged from minor (space for the disbursing office) to major (the risk of concentrating aircraft and carriers in San Diego). A number of snippy letters exist between Rear Admiral Jack Towers, then chief of the Bureau of Aeronautics, and Captain McCain about issues such as office and barracks space. In one letter Towers berated McCain: "It appears to me that you are still obsessed with the idea that San Diego will continue to be the aviation center of the Navy." One can imagine the strain between an energetic commander on one coast and a stern boss far across the country. But beyond that, Towers was not likely to be favorably disposed toward classmate McCain because McCain was a newcomer to aviation, not one of the old-timers; and because he was moving into the orbit of Admiral Ernest King, with whom Towers had a strong rivalry.

Although he was now out of the loop on officer personnel matters, his specialty in Washington, McCain kept up a lively correspondence with friends and superiors. A lot of this pertained to the equalization principles he had developed to achieve a balance in numbers and promotions between the general line officers and the specialist staff officers.

On the lighter side, an anecdote about Slew recounts that he was in his office on the base one day when he heard the fire siren. He waved out the window to stop the fire truck. Then he ran out and jumped into the driver's seat, elbowed the driver aside, and drove off to the emergency himself.[20]

Armored Decks

A continuing campaign for McCain during this period was his recommendation that carrier flight decks be armored. He wanted the decks to stop a 500-pound bomb. Further, McCain recommended that all planes should be carried on the protected hangar deck except for two or three manned topside for emergency launching. Massed planes on the flight deck, he felt, were an invitation to disaster. While this scheme required the fitting of catapults and high-speed cantilevered elevators, Slew pointed out that an armored flight deck had saved the HMS *Illustrious* from destruction in battle off of Norway.

Earlier McCain had championed the small carrier. Now he took heed of the Navy's experience with the limited design of his baby, the 14,500-ton *Ranger*. Navy leadership was convinced that carriers should be larger—20,000 tons and up. Because of treaty limitations, the *Wasp* (CV-7) was built at 14,700 tons, but she was superior to *Ranger* and was used as a full-fledged fleet carrier. Later the escort carriers were built on cargo hulls to meet urgent needs during the war, and light carriers were built on cruiser hulls; but larger carriers were favored as the basic design.

Now McCain proposed an even larger carrier of sufficient size to absorb the additional weight of an armored deck located some forty feet above the waterline, thus not compromising stability. His proposal spoke of operating against shore-based enemy planes (an anathema for carriers even through World War II) in a future war. He suggested: "For instance, if we were moving westward, the fleet could lay on the northern flank of the Mandated Islands while armored flight deck carriers and light forces, plus an occasional heavy vessel, cleared out all the opposition in those islands—and it wouldn't take long either." The "Mandated Islands" he mentions were the Japanese-controlled Carolines, Marshalls, and Marianas.

McCain lost that round, writing "I suppose I am beaten in this matter for this time, but I still am not convinced . . . I shall not quit, but feel unable to do anything more at the present moment." His dream was fulfilled, however, in 1942 when the Navy placed the order for the USS *Midway*, a 45,000-ton armored deck carrier. Also, the value of armored flight decks was demonstrated in the closing months of the war when British carriers with armored decks were able to remain in action even when hit heavily by the Japanese suicide planes.[21]

Late in 1939 Captain McCain underwent his annual physical examination for flying. His left eye was going bad about this time. Physical examinations showed 2/20 vision (instead of the required 20/20), but the deficit was corrected by eyeglasses. The physical exam resulted in a letter from Chester Nimitz, who then headed the Bureau of Navigation, setting limits on Slew's flying. It might be thought that this letter had a humorous vein: "The Bureau of Navigation considers you physically and temperamentally qualified for duty involving flying in actual control of aircraft only when accompanied by a co-pilot. In view of a certain defect of vision which the Bureau of Medicine and Surgery has noted in your case, you are hereby directed to utilize fully the services of this co-pilot. You will not only fully indoctrinate him, but you will turn over control of the airplane to him in all situations wherein your defect of vision interferes with safe and efficient control of the airplane."

Slew probably did not get involved in any grandstanding in the air, but this letter certainly made sure that he wouldn't in the future should the spirit move him.

Also about this time, Slew got into another issue typical of his tenacity. He'd get his teeth into something and was loath to let go. This issue was not about the Navy, however. It concerned one of his favorite pastimes—horse-racing. He sent letters to several people, including Captain Dan Callaghan, senior naval aide to the President, about the dissemination of racetrack news. He stated: "Gambling, as you know, is a primal human instinct. I have been following the races for thirty years for many reasons, which I may quote for publication; but actually I'd rather pick a long shot to beat a favorite with $2.00 on the nose than most any other form of amusement." Slew went on to support real-time broadcast of lineups, odds, and race results directly from the tracks. Then he commented: "Don't think I am unacquainted with my subject. I've bet on the ponies for over a quarter of a century. I have done it at the clubhouse, on racetracks with and surrounded by the better element—senators, judges, high social figures. I have done it in other surroundings too, in company with all varieties of human society. So I do know that such a procedure as indicated [broadcasting race results] would tremendously benefit the public morals."

But the signal event during this period was John McCain's arrival in the zone for promotion to flag rank. His name came before a board of admirals to be considered along with officers of similar seniority for promotion to rear admiral. He commented to his close friend Commander Francis S. "Frog" Low, perhaps with some prescience, "If the Board does not select me I shall still maintain that selection is the only method for the Navy."

Passed Over

December 1939 brought the crushing news that Captain John McCain had not been selected for flag rank; he had been "passed over." His files are full of letters from friends questioning the wisdom of the selection board. Slew replied to one such note from his classmate Aubrey Fitch, who had been selected: "At any rate, Jake, whatever may be said of the others, between you and me, they made no mistake in selecting you."

Looking ahead to the selection process in 1940, McCain commented: "I am collecting a bunch of heavy artillery . . . for the next engagement in December. But I refuse to do any hoping."

In February 1940 Slew wrote to a fellow officer with his perspective on the issues: "While all officers passed over have many alibis, I will give mine briefly so that you may use it as ammunition. There is little or nothing on my record to indicate the constructive nature of the personnel work which I did from 1918 through and including the summer of 1935. I can truthfully state that all naval personnel legislation during that period was prepared by myself and most of it was originated by me. This was arduous work. I have gathered the idea that some members of the [selection] board concluded that my tours of duty in Washington were occupied in holding hands. I understand that two members asked if I did not do some important personnel work. There was nothing on the record to indicate such. Probably the distinguished chiefs of bureau who signed my fitness reports during the periods in question, which reports are excellent. . . concluded that everyone knew what I was doing. Possibly the reports were written exactly as they intended they should be. I intend to find out and, if possible, to round out the record. For that purpose I may be east in April and will call on you. The Equalization Bill was passed over many strenuous line objectors. That, I conclude, was my best piece of work; but if the Admirals disagree, I cannot criticize their stand."

And in another letter: "I have given deep thought as to why I was passed over. My record at sea is second to none whatever. On shore I was always mixed up with controversial items necessarily, and made bitter critics as well as firm friends. I somehow feel that I have been punished for my legislative activities, which may or may not be wrong. I can, however, assure your that nowhere public or private is there anything to my discredit."

Because augmenting one's records before a selection board could create an adverse reaction, Slew was very careful that discretion and judgment be used to insure that his record accurately reflected his accomplishments. In essence, McCain asked some of his friends to go to bat for him, and they delivered.

His fitness report for 1940 stated: "I cannot say too much in praise of Captain McCain's command of the Naval Air Station, San Diego."

McCain felt that Admiral Ernest King, although King had given him outstanding reports, could have mentioned more about his conduct of the forces under his command in fleet maneuvers. So Admiral King supplemented John McCain's record with a comment about his command of the Fleet Air Base, Coco Solo: "You have cleaned up a mess down there—and your administration throughout has been a brilliant success."

Admiral King also stated, regarding McCain's performance on the *Ranger*, "You are the most competent and resourceful captain of my acquaintance." Further, regarding fleet exercises, King observed, "Whether with me or against me he handled his forces with skill, decision, and good fortune."

John McCain also enlisted the help of his former boss, retired Rear Admiral R.H. Leigh to supplement his records about his duties in Washington. Admiral Leigh was a close family friend of McCain's and a real Navy heavyweight. He was Commander-in-Chief of the U.S. Fleet in the early 1930s as well as a fast friend of Ernest King's. Leigh's letter added luster to the record of important facts about McCain's accomplishments in Washington.

McCain had also worked for William D. Leahy in Washington in the early 1920s and on the *New Mexico* in 1926. In 1940 Leahy was Governor of Puerto Rico, and he had been Chief of Naval Operations until his retirement in 1939. Admiral Leahy agreed to write a letter to be included in McCain's record, but warned, "I have been on many selection boards and it is my considered opinion that such a letter would do more harm than good to your prospects." McCain did not want the letter "for any effort toward sweetening my record but merely that he [Leahy] state that I was responsible for the Equalization Bill, the Britten Bill, and other constructive personnel plans." The final product from Leahy, however, didn't look right to Slew. So he prevailed upon Admiral Nimitz, then chief of the Bureau of Navigation, to look it over. Nimitz agreed that the letter wouldn't do the job and, inasmuch as McCain had requested it in the first place, he had it set aside.

Selected!

All of this worked. McCain's friends and mentors came through. His records were supplemented to fully reflect his work. On December 2, 1940, John S. McCain's name appeared on the list for promotion to rear admiral.

6

FLAG RANK

When the flag officer selection board saw the error of its ways and finally selected John Sidney McCain, it seemed like the whole Navy rejoiced. McCain's records contain a file of congratulatory messages two and a half inches thick, with more than 250 letters and cards.

Among the replies to these messages was a note from McCain to Admiral Harold Stark with the words, "Your telegram was my first notification. I am deeply honored that the Chief of Naval Operations should have thus remembered me, and I am saving the telegram."

McCain related to his friend Commander Frog Low, "It was more 'chancy' in my case than it was in yours," and to Commander Matt Gardner, "I was surprised last time when they passed me and I was equally surprised this time when they promoted me." Soon Gardner would receive orders to be McCain's chief of staff.

Handwritten notes came from classmates Frank Jack Fletcher and Isaac "Cap" Kidd. Another note said, "Last year it appeared to be a matched race between you and Fitch with a toss of the coin to decide the winner. This year in an open race you came through in grand style to the deep gratification of all your friends."

Also among the congratulations was a note from Chester Nimitz that stated: "The result, when your name was reached, was never in doubt in my mind." There was also a cryptic postscript regarding $1.00 [a wager?] that had arrived and already had been spent.

Captain McCain thought he would "make his number" in February 1941 and be detached from North Island in June. Things moved much faster than that. He received the following radio message from the Bureau of Navigation: "Executive order signed January twenty three designates Captain John S. McCain as ComAirScoFor with rank of rear admiral effective on date he assumes command of ComAirScoFor and directs him to assume rank and hoist flag of rear admiral on date he assumes above command."

The appointment letters as Commander, Aircraft, Scouting Force, Pacific Fleet (ComAirScoFor) that followed were signed by Franklin Roosevelt, Secretary of the Navy Frank Knox, and Chester Nimitz. McCain expressed his thanks for a "splendid detail" to Nimitz and told King, "I hope I assimilated enough under you to make a success of this job."

What a thrill it must have been for John McCain to carry out President Roosevelt's order to "hoist the flag of a rear admiral."

With flag rank, everything changed. Flag rank was the culmination of McCain's naval career—although more glory lay ahead. His relationships with more senior officers such as Jack Towers changed. He was now part of the club. He had a personal staff, and aides on that staff would make life easier for John Sidney by taking care of many of life's ordinary details and chores. But along with the honors and perquisites came the crushing level of responsibility. From now on the effects of McCain's decisions would ripple through his command, through many other parts of the Navy, and even into civilian life.

Patrol Plane Commander

Rear Admiral John S. McCain reported as Commander, Aircraft, Scouting Force, United States Pacific Fleet, on January 23, 1941, with additional duty as Commander, Patrol Wings, United States Fleet. He had under his administrative command the patrol planes based on the West Coast, Alaska, and Hawaii. His flagship was the USS *Hulbert*, but his headquarters remained in the administration building at North Island. He inherited a staff, but had to work with Jack Towers to select a new chief of staff. After sorting through a half-dozen candidates, he selected his friend Commander Matthias B. Gardner. Gardner was then executive officer on the seaplane tender USS *Wright*, which was penciled in as McCain's new flagship.

Lieutenant Herbert D. Riley became his aide and flag lieutenant. Riley appears many times through the balance of McCain's life.

Interestingly, Riley (a McCain supporter) married the beautiful and talented Marjorie Towers, the daughter of Admiral John Towers (a McCain rival and detractor).

Admiral McCain's assignment was what the Navy termed a "type" commander. He had administrative and logistical control over the patrol wings and squadrons. He occasionally could have day-to-day operational control, but more often operational control was assigned to fleet and area commanders on the scene, such as at Pearl Harbor.[1]

As Admiral McCain moved into his job, his force consisted of about forty-two Consolidated PBY Catalina patrol planes in Patrol Wing 1 in San Diego, sixty planes in Patrol Wing 2 at Kaneohe, Hawaii, and twenty-four PBYs in Patrol Wing 4 in the Pacific Northwest. Aircraft moved in and out of McCain's Test, Acceptance, and Indoctrination Unit in San Diego for transition training.

One of the new rear admiral's first official duties was a trip to Seattle to inspect Patrol Wing Four. "PatWing-4" was beginning to develop bases and move planes out to Sitka and Kodiak in Alaska.

But all was not work alone. Slew found time to visit horse race-tracks in Aqua Caliente and Los Angeles, as well as time to counsel son Jack: "Do not get yourself all worried and beat up about your prospective change of duty. If the captain wants to keep you on board, he is paying you the highest compliment he can pay you!" And to brother Joe: "The ham arrived on the same day as your letter. [We] have been eyeing it hungrily ever since."

In February, John Sidney had a one-day stay in the hospital to have a growth removed from his left eye. This was the eye that kept giving him problems. He also corresponded with son Gordon in Washington, D. C., with advice about obtaining a commission in the Navy, possibly in the legal or intelligence branch.

McCain's widespread command required substantial travel. In April he flew to Pearl Harbor, Midway, Johnston Island, and Palmyra Island to inspect Patrol Wing 2. Then it was off to a conference in Washington, DC in May. In July he toured the Alaskan bases, visiting Sitka, Kodiak, and Dutch Harbor. On this trip he inspected the proposed site of the future Whidbey Island Naval Air Station in Washington State, and was impressed with both the need for the station and the advantages of the site.

He conferred with Admiral Husband Kimmel, Commander-in-Chief of the Pacific Fleet, at Pearl Harbor in August. In September he was in Washington again, this time as senior member of a line selection board. Then it was back to Pearl Harbor in October for inspections of Patrol Wing 2 and the base at Kaneohe.

As a flag officer, McCain dealt with a wide range of issues and problems. He was concerned about getting personnel together before new planes were delivered. Training always required attention. The admiral corresponded with Jack Towers (still head of the Bureau of Aeronautics) about extending seaplane ramps using wooden platforms.

He worked with his commanders and the Bureau of Ordnance in an attempt to develop the practical use of aerial torpedoes by patrol planes. McCain was concerned that the Navy's current weapons could only be dropped from a very low altitude—75 feet—placing the launching patrol plane in a very vulnerable position. His conviction was that patrol planes were of the greatest value as long-range scouts, and he did not want them sacrificed in low-level torpedo attacks unless the need was critical. So he urged development of a torpedo that could be dropped from safer higher altitudes, as could the Italian and British weapons.

Obtaining spare parts for PBYs stationed in Hawaii was an ongoing problem. McCain wrote Rear Admiral Pat Bellinger, who commanded Patrol Wing 2 at Pearl Harbor:

> We are raising heaven and earth, not to say hell, to get the stuff you need. It seems at present there are only six generators in the whole damn United States. As they come in we will ship them out air-express.
>
> Our position here is very difficult. Just to let you know that other people have troubles, our planes are flying 12 to 14 hours a day, and this week I have got to let up because of impending exhaustion of machines and pilots . . . We are managing to train some mechanics on short hops. The pilot and radio training, except on the ground, is poor pickings.

Rear Admiral Pat Bellinger was an interesting character in the McCain story. He had been a member, with John Towers and Marc Mitscher, of the famous "NC" flight team on the first transatlantic flight in 1919. Bellinger commanded the NC-1 which made an emergency landing at sea. He and his crew were rescued by a passing freighter, and NC-1 sank three days later. McCain and Bellinger, who had graduated from Annapolis one year behind McCain, were on the friendliest of terms. They exchanged visits and copious correspondence during their duty together. As mentioned earlier, McCain had relieved Bellinger as captain of *Ranger,* and the pair undoubtedly exchanged a friendly word or two during the time Bellinger served as chief of staff to Admiral King when King was commanding the air component of the Battle Force.

Although McCain dealt with him as subordinate commander of Patrol Wing 2, Bellinger wore many hats. Simultaneously he held three assignments as a force commander plus an assignment as liaison to the Fourteenth Naval District. He was responsible to five superiors, including McCain, and various task force commanders. Bellinger noted in January 1941: "I was surprised to find that here in the Hawaiian Islands . . . we are operating on a shoestring and the more I looked the thinner the shoestring appeared to be."

Bellinger co-authored the Martin-Bellinger Report, dated March 31, 1941, which presented a plan for joint action in the event of an attack on Oahu. The report was right on the money. The document pointed out that the most likely and dangerous form of attack would be a carrier-based air attack preceded by a surprise submarine attack. The report noted: "The aircraft at present available in Hawaii are inadequate to maintain, for any extended period, from bases on Oahu, a patrol extensive enough to ensure that an air attack from an Orange [Japanese] carrier cannot arrive over Oahu as a complete surprise."[2]

Through the summer of 1941, McCain fought big battles about personnel. Many Pacific Fleet radiomen and machinist mates were ordered to the Atlantic fleet, leaving McCain and his patrol wing commanders without sufficient radiomen to man their 110 planes. McCain wrote to Admiral Kimmel, Commander-in-Chief of the Pacific Fleet:

I enclose herewith a letter from the Fleet Personnel officer directing transfers which, if effective, will strip the Pacific Forces . . ."

There was no intimation of this blow coming . . . It had been my hope if not a precise understanding that the Atlantic wings would train for new Atlantic squadrons; evidently this is not the case.

The loss in radiomen and machinist mates is a body blow to our proposed pre-fleet and transitional training. However, we do not intend to quit on the job; we simply intend to make new plans and push them as energetically as possible.

Washington had declared a "Europe first" policy to save England. The Pacific Fleet, facing a *potential* danger from Japan, was robbed to build up the Atlantic Fleet, which faced the *demonstrated* danger from Germany. Newly constructed ships would be manned with 72 percent of the crew from the Pacific and 28 percent from the Atlantic.[3] There simply were not enough experienced pilots and aircrew, nor parts and armament, for McCain's and Bellinger's patrol planes.

In June 1941, Slew sent a letter to Nimitz to complain about training and this serious loss of personnel. He received a note in return from his old skipper on the *Panay* with the following handwritten note at the bottom: "Cheer up! Kindest regards and best wishes."

During this period McCain expressed his confidence in Pat Bellinger (and showed his own leadership style): "You may speak your piece whenever your opinion is asked without regard to agreement with me. I haven't seen your letter yet, nor indeed any of the letters, but you can rest assured that I will find no fault with you."

Pearl Harbor

Friday, December 5, 1941, was a routine day. McCain wrote to his boss, Vice Admiral Wilson Brown, Commander, Scouting Force, about assigning twelve planes to work with the Army on an air attack and interceptor exercise scheduled for December 11–16. The exercise was to test the air attack warning system on the West Coast. McCain could only provide three planes due to the meager resources available to him in Alameda and San Diego. Even though he wanted to assist the Army, he regretted losing even those three planes from the training schedule.

On Sunday, December 7, Sidney and Kate were at the veterinarian's office. When they returned home, McCain's aide was waiting with the news of the attack. McCain was not surprised. Not many in the Navy were surprised that Japan had attacked.

In a brief mention in a late-December letter to his daughter-in-law, John Sidney wrote: "Tell Gordon the Pearl Harbor incident missed me altogether." But it didn't miss Admiral McCain's planes. Dramatic photos show shredded and burning PBY patrol planes on Ford Island and at Kaneohe. Pat Bellinger, wearing his hat as Commander, Task Force 9 (which included both Patrol Wing 1 and Patrol Wing 2), reported his damages to Admiral Kimmel on December 20. Of the fifty-four task force patrol planes not in the air and quickly available to him at Pearl Harbor and Kaneohe, only one escaped damage. Squadron personnel put forth heroic efforts during and after the attack. The crews quickly patched up one of a group of planes that were undergoing repair plus three of the freshly damaged aircraft and threw everything they had into searches for the Japanese.[4]

Meanwhile, on the West Coast, there were fears of Japanese air and submarine attacks, and even invasion. Some could envision the enemy landing on the California coast and, with little opposition, marching straight to the White House to dictate surrender terms. McCain didn't waste any time getting into action. In a subsequent report to Admiral John W. Greenslade, commandant of the Twelfth Naval District (headquartered in San Francisco), McCain summarized his initial actions: "By 12 o'clock on Sunday, the 7th, it was apparent to me that immediate and effective measures must be taken to organize and deploy available forces at San Diego. I called a conference of fleet unit commanders and also requested the presence of the chief of staff and operations officer of the Eleventh Naval District. An agreement was reached and plans placed into effect."

McCain reported forces available as four submarines, nine destroyers, fourteen patrol planes, seventeen fighters and scout bombers, four Army bombers, and ten to twenty-eight Army fighters. He also reported his own status as "sea-going." War plans provided for Bellinger to shift his command to Midway and McCain to shift to Pearl Harbor, but those moves were placed on hold.

On December 10, Admiral Greenslade formally designated McCain as Commander, Southern California Sector, Southern Coastal Frontier. He directed McCain to continue operations under his own initiative. At the same time, McCain served as acting commandant of the Eleventh Naval District from December 9 through 18 as officers were reassigned.

On December 17th McCain recommended to Admiral Kimmel that each capital ship carry one or more catapult fighters, and that they be loaded in secrecy "in view of the efficient spy system there will be in Hawaii." He also reminded Kimmel to "get me into the fight as soon as possible."

With his eye on coastal defense, McCain corresponded with Jack Towers at the Bureau of Aeronautics about getting long-range land-based heavy bombers for the Navy, and using San Clemente Island as a fog-free patrol base. Towers assured McCain that the bombers were in the program but lamented that training had stopped. He also stated his personal opinion that a great deal of hysteria had been evident on the West Coast. Slew replied: "There is no hysteria or even fear . . . on the contrary; the civilian attitude here is one of polite curiosity and concern as to what is going on, intermingled with absolute confidence in the Navy."

In early January 1942 McCain submitted a letter citing the out-standing performance of Captain Earnest L. Gunther, McCain's relief as commanding officer the Naval Air Station, San Diego. McCain lauded Captain Gunther's work in berthing, feeding, and supplying some 4,000 additional personnel from the Marine Corps and the Army assigned to North Island. Gun emplacements were built, communications set up, and command posts established. Revetments for plane protection and trenches for the shelter of personnel were constructed on North Island and outlying fields.

During January 1942 McCain kept the screws down on his patrol planes. By directive he made it clear that while the "primary mission of patrolling aircraft is to inform proper authority of the presence, action, and movements of enemy forces . . . against enemy submarines the patrol planes should . . . attack first and report immediately afterwards." He saw the difference between success and failure as being a matter of split seconds.

There was a lot of correspondence in January between McCain and Pat Bellinger to discuss scouting tactics and search patterns. After plotting Bellinger's air search plans for the Hawaiian area, McCain suggested that the morning sortie begin shortly before daylight and extend out to a 400 mile range by eleven o'clock. That search and the return trip would provide coverage until nightfall. McCain didn't believe that a night attack on Hawaii had much chance of success. He pointed out that although the scheme exposed the Islands to a dawn attack, Bellinger had a good chance of picking up an enemy flight coming in, and could find and destroy the attacker's carrier bases.

McCain gave two reasons for his strategy. First, it would give much-needed rest to Bellinger's hard-pressed pilots and planes. He admitted that his second reason was a bit more far-fetched. He believed that if this form of search was kept up regularly for three or four weeks, leaving at the same time and coming back at the same time, the Japanese might be tempted to make another try at Hawaii. In McCain's words: "As a cold-blooded proposition and if the decision rested with me alone, I would endeavor to try to invite an attack in order to make certain of getting the attacking carrier or carriers. Therefore, the second reason is that a form of search of this kind might be used as a ruse."

McCain told Bellinger to use his suggestions as his judgment dictated, and he also sent his regards to Admirals Brown and Nimitz.

McCain added to Bellinger a few days later: "I agree that our lack of the sinews of war is deplorable, particularly in view of our long anticipation of such event. This disadvantage however has been due in a large measure to a policy which has been entirely beyond our control and certainly should occasion no surprise among those who have thought of its inevitable result. I believe, therefore, that we would all be more effective and certainly much happier if we forewent vain regrets and based our actions on the ultimate which we can wring from the equipment available to us . . ."

On January 13th McCain commented to Captain Arthur W. Radford at the Bureau of Aeronautics: "We have had antisubmarine flurry here with three surface and one submerged contact by patrol planes—no hits, no runs, no errors, due largely I believe to lack of proper bomb equipment . . ."

McCain was back on the road again in February, March, and April with trips that included conferences with the commanders of the Western Sea Frontier and Patrol Wing 8 (which had been transferred from Norfolk, Virginia), the commander of the Northwest Sea Frontier, and the commander of Patrol Wing 4.

In late March Sidney commented in a letter to sister Jimmie Spencer that he "just came back from Pearl Harbor yesterday. Saw the remains of the *Arizona* and the bottom of the *Oklahoma*. Sad sight."

All through the spring of 1942 Admiral McCain was fighting for supplies as well as trained and experienced patrol plane commanders. He felt that "It is murder to send PBYs and like types into combat zones" and "It is criminal waste and stupid folly not to use our magnificent trained crews and pilots in B-17s and 24s (with superchargers)."

On April 27, 1942, John McCain was detached as Commander, Aircraft, Scouting Force, and reassigned as Commander of Patrol Wings, Pacific Fleet, effective April 10th. This was simply the result of a reorganization of the Pacific Fleet in which commanders were assigned to specific forces (battleships, cruisers, submarines, etc.). McCain had the patrol planes and Bill Halsey had the aircraft carriers.

For his efforts during this period in organizing and conducting offshore and coastal air patrols, utilizing Army Air Force planes at times, McCain was awarded a Letter of Commendation by Secretary of the Navy Frank Knox.

Also throughout this hectic period, McCain's correspondence reflected a deep reverence for home-grown corn meal. In late November 1941 Sidney wrote to brother Joe: "I received the corn meal a couple of days ago. It is excellent. However, considering the many times I have carried five pounds of corn meal it is queer I don't remember how much it was. I'll never eat it before it spoils."

In a December letter to sister Katie Lou, Sidney complained that the corn meal had developed black specks, and she should ask Joe to send a one-pound package once every two or three weeks. Joe replied in January: "Our grist mill has been frozen for two weeks and as soon as we have a thaw, I will send you some meal."

To which Sidney replied: "for God's sake unfreeze the grist-mill."

Westward Bound

Everything changed for McCain in May 1942. He got his wish and headed west to the war. His job was a brand new command. He was to direct the operations of tender-based and land-based aircraft in the South Pacific under Vice Admiral Robert L. Ghormley.

In gratitude he wrote to classmate "Hook" Ghormley, now the commander of the South Pacific Area and the South Pacific Force: "The only way I can thank you and Admiral King is to do a bang-up job, upon which we stake our lives and our fortunes. The enclosed list is the members of my staff who desire to go, and whom I earnestly wish to take along. I not only want, but will need every one of them. [I] and my staff have already given considerable thought to the area in question, though necessarily our information is very meager . . ."

McCain already had specific suggestions about what he needed to get his job done. "Every PBY in the area in question should be relieved by B-24s fitted with superchargers and with radar and manned by naval crews. This is the most important thing of all, and if you put this one thing over, your country will never be able to repay you."

This recommendation about the B-24s [four-engine Consolidated heavy bombers] likely had its origin in a report made to McCain and Nimitz by Commander Norman Miller, who had just returned from a trail-blazing flight to Australia and Java. There, the men flying the old PBYs asked for four-engine land-based bombers with heavier armament, such as the B-17E and the B-24 with superchargers [to gain better high-altitude performance].[5]

McCain went on: "Further, we should have some fighter squadrons equipped with extra tanks. I understand that such were in production but do not know. In this connection I feel that the Lockheed P-38 (Lightning) is as good a fighter as there is in current production for long-range over-water work . . . I can not thank you enough for this opportunity and the same goes to Admiral King. As a matter of fact, I feel as lucky as I did on the day that Bayview won the Santa Anita at 60–1 in the mud and the rain."

7

WAR IN THE SOUTH PACIFIC

When Pearl Harbor was hit by the Japanese, Ernest King was Commander-in-Chief, Atlantic Fleet, and Chester Nimitz was in Washington as chief of the Bureau of Navigation. Bill Halsey, commanding the Pacific Fleet carriers, was at sea with the USS *Enterprise* and Task Force 8 returning to Pearl Harbor after delivering Marine fighter planes to Wake Island.

Before the end of December, King had taken over as Commander-in-Chief of the U.S. Fleet, and he added the job of Chief of Naval Operations—CNO—two months later. Nimitz was reassigned as Commander-in-Chief of the Pacific Ocean Areas and the Pacific Fleet. Both King and Nimitz held those jobs for the duration.

Also, on December 7 McCain's classmate Jake Fitch was at sea aboard *Saratoga* as commander of Carrier Division 1. However, Fitch was displaced by more senior 1906 classmate Rear Admiral Frank Jack Fletcher when Fletcher's force of cruisers and destroyers was ordered to form Task Force 14 and escort *Saratoga* in an abortive mid-December attempt to deliver more Marine fighters to embattled Wake Island. Although he was not an aviator, Fletcher remained in command of carrier operations over the next ten months.

The Strategy

Actions that shaped McCain's future came as early as December 23, 1941, when the first Washington Conference—Arcadia—was convened. Roosevelt, Churchill, and key staff met to discuss strategy and combined operations. Although the "Germany First" policy continued

71

to be endorsed, Admiral King secured agreement that Australia and the line of communication between Australia and Hawaii must be held.

Early in March 1942 the brand-new Joint Chiefs of Staff heard King's concept of operations to protect the Australia–Hawaii sea lanes and plan for a step-by-step advance through the New Hebrides, the Solomons, and the Bismarck Archipelago. By the end of the month, the Joint Chiefs and Roosevelt approved the plan as well as the division of the theater into the Southwest Pacific commanded by MacArthur; and the North, Central and South Pacific areas commanded by Nimitz. Admiral Nimitz now wore two hats: Commander-in-Chief, Pacific Ocean Areas, and Commander-in-Chief, Pacific Fleet. King's marching orders to Nimitz were to hold onto what we had, and prepare for the eventual assaults through the Solomons.

King also assigned Vice Admiral Robert L. Ghormley to command the South Pacific area under Nimitz. Ghormley's assignment, as commander of the South Pacific Area and the South Pacific Force, united the administrative area command with the operational force command. Thus Ghormley was in a position to efficiently keep his fingers on both the logistics and the fighting.[1]

Although King may not have consciously realized it at the time (although he probably did), his appointment of John McCain as one of Robert Ghormley's key commanders struck a critical balance. On one hand he had cautious Ghormley, and on the other, action-oriented and visionary McCain.

Battle Action

After Pearl Harbor the Japanese advanced rapidly through the Southwest Pacific. Wake Island, Hong Kong, Manila, Singapore, and Rabaul all fell. In February 1942, Halsey took the *Enterprise* and the *Yorktown* carrier forces to attack the Gilbert and the Marshall Islands, and followed up with raids on Wake and Marcus. Rear Admiral Wilson Brown took *Lexington* and *Yorktown* into action against Rabaul in February. Although the actual strike against Rabaul was cancelled when the Japanese spotted the carrier task force, fighter pilot Butch O'Hare scored five victories and won the Medal of Honor in the following air action.

In March planes from *Lexington* and *Yorktown* carried out a successful raid against Lae and Salamaua, New Guinea. Army Lieutenant Colonel Jimmy Doolittle's Tokyo raid was launched from *Hornet* in April with Halsey in command of the two-carrier task force. The Battle of the Coral Sea followed May 4–8 under Fletcher's overall command. In this carrier battle, history's first when opposing fleets did not come within sight of each other, the *Lexington* was sunk and the *Yorktown* damaged.

While McCain was setting up his new command in the South Pacific, the Battle of Midway was won by carrier task forces under Raymond Spruance and Frank Jack Fletcher. All four Japanese carriers involved in the battle were sunk, while the Americans lost the *Yorktown*. Spruance, a 1907 Naval Academy graduate and a non-aviator, had taken over Task Force 16 when Halsey was hospitalized for treatment of dermatitis.

McCain Arrives

Admiral McCain received dispatch orders and was detached from his West Coast command on May 1. His replacement as patrol plane commander was Pat Bellinger, the obvious and logical choice. On May 2 McCain reported to Nimitz at Pearl Harbor. After a few days of consultation, he hop-scotched to Palmyra on May 13, Canton on May 14, and then to Suva in the Fiji Islands. After two days there, it was onward to Noumea, New Caledonia, where he established his headquarters. McCain arrived there on May 18 and assumed command of Aircraft, South Pacific Force (ComAirSoPac), on May 20. Initially his flagship was the seaplane tender USS *Tangier* (AV-8); then *Tangier* was relieved in mid-June by the USS *Curtiss* (AV-4).[2]

Slew McCain walked into a mountain of difficulties. The South Pacific in the summer of 1942 was a commander's nightmare—just the kind of challenge he relished.

His job was complex. He had a brand-new multi-service, multi-national command operating from Free-French territory. He had to protect the vital sea lanes—the lifeline—between Hawaii and Australia. He had to establish patrols to catch the Japanese if they approached from the Solomons as well as search a huge area north of Australia for threats from the Marshalls and Carolines.

At the start his staff was a two-man operation—Captain Matt Gardner and Commander Frederick Funke, Jr. He didn't even have a yeoman to type reports. It was to be more than a month before any other help arrived.[3] In the meantime, his letters were typed on the *Tangier's* letterhead.

McCain's aviation assets were varied and widely dispersed. In the Noumea area of New Caledonia he had 22 Navy PBY patrol planes, 3 Navy scouts, 38 Army Bell export model P-400 fighters, 6 Royal New Zealand Air Force Lockheed Hudson light bombers, 27 Army B-17 heavy bombers, 10 Army Martin B-26 medium bombers, and 17 Grumman F4F Navy fighters. The inventory at Efate in the New Hebrides was 6 Navy scouts and 18 Marine F4F fighters. Stationed in the rear areas of Fiji, Tonga, and Samoa were 9 PBY patrol planes, 16 scouts, 59 fighters, 21 Royal New Zealand bombers, 3 Royal New Zealand patrol planes, 12 B-26s, 8 B-17s, and 17 old Curtis SBC biplane dive-bombers. Douglas MacArthur would add to the pot intermittent use of Royal Australian Air Force reconnaissance planes and Army B-17s.

These assets, with the exception of the PBYs and the B-17s (if the B-17s were lightly loaded), could not reach nor operate beyond the Japanese-held eastern Solomon Islands. Auxiliary belly tanks would have helped for some of the planes, but there were none available.[4] McCain really wanted some Army B-24 bombers, which could reach the eastern Solomons with a full load.

Communications were wretched. During many hours of the day, weather conditions limited direct communication among the commands at Noumea and Espiritu Santo, McCain's location from August 5 onward.[5] Further, the command organization itself created indirect communications paths that later had disastrous consequences.

The dividing line between MacArthur's Southwest Pacific U.S. Army command to the west and Nimitz's U.S. Navy command to the east was initially set at longitude 159 degrees east. This was subsequently modified so that the patrol responsibilities were split at 158 degrees, 15 minutes east, a line just west of Guadalcanal in the Solomons.[6] MacArthur's planes were to patrol to the west of this line (where the major Japanese bases were located) and McCain was to patrol to the east.

McCain rolled up his sleeves and got to work. He reported progress directly to Nimitz on May 26. Ghormley would normally receive this report, but he did not formally take over as area commander until June 19, although he had arrived in the South Pacific earlier. McCain related to Nimitz:

Have just returned from Nandi [in the Fiji Islands]—situation not the best for the long haul.

The Efate flying strip [in the New Hebrides Islands] looked hopeless on my first visit, however they have spared neither brain nor brawn. [Marine Lieutenant Colonel Harold] Bauer, who commands the Marine VFs [fighters], has practiced his people almost exclusively in short-field landings and takeoffs. Hence, all flyable planes will be in Efate by the 29th of this month.

The Marston Mat [perforated steel plates laid to form as a hard surface on dirt airfields] . . . will save months in getting ready for the bombers. Large supplies of this matting should be sent down here for two additional fields on Efate and in anticipation of perhaps three more on Espiritu Santo.

McCain went on to discuss at length Army personnel, the need for additional radar, potential citizen volunteers, delays in getting Army bombers, carrier replacement groups, and the need for base personnel to free up combat personnel.

Nimitz replied on June 24, starting his letter with a nice insight into the Battle of Midway. It is interesting to see what the big boss had to say about one of his greatest victories:

Dear McCain:

Your letter of 26 May arrived in the middle of our Midway job. As you may well suppose, there has been little time for other interests while that was going on.

No doubt you already know, at least in general terms, how successfully the Midway battle turned out. I can't go into detail in this letter, but I know you will be glad to hear the reports of damage and sinkings have not been exaggerated. I

regard the entire operation as a wonderful example of coordi-
nation and utmost determination by all concerned. Our aviators bore the brunt, but decidedly not in vain.

McCain liked the potential of what he saw in his area. He told his
pal, Frog Low, "Have been over some but not all of this vast area of
anchored carriers [the islands] and am impressed by the ease with
which it can be made impregnable with a minimum of air. Air, among
these interlocking islands, can in a large measure, substitute for ships,
guns, and infantry." He also commented to Nimitz: "It is apparent
that the New Hebrides and Santa Cruz Islands must be built into a
great boulevard for planes."

Within a month of taking command, McCain issued a plan entitled "Organization of Aircraft, South Pacific Forces." The document
indicated some of the problems he faced. He directed: "In view of the
wide dispersion of the air units under this command, their dissimilar
composition, the variation of available facilities, the inherent difficulties in communication, and the differences in defense problems con-
fronting the commanders addressed, the Commander, Aircraft, South
Pacific, considers it entirely impracticable . . . to exercise command
directly."

He went on to say that he would conduct training and operations
by specifying the types of operations he expected and laying out a general doctrine of force employment. Implementation would be delegated to the local commanders.

Setting the Target

The Japanese offensive into the Southwest and South Pacific areas
exceeded all their expectations. However, they realized that the occu-
pation of Australia was, at that point, beyond their reach. The
Japanese could, however, isolate Australia by seizing Port Moresby in
New Guinea as well as by advancing through the Solomons, New
Hebrides, New Caledonia, Fiji, and Samoa to block the sea lanes from
Hawaii.

The Japanese landed on the north coast of New Guinea in March,
and by early May they occupied Tulagi in the Solomons with its fine
anchorage. They then started restoring and expanding the captured

Royal Australian Air Force seaplane base on nearby Tanambogo Island.

After the Japanese seaborne invasion force headed for Port Moresby was turned back in May as a result of the Battle of the Coral Sea, they pulled in their horns a bit. They cancelled their ambitious plans for New Caledonia, Fiji, and Samoa, and focused instead on parallel thrusts. One was an overland move against Port Moresby. The other was development of the naval and seaplane base at Tulagi and construction of an airfield on nearby Guadalcanal. These facilities would provide the springboard for a Japanese move on the New Hebrides.

All through June, Admiral King lobbied General George C. Marshall, Chief-of-Staff of the Army, for his plan to move through the Eastern Solomons. King ordered Nimitz to prepare to seize Tulagi. Marshall finally agreed to the plan. The operation was set to begin on August 1, 1942.

Major General Alexander A. Vandegrift, commander of the 1st Marine Division, arrived in Wellington, New Zealand, in mid-June. He met with Ghormley in Auckland on June 26. There he was informed that he and his men were headed for the Solomons with D-day set for August 1. He had one month to prepare plans, unload and reload his ships, rehearse the landing, and move to the target area.

All through the last days of June and into July word was filtering in about Japanese activity on Guadalcanal. McCain mentioned the Japanese activities in a letter on June 24, and mentioned the Japanese airfield construction in a letter on June 27. A coast-watcher reported that a pier had been constructed near Lunga Point and that earth-moving equipment had been unloaded.[7] Nimitz's orders to Ghormley included establishing air bases at Guadalcanal and Ndeni (in the Santa Cruz Islands), so seizing the airfield under construction on Guadalcanal would not only deny the base to the enemy but would be a head start on achieving what was rapidly becoming the key objective of the whole operation.

Building Bases

A major early effort for McCain was the construction of airfields at Efate and Espiritu Santo. McCain kept himself in or near each base until any problems were solved or were on the road to solution. He called his job pioneering in the roughest and rudest sense, but of intense and ever-changing interest.

Espiritu Santo was being turned into a major port, and two airfields were completed there in twelve days and seventeen days, respectively.[8] By the end of June the airfields at Efate were ready for the operation of heavy bombers. McCain hoped to have B-17s and B-24s assigned to "annoy . . . considerably" the Japanese and their airfield construction on Guadalcanal. Airfields suitable for heavy bombers were also developed at Plaines des Gaiacs and Koumac on New Caledonia. Bases for the PBY patrol planes were readied at Havannah Bay, Efate, and Segond Channel, Espiritu Santo.

As early as June 30 McCain's PBYs attacked the enemy on Tulagi. These attacks continued into July, but daylight attacks were curtailed when Matt Gardner discovered that float-plane Japanese fighters were active in the Tulagi area.

A new problem arose about this time when the high command raised strong objections to the Eastern Solomons operations. After conferring in early July, MacArthur and Ghormley sought a postponement of the Tulagi and Guadalcanal invasion, stating, "The initiation of the operation at this time without reasonable assurance of adequate air coverage would be attended with the gravest risk." Their request was denied by Admirals Nimitz and King.[9]

A brief word reached home about Slew during this busy period. Rear Admiral Richard E. Byrd, Jr., the great explorer, was back from an inspection trip that included stops at Efate and Noumea. In a letter to Kate he said:

I had the great pleasure of seeing John in the Far Pacific, and I am glad to be able to tell you that he is very well, indeed, and, incidentally, is doing a perfectly grand job; one that we are all proud of.

If you don't know where John is and would like to know, please write me and I will see if I can get an O.K. on giving you the information. I think I can.

John has very little to work with, but he has done wellnigh superhuman things in getting established and organized.

If I can do anything for you while John is away I would consider it a privilege, so please call on me.

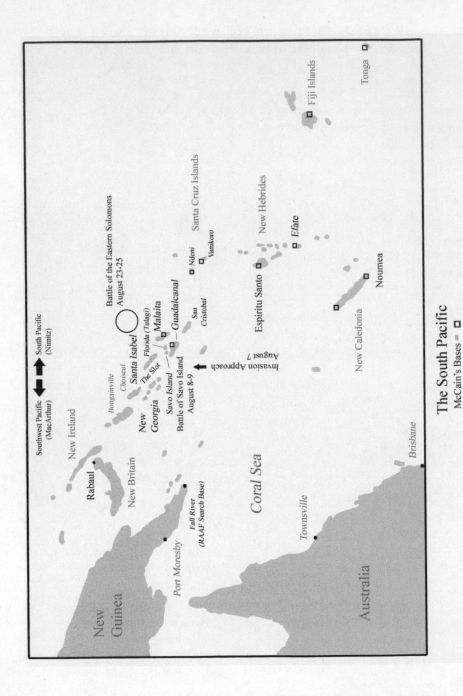

The South Pacific

McCain's Bases = □

8

GUADALCANAL

As the invasion D-day approached, Nimitz was able to supply McCain with thirty-five B-17's from Hawaii. But he told McCain a sad truth: "I think we must face an indefinite period during which calls for help will get little response from home." Further, Nimitz told Slew that there would be delays in forming and training new Marine fighter and dive-bomber squadrons.[1] Nevertheless, McCain thanked Nimitz for his "word of encouragement in the action being taken to fulfill our crying needs."

Next, Ghormley told his aircraft commander that he could expect very little air help from MacArthur.

Facing all these problems, John McCain persevered. When asked what he considered to be Admiral McCain's outstanding characteristic, Captain Gardner thought a minute and commented, "When there isn't anything to be done, he's the kind of fellow who does something."[2]

Invasion Planning

Ghormley issued his operations plan on July 16. The first phase was the rehearsal in the Fiji Islands, and the second was seizure and occupation of Tulagi and Guadalcanal. Occupation of the Santa Cruz Islands—specifically Ndeni—was pushed into the third and final phase.[3]

The expeditionary force to Guadalcanal, Task Force 61, was commanded by Vice Admiral Frank Jack Fletcher. Rear Admiral Richmond Kelly Turner commanded the amphibious force (Task Group 61.2), and the troops that would actually make the landing

81

were the 1st Marine Division, commanded by Archer Vandegrift. Air support was furnished by three carriers (*Enterprise, Saratoga* and *Wasp*) in Task Group 61.1 under another of McCain's 1906 class-mates, Rear Admiral Leigh Noyes.

The land-based Navy, Marine, and Army air units under McCain's command were designated Task Force 63. Noyes and Turner reported directly to Fletcher, and Fletcher and McCain reported directly to Ghormley.[4]

McCain's job was to cover the amphibious force approach to Guadalcanal and Tulagi, and then to patrol from new bases at Ndeni and Malaita after moving his tenders forward. His planes would search the area between New Caledonia to just north of the Solomons, as well as points east and south as far as the Fijis. MacArthur's search planes would cover areas north and west of the target islands.

McCain issued his own set of orders for Task Force 63 on July 25. He broke his task into seven elements. These included search opera-tions from New Caledonia by Navy PBYs, Army B-17s, and New Zealand Hudsons; and scouting and bombing missions against the enemy on Tulagi and Guadalcanal prior to D-day conducted by B-17s from Espiritu Santo. He also ordered the forward movement of the aircraft tenders *Curtiss, MacFarland,* and *Mackinac* to Espiritu Santo, Ndeni, and Malaita (close by Guadalcanal), respectively.[5]

In the middle of his planning for the operation, McCain got the news that he had been promoted from the "lower half" of the list of rear admirals to the "upper half," dating from July 13, 1942. The Navy's system skipped the one-star rank but divided the two-star admirals into "lower" and "upper."

On July 26, during the invasion rehearsal in the Fijis, Admiral Fletcher called the only meeting held by the principal commanders. Turner, Vandegrift, and McCain attended. Ghormley did not. In his stead he sent his chief of staff, Rear Admiral Daniel J. Callaghan. This sometimes acrimonious meeting was aboard Fletcher's flagship, *Saratoga*, and gave rise to another of the many stories about Slew McCain. As he was climbing up a Jacob's ladder on the *Saratoga's* side, someone on the carrier opened a garbage chute by mistake and doused him with sour milk.[6] Maybe this (and Ghormley's absence) was a forewarning.

Also notable on July 26 was the arrival of recent aerial photos of the objective area. Obtaining this intelligence took a strenuous effort involving many days of travel between New Zealand and Australia and a long B-17 flight out of Milne Bay, New Guinea.

Fletcher planned to keep the carriers in the landing area for only two and a half days. This was less time than required to unload the amphibious force cargo ships. So McCain's Task Force 63 had to provide air support for the Marines ashore and the ships off the beachhead between the time the carriers pulled out and the time when land-based planes could be pushed forward to the airfield on Guadalcanal (which the Japanese were still building).[7]

Admiral McCain scrawled out a plan for air support during this period. He based his plan on the aircraft carriers' planned withdrawal on D-day plus 2. The auxiliary carrier *Long Island* was scheduled to arrive from Hawaii with a small load of Marine fighters and bombers on D-day plus 6, August 13. Thus McCain had to plan for four days of exclusive air coverage from his meager resources; and his closest base was more than 700 nautical miles away on Efate.

McCain's ideas involved shifting Marine and Navy squadrons among his bases, but none of the potential moves seemed to meet the needs. The biggest problem was that, with the exception of the B-17 and PBY reconnaissance planes, his bombers and fighters in Efate and Noumea didn't have the range to reach Guadalcanal without auxiliary fuel tanks, and there were few if any such tanks around.[8]

Starting on July 31, McCain's B-17s conducted daily bombing raids on Guadalcanal and Tulagi in an effort to delay construction of the airfield and soften the beach defenses. These heavy bombers operated under the command of Colonel LaVerne Saunders, who ran the Army's 11th Heavy Bombardment Group, and was one of McCain's key deputies.

Before D-day Ghormley moved his headquarters (on the *Argonne*) forward to Noumea. McCain also moved forward on the *Curtiss* with nine PBYs to Espiritu. As called for in his plan, McCain extended his PBY patrol range by moving the tender *Mackinac,* with nine PBYs, northward to the east coast of Malaita on August 7. The next day he shifted *MacFarland,* an old four-stack destroyer converted to a tender, north to Ndeni in the Santa Cruz Islands with five PBYs.

Desperate Days

D-day on Guadalcanal and Tulagi was August 7, 1942. Fletcher, Turner, and Vandegrift ran the show. Task Force 61—*Saratoga*, *Enterprise*, and *Wasp*—provided air cover. The difficulties of those first days, ashore and at sea around Guadalcanal, are a well-known and documented story.

From Rabaul, the Japanese sent three land-based bomber raids against the invasion force on August 7 and 8. Little damage was done to the invasion fleet, and the enemy air force suffered serious losses. But the defending carrier-based planes of Admiral Fletcher suffered as well. Fletcher was down to seventy-eight fighters from the ninety-eight he started with. Under the threat of enemy land-based air attack, the fighter losses, tired air crews, and the low fuel supplies, Admiral Fletcher withdrew his three aircraft carriers early in the morning of August 9 south to the Coral Sea. They would not return for two weeks.[9]

Savo Island

The campaign for Guadalcanal involved a series of savage battles on land, in the air, and on the sea. Historians agree that the United States Navy suffered one of its worst defeats in history at the Battle of Savo Island. A discussion of this action is needed because some analysts have placed part of the blame on Admiral John McCain.

A Japanese force of five heavy and two light cruisers plus one destroyer, under the command of Vice Admiral Gunichi Mikawa, assembled off Rabaul early on the morning of August 8. The force moved southeast along the east coast of Bougainville and reached a waiting area at about 6:00 a.m. They lingered there, and around mid-morning were spotted twice by Royal Australian Air Force Hudson bombers flying from their base at Fall River on Milne Bay in New Guinea. The enemy force moved south about noon and then headed down The Slot—the channel between two island chains pointed directly at the invasion force off Guadalcanal and Tulagi. They approached Savo Island undetected about midnight, slipped past patrolling destroyers, and sank one Australian and three American cruisers. Another American cruiser was heavily damaged. Only one enemy ship was damaged, and that pretty minor in comparison.

Fortunately the Japanese did not follow up on their victory. They withdrew to the north without attacking the unprotected transports. Had they done so, the Allied South Pacific offensive would have been effectively sidetracked and the Marines cut off from supply and reinforcement.

Lots of blame was passed around for the fiasco, but much of the analysis and speculation after the battle (and there has been plenty) focused on the problems of aerial reconnaissance. Air searches for enemy ships approaching Guadalcanal were a split responsibility between Ghormley's South Pacific command (i.e., McCain) and MacArthur's Southwest Pacific forces.

McCain sent his PBYs far to the north to watch for Japanese carriers that might move south from the Marshall Islands and Truk in the Carolines. The PBYs timed their flights to reach the outer search limit (near the Equator) at sunset and then return at night using radar to detect any carriers. McCain's B-17s could reach only about 200 miles northwest of Guadalcanal, as far as New Georgia. Radar limitations forced these B-17s to time their searches in daylight hours. This pattern left most of the southern portion of The Slot uncovered, particularly at night. In addition, on August 7 and 8, weather interfered with the search of the area between Guadalcanal and New Georgia. On the 8th one B-17 had to abort and the other turned back early.[10] Mikawa's force was missed by only about sixty miles.[11] The Japanese air searches had faced similar weather problems, which was one of the reasons they were completely surprised by the appearance of the American invasion fleet on August 7.[12]

McCain's orders called for the patrol squadrons to report the day's search results after all planes had returned. So it was almost midnight before amphibious force commander Turner received McCain's summary and realized that the northwest approaches had not been completely searched.

Also, on the day before, Turner had asked McCain for an additional search to the northwest. The record is not clear about whether this flight was made or not. In fact, it's not certain if the request was ever received. Turner's flagship chose to send the message without requiring a receipt. It is possible that the *Curtiss*, McCain's flagship, was not listening to the radio net when the message was transmitted because it was not part of the expeditionary force at Guadalcanal.

The other half of the reconnaissance picture was MacArthur's Australian Hudsons operating from New Guinea. Their search pattern covered the northern reaches of The Slot beyond McCain's reach. And, in fact, one of the Hudson's *did* spot the Japanese force shortly after 10:00 a.m. on August 8. The Hudson's crew attempted to send an immediate report to its base at Fall River on Milne Bay, but without luck. The radio at Fall River may have been shut down at the time due to an alert. Although the search plane immediately headed back to base with the sighting report, it wasn't until after noon that the plane landed and delivered the news. The message went out about two hours later and, for unexplained reasons, didn't reach the duty officer in Brisbane for another six hours. Another version of events has the sighting report passing from Fall River to Port Moresby, to Townsville, to Brisbane, to Canberra, and to Pearl Harbor before being broadcast out to the invasion fleet.[13]

Either way, Turner did not receive the sighting report until between 6:00 and 7:00 p.m. on the evening of the attack, and the details of the message left doubts about the sailing direction of the enemy force and its composition. The report identified two destroyers, three cruisers, and two gun boats or seaplane tenders. To Turner this sounded more like an expedition to establish a seaplane base than a threat to the invasion fleet.[14]

Were these search plans inadequate, as charged by some? Clearly, in hindsight, they were. The enemy was not detected that night in the lower reaches of The Slot. Mikawa, by luck or design, was able to thread his way among the search patterns both in distance and (most critically) timing. But wherein lies the fault? The Australians were preoccupied and overextended with the fighting in New Guinea. The communications set-up was clearly not up to the task due to weather, lack of equipment, and command organization. McCain's PBYs were an overworked force with primitive facilities. From August 1 through August 8, McCain lost four PBYs from grounding and sinking, and one failed to return from a mission.[15] The B-17s operating from the New Hebrides and New Caledonia were handicapped by inadequate airfields (for one thing, lacking runway lights) and hand-pumped refueling facilities.[16]

McCain was later criticized for not adapting his patrol plan to cover The Slot, for not asking Turner to search with catapult-launched scouts from cruisers, and for not asking Fletcher to step in with carrier planes. Turner felt that McCain's patrol reports were "unjustifiably tardy." Further, he believed it was inexcusable for McCain not to have told him earlier about search failures due to weather, and that McCain did not make the special search that Turner had requested (in a message that McCain may not have received).[17]

John McCain was not exactly a neophyte at patrol plane operations. Now he was stretching his meager resources to the limit. One of McCain's squadron officers later observed that the officers and men flying the PBYs "were worthy of the highest praise and credit for the outstanding manner in which they carried out 'routine' operations under such exacting and often dangerous conditions. Their physical and moral stamina, their courage and devotion to duty was of the highest order."[18]

One could easily conclude that any air reconnaissance failures were simply the fortunes of war as well as the fruits of trying to do too much with too little.

Henderson Field

With the carriers gone, the only aircraft in the invasion area were McCain's PBYs, his B-17s flying up from Espiritu Santo and Noumea, any B-17s sent by MacArthur, and the scouting planes on the cruisers. The airfield—which would become hallowed Henderson Field—was not operational until after August 17. So the Marine planes from the *Long Island* didn't fly ashore until August 20. Instead of four days, McCain was responsible for air cover of the target area for twelve long days.

On August 9, without carrier air cover, Admiral Turner withdrew the amphibious force. The ships had unloaded only half their cargo.

Because of the increased risk brought about by the heavy losses of protective combat ships at the Battle of Savo Island, *Mackinac* and her PBYs were ordered to withdraw from Malaita and set up shop at Espiritu Santo.[19] Also, early in the campaign, McCain's tenders were chased out of Ndeni when they were shelled by a submarine and when a Japanese destroyer was sighted moving south. The Japanese shelled the base, but the tenders had already left. A new base was set up at Vanikoro in the Santa Cruz Islands. The patrol planes shuttled in and out, staying overnight between searches.

Interestingly, as late as August 12, McCain did not know the complete outcome of the Battle of Savo Island. He messaged Ghormley, "Please let me know losses our side and losses enemy side in late encounter."

The Marines held on to their gains ashore and set about completing the airfield. They finished the 2,600-foot runway left under construction by the Japanese, filling in a depression remaining in the center and adding 1,178 feet. On August 10 General Vandegrift announced that the field would be named after Major Lofton R. Henderson, a Marine squadron commander lost in the Battle of Midway.[20] Two days later, on August 12, Lieutenant William Sampson, McCain's aide and pilot, radioed the ground controllers at Henderson Field that his PBY (McCain's personal plane) had suffered a serious mechanical malfunction and he had to set down. He was allowed to make an emergency landing in the middle of runway construction. Mechanics checked the plane thoroughly, but could not find any problems. Thus Sampson had cleverly conned his way into history as the first pilot to land on Henderson Field. On the way out, he evacuated two wounded men. This was another Pacific Theater first—the maiden aerial evacuation of wounded from a combat area. Sampson told McCain that the field was in excellent condition and ready for fighter operations. But that was optimistic. The field was muddy and there were too many trees at either end.[21]

That same day Ghormley told McCain to load all available transports with fuel and supplies and get them on their way to Guadalcanal.[22] McCain responded that "[I] don't know how well we will do it but we're certainly going to put everybody's foot on the throttle." McCain put together a convoy of four old World War I four-stacker destroyers that had been converted to fast transports. They arrived at Cactus (the code name for Guadalcanal) three days later with aviation gas, bombs, ammunition, tools, and spare parts, plus 120 men from a Navy air base unit.[23] Additional shipments arrived at Guadalcanal every few days thereafter, but it was always a chancy business.

McCain still had his eyes on the main target of getting the planes into Henderson Field. He sent a letter off to Vandegrift on August 16 carried by hand in the convoy of destroyers (followed by a back-up copy via a PBY flight): "The use of PBYs for daylight patrol your area highly undesirable and not to be done unless absolutely necessary because of the ease which they can be shot down . . . The best and proper solution, of course, is to get fighters and SBDs [bombers] onto your field. *Long Island* arrives Vila [Efate] the early morning of the 17th. Trained pilots will be put aboard and she will proceed to fly-away positions off the south tip of San Cristobal." This was just the first act in McCain's never-ending quest to provide support for Guadalcanal.

McCain's responsibilities for logistics were eased somewhat on August 17 when Ghormley shifted the responsibility for the operational control of the supply ships from McCain to Turner. McCain would let Turner know when he had supplies ready to ship by sea and Turner would make the arrangements for the vessels.[24]

The Planes Arrive

The auxiliary carrier *Long Island* arrived at Suva, Fiji, on August 13. From there, the skipper informed Ghormley that the pilots aboard had only limited training. Ghormley passed the problem on to McCain, who found a solution. *Long Island* reached Efate on August 17, where eight of the more-experienced fighter pilots from the Efate-based Marine fighter squadron were exchanged for eight of the greener pilots aboard the carrier. But whatever their level of training, green or not, the pilots and planes on *Long Island* were the first installment of the heroic and effective "Cactus Air Force."[25]

Finally, on August 20, the *Long Island* launched nineteen Marine F4F Wildcat fighters and twelve Marine two-seater Dauntless SBD dive-bombers for Henderson Field. This was the initial echelon of Marine Aircraft Group 23, part of Brigadier General Roy S. Geiger's 1st Marine Aircraft Wing. Merrill Twining (then a lieutenant colonel and an assistant operations officer for the 1st Marine Division) put it this way in his 1996 memoir: "Working against the atmosphere of apathy and indecision that prevailed at ComSoPac, the always effective and dedicated Admiral McCain, with his unlimited initiative, somehow managed to open the gate."[26]

This not only was cause for cheering by Vandegrift's embattled Marines, but opened new worlds for Slew McCain. He now had fighters on Guadalcanal to defend against the enemy bombers who came down from the north to strike Henderson Field and the Marine positions. He had fighters and dive-bombers to strike Japanese troops on Guadalcanal and the enemy ships in surrounding waters. In fact, on the day after their arrival, four of the F4Fs conducted a successful strafing mission against Japanese troops on the Henderson perimeter in the closing phases of the Battle of the Tenaru River.

McCain also extended his search and patrol coverage significantly. In the scouting half of their dual role, the SBD scout-bombers could patrol up The Slot for another 300 or more miles, filling a big gap. The potential also existed for B-17s to refuel at Henderson and then search 800 miles northwestward in the direction of the enemy bases, but this possibility was limited by the short fuel supply and primitive, sometimes hand-powered, re-fueling facilities at the field.

McCain wrote to Ghormley on August 21, emphasizing the need to supply Guadalcanal: "The situation up north is vexatious. The PBY is of little use in combat, as you know. As for the B-17s, they must be back by nightfall since the weather is generally rotten in darkness and the field has insufficient night landing provisions. Also, with a bomb load, they can only cover the active vicinity for about two hours . . . *We have got to get food and guns and gas into Guadalcanal, and we have got to take chances to get them there. I fully expect the enemy's big push in the next two or three days. Hope to meet it with a fresh striking force.*" [Emphasis added]

With the arrival of the planes, a battle pattern evolved. The Japanese priority was to shell, bomb, and recapture Henderson Field. The "Tokyo Express" of destroyer-transports and their escorts ran regularly at night to bring in reinforcing Japanese troops and subject Henderson and the Lunga perimeter to murderous bombardment. The Japanese bombers hit Henderson Field about noon each day on a regular basis.

The American priority was to defend the airfield and move in more planes, pilots and crews. Vandegrift concentrated on improving air defense while waiting for reinforcements.

The Japanese conducted their troop landings at night when American planes were not effective, and the American transports unloaded only by day when friendly aircraft could provide cover.[27]

On August 22 the second "wave" of planes, five Army Air Force P-400 fighters, arrived at Henderson. McCain sent his personal PBY to Henderson on August 23 with a full load of oxygen bottles for the fighter planes, thus relieving a serious shortage that had halted or threatened to impede the fighters' ability to defend the base.[28]

The Battle of the Eastern Solomons

In early August a major enemy force sortied from Japanese ports on the long journey to the South Pacific. Their objectives were to land 1,500 troops on Guadalcanal, hopefully meet and defeat the American fleet, and take a swipe at Henderson along the way. Moving southward, the enemy force included the transports and their escorts; several battleships, cruisers, and destroyers; and the carriers *Shokaku*, *Zuikaku*, and *Ryujo*. Facing them was Fletcher's Task Force 61 maneuvering east of San Cristobal with *Saratoga*, *Enterprise*, and *Wasp*.

Early air search efforts from both fleets missed each other's main forces. On August 20 the Japanese spotted *Long Island* on her mission to deliver planes to Henderson Field. On the 21st one of McCain's PBYs from Ndeni sighted enemy cruisers and destroyers 300 miles north of Tulagi.

When American air searches on August 22 produced no firm enemy contacts, Fletcher obtained Ghormley's approval to detach *Wasp* for refueling. *Wasp* left late the next day.

Finally, on August 23, one of McCain's PBYs sighted the enemy transports 300 miles northwest of Task Force 61. Air searches were launched from both the task force and from Henderson Field. A new tactical wrinkle played out when planes launched from *Saratoga* on a mission to locate and attack an enemy force of cruisers, destroyers and transports returned to Henderson Field rather than returning to the carrier. The availability of Henderson Field added tactical flexibility and search range to the task force planes. The *Saratoga* group refueled and returned to *Saratoga* the next day.

The battle was joined on August 24. McCain's B-17s, PBYs, and

Henderson-based scouts were all out working. Finally the light carrier *Ryujo* was sighted by several PBYs on her way to attack Henderson, which she did shortly after noon. The attack was beaten off by the Marine flyers.

Shokaku and *Zuikaku,* the enemy's mainstays at the Coral Sea, were also spotted, and the carrier forces traded blows. *Ryujo* was sunk; *Shokaku* and *Zuikaku,* although unharmed, lost most of their pilots and planes. In spite of inspired damage control efforts, *Enterprise* suffered heavy damage that put her out of action until mid-October.

McCain's planes based at Henderson Field got back into the battle on August 25. Several unsuccessful night strikes were launched against marauding Japanese destroyers. Then, acting on a sighting report from one of the PBY search planes, a force of SBDs and F4Fs took off after dawn to strike what turned out to be the transport force. Hits were scored on a transport and a light cruiser.[29]

Eight of McCain's B-17s from Espiritu Santo got in on the tail end of the action as well, sinking the transport and the light cruiser that the Henderson Field planes had left dead in the water.[30]

As a result of the battle, the Japanese troop transports withdrew, delaying their reinforcement effort, and Henderson Field received a badly-needed transfusion of aircraft orphaned by the damage to *Enterprise.*

On Cactus

John McCain never stopped fighting for adequate air support for the beleaguered Marines, but it was a catch-as-catch-can proposition. He quickly grasped the opportunity presented by the Eastern Solomons carrier battle. Eleven dive bombers from the damaged *Enterprise,* Flight 300, arrived on August 24 when the carrier left for repairs. They would remain for a month. Nine more P-400's landed on August 27.[31]

On August 30 Admiral McCain flew into Henderson Field in a B-17 for a short visit with General Vandegrift. The Marine commander had told McCain earlier in the Fijis that he had one bottle of bourbon and would save it to celebrate McCain's visit. Vandegrift related that the bottle was enough for about one drink each for the two commanders and their staffs. "We were toasting his visit when the siren announced enemy bombers. Later that night a Japanese cruiser tossed in the normal ration of shells, and the next morning enemy air struck again. . . . At the height of the bombing he [McCain] fixed me with his eyes 'By God, Vandegrift, this is your war and you sure are welcome to it. But when I go back tomorrow I am going to try to get you what you need for your air force here.'"[32]

McCain spent the night under a Japanese blanket in Vandegrift's tarpaulin tent. During his visit he talked to squadron leaders, pilots, and crew chiefs. McCain told everyone he saw that Guadalcanal was not just a dirty little local fight, but a rampart, and that successful defense of the island would lead to the destruction of Japanese naval power in the Pacific. On the other hand, he pointed out the loss of Guadalcanal would forfeit all the gains of Coral Sea and Midway. John McCain did his best to make the men on Guadalcanal feel good about themselves and understand the importance of their battle.[33]

During his visit to Guadalcanal, McCain gleefully witnessed the arrival from Espiritu Santo of nineteen more Marine fighter planes and twelve more Marine dive-bombers.

McCain's visit to Vandegrift was his first taste of down-and-dirty combat. The visit added exclamation points to his thinking about the importance of Guadalcanal to the Pacific war and what was needed to support the Marines. When he saw how much the Japanese dominated the night with ships and the day with bombers, he fired off a bold message to Ghormley, MacArthur, Nimitz, and King, laying out the plain facts that additional aircraft and crews must be provided immediately. He reported that the sleep-deprived pilots were "very tired," and urged that "Two full squadrons of P-38s or F4Fs in addition to present strength should be put into Cactus at once . . . The situation admits of no delay whatever. No help can or should be expected of carrier fighters unless based ashore."

McCain told his bosses: "*With substantially the reinforcements requested, Cactus can be a sinkhole for enemy air power and can be consolidated, expanded and exploited to the enemy's mortal hurt. The reverse is true if we lose Cactus. If the reinforcement requested is not made available Cactus can not be supplied and hence can not be held.*" [Emphasis added][34] This lightning bolt laid out the strategic truth, and articulated the aggressive tone that high command must adopt to ensure success of the campaign.

McCain picked up an ally in his crusade when Undersecretary of the Navy James Forrestal, who was in the South Pacific studying the supply situation, told Washington that it was "imperative" to send more planes.[35]

When *Saratoga* was damaged by a Japanese submarine torpedo on August 31, she was out of action for three months. She sent all planes that could be spared from her own protective patrols to Espiritu and Efate. McCain jumped on the bonanza, and sought and received permission from Nimitz (who had received approval from King) to assign *Saratoga's* stranded fighters and dive-bombers for duty at Henderson Field. Over the next weeks, the *Saratoga* air group added twenty-four fighters and twenty-four bombers to the force on Cactus. During the same period, *Wasp* and *Hornet* ferried eighteen more fighters to Henderson.

An important addition to Vandegrift's command and significant new help for McCain was the September 3 arrival on Guadalcanal of Brigadier General Roy S. Geiger. He took control of the air defense of the island. Like McCain, Geiger was a fighter. He threw every plane he had into the battles above Henderson Field.

The Ubiquitous Patrols

McCain, although focused on Guadalcanal, still had a larger air operation to run. On August 26 one of McCain's PBYs had been lost to a patrol of enemy fighters, and on September 5th another PBY attacked and shot down a Japanese flying boat. Then, on the next day, two PBYs took on another enemy flying boat. One of the PBYs was lost in the encounter, but the crew was saved. McCain reminded his crews that their first order of business was finding the enemy ships and that they were not to seek combat with enemy aircraft.[36]

McCain also had a few remarks about the patrol plane business for Rear Admiral Marc "Pete" Mitscher, at that point commanding Patrol Wing 2. Mitscher offered some assistance and McCain replied: "We appreciate all that you try to do for us, and having been on that end of the job myself, I know your troubles and the headaches connected with it. We too are having our troubles here, and plenty of them, and don't you forget it. However, it is much more interesting than shoving papers."

Back to Cactus

But McCain's focus remained on Cactus. He reported to Ghormley on September 10 about his activities:

> At the moment the air situation in Cactus is critical because the rains of the past three days have put the field out of commission. If it isn't one thing it seems to be another! Work on the field is going ahead on a twenty-four-hour basis, but the outcome depends on a few days of dry weather plus the early arrival of Marston Mats. This contretemps has lost us the opportunity of two promising strikes at Jap light forces and has delayed an all-out B-17 raid on Bougainville area.
>
> As soon as I see Kelly Turner and the weather permits, will take passage on a B-17 escorting fighters to Cactus. Expect to stay there at least two days. My objective will be, first: To detect and strike enemy forces before they effect a raid and, second: If we fail in that, to strike them the next morning.

As he planned, on September 11 McCain and Rear Admiral Kelly Turner flew into Guadalcanal in a Douglas R4D transport plane to confer with Vandegrift. They carried with them Ghormley's gloomy estimate of the situation on Guadalcanal. In essence, Ghormley said that in view of the increasing Japanese strength and American weaknesses, he could no longer support the Marines. In spite of McCain's entreaties and specific requests, the ever-cautious Ghormley was not convinced that Guadalcanal could be held. He left the three sub-commanders to save Guadalcanal on their own. And so they would.

After conferring, the three agreed that Turner would bring in the 1st Marine Division's uncommitted infantry regiment to provide the much-needed reinforcements. They strongly recommended this action to Ghormley.[37] He approved, and Turner landed the 7th Marine Regiment and an artillery battalion on September 18.

A New Threat

Sightings were made by McCain's PBYs of a large Japanese fleet on September 13 and 14. The enemy was reported as various mixes of battleships, carriers, cruisers, and destroyers. The sighting reports prompted offensive sorties by the carrier Task Force 61 and evacuation of the harbor at Espiritu Santo under McCain's orders. The enemy reversed course, however, before contact could be made. One PBY was lost to Japanese Zero fighters.[38]

Change of Command (I)

On September 21, 1942, John McCain was relieved by Aubrey Fitch at Espiritu Santo, New Hebrides. This was not a complete surprise. McCain had been aware of the upcoming change in duty since early in the month.

McCain's replacement as ComAirSoPac was part of a proposal for a rather grand reshuffling of air admirals in and out of the war zone. The idea came to light on September 7 at a meeting in San Francisco between Admirals King and Nimitz. Earlier, Nimitz had prevailed upon King to transfer Rear Admiral Claude C. Bloch, commandant of the 14th Naval District, out of Hawaii. Now King was ready for Nimitz to return the favor. King wanted to transfer Rear Admiral John Towers out of Washington, where Towers was the chief of the Bureau of Aeronautics. Nimitz would take on Towers at Pearl Harbor as his top aviation commander.[39]

King and Towers had been dueling for years, perhaps as far back as 1929, when King was transferred out of the Bureau of Aeronautics by bureau chief Admiral William A. Moffett and replaced by then-commander Towers. The rivalry intensified in 1933 when King was appointed to head the bureau instead of Towers.[40] For his part, Towers regarded King (undeservedly) as one of the greatest enemies of all.

But King had other motives as well. He wanted to move aviators into higher command positions because he recognized the critical importance of aviation and aviators in fighting the Pacific War. King wanted to start at Pearl Harbor, and the efficient and visionary Towers was the obvious and best choice for the job. Beyond that, as chief of the Bureau of Aeronautics, Towers was not under King's thumb.

Although King was Commander-in-Chief of the Navy, the bureau chiefs reported directly to the Secretary of the Navy. Thus King had no direct control over Towers in his job as a bureau chief.[41]

King's solution was to offer Towers the post of Commander, Air Force, Pacific Fleet, and a promotion to vice admiral (or Towers might have demanded the promotion as part of the deal). King could then put one of his own men in as chief of the Bureau of Aeronautics. There was another twist. Nimitz and Towers were also rivals dating from the days when Nimitz ran the Bureau of Navigation and Towers ran the Bureau of Aeronautics. Nimitz could not have been happy to have his old rival on the way to Pearl Harbor.[42]

The result of these machinations was that Rear Admiral Aubrey Fitch, the current ComAirPac, would be sent to relieve McCain in the South Pacific. McCain, a King man, would then go to Washington as the new chief of the Bureau of Aeronautics. Thus King would be rid of Towers, who was a major irritant, and get some de facto control of BuAer.[43]

Towers was not completely happy with all this. He did not feel that McCain was qualified either in administrative work or procurement. Towers wanted one of his own boys—one of the young aviators—to have the job as bureau chief.[44]

Navy Secretary Frank Knox did not share Towers's opinion. He felt that the Bureau of Aeronautics would benefit from the change from Towers's leadership to McCain's. Knox felt that McCain was a better administrator and coordinator.[45] Clearly John McCain had done very well in Washington in earlier assignments, and he had the confidence of Congress as well.

As a further result of the same meeting, Bill Halsey, now cured of the dermatitis that had kept him out of the Battle of Midway, was to relieve Fletcher of his carrier command in the South Pacific. Fletcher had been sinking in the esteem of Admiral King because of a lack of aggressiveness in battle, plus, probably, some plain old bad luck. King wanted him back in Washington for a look-over. The aggressive and popular Halsey was available and rarin' to go.[46]

There are usually at least two sides to most stories and this episode with McCain was no exception. As discussed earlier, the finger of blame was pointed by some analysts at McCain for failures in the air-search system that led to the surprise defeat at Savo Island. Of course, John McCain would shoulder blame, if there was any, as one of the risks of command.

This other slant on the story says that, because of Savo Island, Admiral King wanted a change of command. Fitch was available because Towers was relieving him as ComAirPac. McCain could thus be sent back to Washington so King could look him over and decide if he should have another battle command or not.[47] The truth may be the one, the other, or a combination of both. Certainly it seems like a stretch to consider that moving McCain to head the Bureau of Aeronautics was done simply to create an opportunity for King to assess his capabilities as a battle commander.

McCain had already demonstrated his fighting capabilities though his recognition of the critical importance of the South Pacific Theater and his aggressive posture about holding and expanding U.S. positions on Guadalcanal. But this merry-go-round of command changes had too many benefits for everybody to allow an exception for McCain, even though Slew was ready to stick it out until the enemy was defeated at Guadalcanal. Another factor may have been that McCain was worn out from scratching and fighting to launch and support the offensive. Undersecretary Forrestal, after his inspection tour of the South Pacific, felt that both McCain and Ghormley were exhausted.[48] Fitch, a battle-hardened air admiral, was available to relieve Slew. McCain certainly met the needs of his mentor, Admiral King, for a loyal fighter to take command of the Bureau of Aeronautics at a critical time of the war.

Farewells

Admiral John Sidney McCain left many friends behind in the South Pacific; and it was fortunate for the aviators and the Marines that they would have a friend in Washington who would remain dedicated to getting pilots, aircraft, crews, and supplies to the battlefield. In his brief tenure in the South Pacific, McCain had foreseen that Guadalcanal would become the bottomless pit into which Japan would hurl her naval and air strength. He championed Henderson Field as the key to the island's striking power as well as its very survival. He provided a sorely needed aggressive tone to the campaign.

McCain carried back with him to Washington a lasting respect and love for the Marines. It was mutual. Upon hearing about Slew McCain's reassignment, Vandegrift wrote, "I think too much of you to congratulate you. I can think of nothing worse than to be in Washington at this time. Your friends here will miss you, but we will know we have a friend in court who will render a sympathetic ear when told that we need more fighter planes."[49]

Slew's feelings about his service in the Guadalcanal campaign are reflected in this moving reply to General Vandegrift:

> I received your nice letter yesterday. I am at a loss whether to like the new detail or not. I hate Washington thoroughly and all the stuff that goes on there nauseates me. However, I feel that I may be of some use to the boys on the front in my new detail. What I hate the most is the breaking off of my close association with yourself and the tough eggs under you . . .
>
> I hope you and Geiger will feel free to write me in my new capacity, giving me whatever information may be necessary to help me help you.
>
> Best regards and all good wishes to you and all your people.
>
> J. S. McCain
>
> P.S. The planes must find these ships that come in and hit you at night and must strike them before dark. Should I die now, those words will be found engraved on my heart.

Slew also wrote to Geiger and the pilots: "It is with sadness and regret that I go to other duty. Until the day I die I will take intense pride in my association with you brave and gallant men."

McCain promoted the skip-bombing concept to Aubrey Fitch and Major General Millard Harmon, the Army commander in the South Pacific, and also praised the B-17 four-engine bomber: "The B-17 is the best fighter in the sky. It shoots down all comers with relative ease, and controls the air it flies in." He went on to General Harmon: "For my part I wish to state that I have never served with abler or bolder men than these Army pilots."

Slew McCain left his successor, Jake Fitch, with a better inventory

than he had walked into four months earlier. The number of airplanes
went up from 291 in May to 468 in September. They were still spread
all over the South Pacific, but at least 80 or more of them were on
Guadalcanal. McCain had also built up significant strength on
Espiritu Santo, the staging ground for Henderson Field.

If Savo Island was a blot on McCain's copybook, he more than
made up for it with his visionary and relentless support of the Marines
on Guadalcanal. He was awarded his first Distinguished Service
Medal by Secretary of the Navy Frank Knox in the fall of 1942; it covered his service as Commander, Aircraft, South Pacific, from May 19,
1942, to September 21, 1942. The citation mentions his "courageous
initiative," "judicious foresight," and "inspiring devotion to duty."
The citation further states: "His tireless energy and extraordinary skill
contributed greatly to occupation of the Guadalcanal-Tulagi area by
our forces and to the destruction and serious damaging of numerous
aircraft and vessels of the enemy Japanese Navy."

9

WASHINGTON AGAIN

John McCain left Espiritu Santo on September 22nd. He traveled via Noumea and Suva and arrived on Canton Island on September 24th.

In the meantime, Admiral Nimitz had heard from Ghormley and MacArthur that Guadalcanal could not be held, so he decided he should head south to find out for himself. He arrived on Canton for an overnight stop and to meet with McCain. Nimitz wanted a first-hand opinion from a straight-shooter about what was going on in the South Pacific.

Both McCain and Nimitz were lodged in the Pan American Hotel, which had been built as a tourist attraction and a rest stop for aircraft crews on the eve of the war. Each officer had a bedroom with an attached bath.[1]

Nimitz had a lot of questions for McCain. He asked about the use of the Royal New Zealand Air Force, and he wanted a firsthand account about how Noyes and Fletcher were doing. Slew took the opportunity to push again for more support for the Marine pilots on Guadalcanal: "I want to emphasize the aviation gas supply and relief for pilots at Cactus. We can fly VF [fighters] up but not back. It is a one-way wind. The Marine VF pilots are very tired. A relief for them is there now and the SBD pilots will be next. They have had no rest; they are just tired. They had to work during the day and could get no sleep at night."

McCain went on: "The Marines are not worried about holding what they have on Cactus, but you have got to stop the Japs coming in. On these moonlight nights we will try torpedoes but we haven't

101

many of them. We lost two SBDs trying to bomb ships at night."[2]

Regarding Fletcher, a classmate and friend of McCain's, Slew told Nimitz: "Two or three of these fights are enough for any one man. A rest will do him good." McCain saw Fletcher a few days later in San Diego, and Fletcher said virtually the same thing about himself. After nine months of strenuous combat, including command of the carrier forces at Coral Sea, Midway, and Guadalcanal, Vice Admiral Frank Jack Fletcher finished the war in the Northern Pacific.[3] He retired in 1947 with the rank of full admiral.

The night of the Nimitz-McCain meeting, an air raid alarm sounded. All hands reported to the air raid shelter except for McCain. Nimitz sent his aide, Arthur Lamar, back to the blacked-out hotel to find Slew. As Lamar recalled, "When I got there, I knocked on the door and asked Admiral McCain if he was all right. I could not understand his mumbled reply, so I opened the door and walked in. Admiral McCain had false teeth, which he had put in a glass on top of the toilet in his bathroom. In the excitement of getting out in the air raid, the teeth had gone into the toilet. I fished them out, and we went on to the air-raid shelter until the all-clear signal was sounded." The next morning McCain had the medical department thoroughly sterilize the teeth before he put them in his mouth.[4]

Slew continued his trip home via Palmyra Island, Pearl Harbor, San Francisco, San Diego, and El Paso. He arrived in Washington on October 2nd. At some point along the way he had talked by phone to Admiral King with a request for fifty high-altitude fighters for Guadalcanal. King's reply was a broadside of shouts: "That's your business. That is why I brought you back!"[5]

Nimitz continued on to Noumea. There he met with Ghormley. After inspections of Espiritu Santo and Guadalcanal, Nimitz returned to Pearl Harbor and made the decision to replace Ghormley with Halsey. Ghormley had lost the confidence of both King and Nimitz as a battle commander. His strengths were in administration and diplomacy. Ghormley went on to command the 14th Naval District and later U.S. Naval forces in Germany.

Halsey's arrival renewed the fighting spirit of the U.S. forces. Halsey went on to drive the Japanese out of the Solomons.

Reporting Aboard

On October 2, 1942, Admiral McCain reported, as directed, to the Secretary of the Navy. On October 9th he was detached from the secretary's office and commissioned as chief of the Bureau of Aeronautics.

Now the world of John McCain was vastly broadened. Although he had been responsible for a huge geographic area in the South Pacific, his focus had been mainly on the struggle for Guadalcanal. Now he shifted his thinking to a truly global scale, including the submarine battle in the Atlantic, personnel procurement and training in the States, the continuing need for planes and pilots in the South Pacific, and the build-up for what would ultimately be the drive across the Pacific to the shores of Japan. His task was to lead the Bureau in procuring tens of thousands of aircraft, pilots, and technicians; and expanding existing bases and building new bases for the new airmen and planes.

Reaction

McCain's appointment as bureau chief caused some misgivings because he wasn't one of the "old-time" aviators. *Time* magazine, on September 28, 1942, editorialized under the heading "Battle Lost" that the reassignment of Rear Admiral John Towers from chief of the Bureau of Aeronautics to commander of the Pacific Fleet Air Forces was a promotion for Towers (to vice admiral) but a demotion for naval aviation. The column continued, "New Bureau of Aeronautics Chief Rear Admiral John Sidney McCain, 58, is a good officer. But like many other so-called air admirals, he got an airman's rating late, is not an airman by profession, but a battleship admiral with pay-and-a-half and a flying suit. Since his air training at Pensacola in 1936, at the age of 52, Battleshipman McCain has had little to do with air developments."

Gordon McCain fired back a letter of rebuttal to *Time* on October 12th: "I believe in justice to my father. It should be pointed out that since leaving Pensacola the only commands he has held have been in aviation."

Citing his father's aviation commands and experience, Gordon concluded: "I would not debate *Time*'s comment that my father has a 'flying suit'—however, I would like to add that all available evidence points most emphatically to the fact that he uses it for its intended purpose."

Gordon's letter was followed the next week by this tribute:

I would like to add my bit to Mr. McCain's defense of his father. You're damn well right the Admiral has a flying suit, and by all that's good and holy he knows how to use it too! I was a student at Pensacola with Admiral McCain, and another old-timer, Admiral Blakely, and there were never two students who pursued their course with such diligence and success as these two gentlemen. They took the entire course with the rest of us including the instructors' cussing when boners became too frequent, and were not spared the tough phases in "deference to their stripes."

They both passed with flying colors the hardest part of the course—the criticism by their fellow students, Naval Reserve cadets, who were merciless in their criticism of all and sundry of the regular Navy.

Later, after graduation, we all found it the greatest pleasure to serve under these admirals because we found that, regardless of the many years of battleships behind them, they were capable of "wearing their flying suits," and deserving of their pay-and-a-half . . .

August D. Watkins
Lieutenant (j.g.) U.S.N.R.

Vice Admiral Charles A. Blakely, mentioned in Watkins' letter, was designated as an observer in 1932 and later won his wings as a naval aviator in March 1936 at age 54. McCain and Blakely were not strangers. In 1935 McCain had, from Washington, assured Blakely that there would be no difficulty about his request for the pilot's course at Pensacola. Blakely went on to serve as Commander, Aircraft, Battle Force, in the pre-war Pacific. Serving under him was Bill Halsey as commander of Carrier Division 1 with the *Saratoga* and *Lexington*. Blakely himself acted as commander of Carrier Division 2 with the

Yorktown and *Enterprise*. Later, as commandant of the 11th Naval District, Blakely endorsed McCain's orders to his first flag command.

This immensely emotional issue—planes versus battleships—lasted through the war and beyond. The conflict was exacerbated by the desire of the Army Air Force to unify all air services. King strongly supported naval aviation and its growth, but on a steady, conservative path.[6] But the old prejudices and hard feelings from prewar days remained, and affected the way aviators viewed Admiral McCain, even though he was one of naval aviation's most assertive salesmen.

The Bureau of Aeronautics

In John McCain's own words, "The sole purpose of the Bureau is to supply our fleet with the kind of airplanes and the kind of aviators that can help destroy our enemies in the shortest possible time."

By December 1942, as McCain took over, there were 1,098 officers on duty at the bureau, a phenomenal growth from 58 in 1939. After the 1941 reorganization under John Towers, the Bureau of Aeronautics had seven principal operating arms for planning, personnel and training, flight, maintenance, aircraft procurement, engineering, and production; plus a photographic section. There were also the usual array of staff offices.[7]

McCain was coming home to the Main Navy and Munitions buildings complex on Constitution Avenue, where he had spent earlier assignments. These so-called temporary office buildings had been opened in 1918 and continued to house the Navy's top command until after World War II, when the Navy brass moved to the Pentagon.

He started his tenure at BuAer with a press conference convened by Secretary Knox in which McCain praised the fighting airmen at Guadalcanal and paid tribute to John Towers. Slew pointed out that the 5-to-1 kill superiority of American pilots in late August and September was evidence that Towers had produced efficient equipment and trained pilots, the measure of success for the air bureau chief. McCain commented further "I hope to do as well as Admiral Towers."

The key Planning Division of the bureau was responsible for developing estimates of overall naval aviation personnel and aircraft requirements. In June 1940, the Navy had 2,172 aircraft in its inventory. The total was up to 7,058 heavier-than-air types by the end of 1942. As the war heated up in Europe, Congress in rapid succession authorized increasing naval aviation strength to 4,500, then 10,000, and then 15,000. In January 1942 this was increased by executive order to 27,500. The next step was in June 1943, when the lid was raised to 31,447 aircraft.[8] The ceiling topped out at 37,735 in February 1944, a level that Admiral King refused to increase.[9] Slew and his staff were busy indeed. They had their hands full meeting these goals.

The bureau had to deal not only with a vast airplane procurement program but also had to initiate the construction of new air stations and the expansion of existing bases. Plans for the maintenance of the expanding aircraft inventory also had to be worked out.[10]

The Planning Division also assisted in carrying out the provisions of the Lend-Lease Act. Commander Herbert D. Riley (McCain's aide in 1940 and assigned to the Bureau of Aeronautics in 1942) reminisced in 1945 about how McCain dealt with our allies: "And on the many deals with the British, 'Russkies' (as McCain called them), etc.: That is the only part of the Washington job he had fun with. I'd fortify him with figures on what they weren't doing with what they already had and when they asked for more, he'd throw figures at them. That would make them writhe. Then when they had about given up and were all whipped down, he'd offer them about a tenth of what they'd asked for and they'd snatch at it and go off happy, thinking they really were getting somewhere. But that was the only fun we had in Washington."

The Personnel and Training Division was charged with procurement, assignment, and training of aviation officers and enlisted men. Although in theory this was a joint responsibility with the Bureau of Naval Personnel, essentially BuAer had operational control of the program. The number of naval aviators topped out at nearly fifty thousand at one point.

The Engineering, Procurement, and Production divisions worked together to get the planes built. Engineering determined technical feasibility and tactical desirability. After planning and design were completed, Procurement awarded contracts. Then, Production dealt with the manufacturers.

Bureau Chief

As chief of the bureau, McCain steadfastly maintained his support of the South Pacific theater, telling the press that we can "Hold the Solomons and more, too." He was full of praise for the pilots and troops on Guadalcanal and told a reporter, "Our people will hold the Solomons . . . if we do our part and get the planes and other supplies out to them."[11]

In mid-October Admiral McCain received a commission from President Roosevelt as a member of the National Advisory Committee on Aeronautics, the predecessor of NASA. A week later, McCain was informed that he had entered the "upper half" of the list of rear admirals on June 27, 1942, instead of July 13th. He had gained sixteen days seniority! Also October and November saw the arrival of household goods and a 1939 Chevrolet from San Diego. John Sidney and Kate settled in at 1870 Wyoming Avenue, N.W., Washington, D.C.

In his job as Bureau of Aeronautics chief, McCain was described as unpretentious, arising every morning at 6:30 to get an early start at the office. Slew was reported as living a quiet life in Washington, although he remained fond of his cribbage and rummy games at the Army-Navy Club. He gave up his expert game of tennis, but he was able to take time out to play golf—not very good golf—with daughter Catherine. He remained an eager horse-player—he loved to place $2 bets—and it was said he played a sharp game of bridge.[12]

McCain was no "swivel-chair admiral."[13] He couldn't sit still long enough. He had lost five pounds in the South Pacific trying to keep the Cactus Air Force in the air, and dropped another six pounds in the first month on the Bureau of Aeronautics job. But he thought he could gain the weight back if he could get away from his desk and out on a carrier or a plane. Slew signed papers at a stand-up desk, and often lunched in the Navy cafeteria.[14]

McCain's office was described to be more like a modern scientific laboratory than the office of a bureau chief. He collected and scattered about gadgets, plane models, and other paraphernalia. He welcomed visitors with friendly cordiality, a powerful handclasp, and cheery informality.[15]

Travel soon showed up on McCain's agenda, and remained there. In November and December 1942, he touched down at Greenwood,

Vicksburg, Memphis, San Diego, Los Angeles, Alameda, and Seattle. On later trips McCain visited Pensacola, Jacksonville, Cherry Point, New York City, San Diego, Pearl Harbor, San Francisco, Burbank, and Memphis. There were inspections of the aircraft factories (where McCain was reported to have had a twinkle in his eye for the lady workers), attendance at various ceremonies, and inspections of air bases where McCain was often able to visit with old friends and colleagues.

Guadalcanal Again

On January 7, 1943, McCain left for an inspection tour of the South Pacific. He flew from Washington to San Francisco via Birmingham, Dallas, Corpus Christi, Midland, San Diego, Burbank, and El Segundo. He left San Francisco on January 12th on a Boeing model 314 4-engined Clipper for Pearl Harbor. Then it was onward in a 4-engine PB2Y Coronado flying boat to Midway, Johnston, Canton, and Suva. He arrived at Espiritu Santo on January 21, 1943. The stated purpose of McCain's trip was to assess the need for pilots and planes in the South Pacific, but no doubt he was eager to get back to the battle zone to see first hand how his boys were doing.

On Espiritu Santo he met with Secretary Frank Knox and Admirals Nimitz and Halsey. Halsey was on a rampage about personnel matters that had McCain gasping and mumbling. Slew resolved the problem (a reassignment of one of Halsey's staffers) by simply rescinding the orders.

The group met aboard Jake Fitch's flagship, USS *Curtiss*. After the evening session split up and all headed for their staterooms, Japanese planes arrived to provide a goodnight lullaby of bomb explosions. The raid was brief and not much damage was done, but such a raid was not a regular occurrence anymore and all were wondering if the Japanese had some inside information about the presence of all the brass.

The next day Knox, Nimitz, Halsey, and McCain flew on to Guadalcanal. The island still had not been secured (that was a month away), but conditions had vastly improved since McCain's last visit. Henderson Field was now an all-weather airstrip, and there were two fighter strips nearby. Although the pilots from Henderson commanded the air over Guadalcanal most of the time the Japanese could still sneak in an attack. They chose that night to unleash a heavy raid that lasted until dawn.

Almost everybody was convinced that the Japanese knew who was on the island and were after the "big game." Knox, Halsey, and McCain abandoned their comfortable hut and dove into the nearest trench. There is some question regarding what sort of trench McCain jumped into. There is an oft-related story that poor Slew dove into a ditch that had been under a latrine. It seems that the work detail had moved the latrine to a new location, but the old ditch hadn't yet been filled with dirt. We will probably never know whether the story is true, but either way, all involved spent an uncomfortable night.[16]

The next day the travelers returned to Noumea. One story relates that when the island's communication officer was prepared to file the routine departure dispatch, his shaken assistant asked, "Do me a favor, will you? Send it in Japanese. I want 'em to know for sure that the high-priced help has left here."[17]

McCain left the party on Noumea on January 24th. He was only able to cautiously promise to Nimitz more planes, which must have galled McCain because he had been pushing hard for that very thing for months. He returned to Washington on February 1st via Suva, Upolu, Pago-Pago, Canton, Palmyra, Pearl Harbor, San Francisco, San Diego, El Paso, and Memphis. This trip stretched for 25 days and included more than 150 hours in the air.

Shortly after his return to Washington, McCain told the press, with the pride of a father, that the men on Guadalcanal were living up to the best Navy traditions.[18]

A Full Agenda

Back at his desk, one of the issues that McCain dealt with was that of night fighters. Japanese reconnaissance planes nicknamed "Washing Machine Charlie" were regular callers at Guadalcanal, dropping bombs just to annoy the troops and keep them awake. McCain requested studies about how to deal with that and other night attack threats. The British felt, as reported by a group of Marine aviators returning from England in June 1943, that a twin-engine night fighter was the best answer.[19] The Grumman F7F Tigercat was a single-seat, twin-engine fighter under development that could fill the bill. The first production model was flown in December 1943. The plane was intended for use as a close support fighter for the Marines, but after thirty-five had been built, the design was quickly modified into a radar-equipped two-seat night fighter. Unfortunately, the first Marine night squadron equipped with F7Fs didn't arrive on Okinawa until the day before the Japanese surrender.[20]

The Navy didn't wait for the Tigercat. A radar-equipped Chance-Vought F4U Corsair single-seat fighter plane was first delivered in October 1942. The dozen night-equipped Corsairs that followed were soon deployed and saw action in the South Pacific. Their first kill was a "Washing Machine Charlie" over New Georgia in October 1943. But the most important night fighter in the Pacific was the single-seat Grumman F6F Hellcat. Standard versions were first assigned to squadrons in early 1943 and became a mainstay of the carrier force.[21] Night-equipped Hellcat F6F-5Ns were assigned to the *Independence* in July and August 1944. Right afterward, in August 1944, John McCain's former chief of staff and friend, Matt Gardner, who had been through the thick of battle as captain of the *Enterprise*, was promoted to rear admiral and set about organizing and training a night fighter task group around his old ship.[22] Gardner's task group saw action under McCain and Mitscher as part of task forces 38 and 58.

Another major problem on Admiral McCain's plate was the German submarine menace in the Atlantic. In 1942 U-boats were operating close to the Atlantic coast and loosing torpedoes at ships as they sailed eastward from the United States. As discussed earlier, McCain had long been an advocate for the small carrier, although as part of the battle fleet. Now he strongly recommended that the escort carriers be deployed to battle the German wolfpacks that operated beyond the range of American and British land-based bombers. McCain's recommendation was at first received coolly. But McCain, in his usual aggressive way, continued to push the idea. He contended that destroyers and destroyer escorts attacking from the surface of the ocean could not meet the threat on their own. But with scouts and bombers in the air, the combination of surface and air (that came to be known as hunter-killer groups) defeated the submarines.

McCain won this time. By 1943, the escort carriers were at work in the Atlantic. Allied ship losses began to drop sharply. As reported in *U.S. Air Services* magazine, naval aviators were credited with sinking sixty-five German submarines, more than half the total credited to the entire Navy.[23]

A significant action approved by McCain was one of the first steps to move naval aviation into turbojet power. In December 1942, the bureau released a proposal for a composite-powered fighter. Ryan Aeronautical was awarded a contract for three prototypes of the FR-1 Fireball. The FR-1 had a piston engine in the nose and a turbojet in the fuselage. Eventually sixty-six were built and assigned to fighter squadron VF-66, but the war ended before they could be deployed.

Numerous other experimental programs were started under McCain's wing. Douglas, Grumman, Curtiss, Martin, and Kaiser Fleetwings all took on the job of developing a new "bomber torpedo" type such as the Douglas Dauntless II (later to become the Skyraider) and the Martin Mauler. Prototypes were also ordered for the McDonnell Phantom and other pure turbojet fighters.

McCain's duties also included public relations, and he did not seem at all averse to promoting the war effort by mingling with movie celebrities such as Veronica Lake, Joan Leslie, and Adolph Menjou. He was always a favorite of the press with his weather-lined face, blue and penetrating eyes, powerful hands, bright smile, keen sense of humor, and even a little cussing to accentuate his thoughts.[24]

All of these were important issues that required action and resolution, but McCain also could claim at least partial credit for another change in direction for naval aviation that paid off handsomely when he returned to the Pacific himself. Slew was convinced that carriers needed an all-purpose plane rather than the mixed complements of fighters, dive-bombers, and torpedo planes. He witnessed the disastrous trials of the Curtiss-Wright SB2C Helldiver dive-bomber in the spring of 1943. In fact, then-captain J. J. "Jocko" Clark, commanding *Yorktown*, obtained McCain's concurrence to send the Helldivers assigned to *Yorktown* back to the factory and replace them with the reliable Douglas SBD Dauntless.[25] Largely through McCain's insistence, experiments and flight tests were made by West Coast training squadrons that demonstrated comparable bombing accuracy between fighter planes and the SB2C dive-bombers. This led to modifications of the Hellcat and Corsair fighters that turned them into all-purpose planes that could carry 2,000 pounds of bombs and rockets in addition to their .50-caliber machine guns or 20-millimeter cannon.[26] The F4U-4 model of the Corsair and the F6F-5 model of the Hellcat first flew in spring 1944, and were true fighter-bombers. McCain kept after this issue all through his time in Washington and during his carrier command.[27]

Even though McCain was considered to be a "King man," he was not spared from the tart attention of the commander-in-chief of the fleet. King detested paperwork. He once sent a note to McCain, "I observed yesterday that the door of room 1909 bore the label 'Duplicating Section, Bureau of Aeronautics' and beside the door the names of two (2) lieuts.(j.g.). I will be interested to know what important factors of duplication require the services of two (2) officers." McCain explained to King that the office sent out instructions and directives to the fleet, and King let the matter drop.[28]

Commander Herbert D. Riley described, in a letter to Kate, how it was to work with McCain in Washington: "He didn't care any more for administrative work than I do, as you know. When he was in Washington and the conniving got him down, his temper would get short and we used to have some of the most violent arguments you have ever heard. One time he got furious at me and I laughed at him. He asked me 'what in hell' I was laughing at—and I said 'you.' 'You ought to know by now that I'm working for you, not against you, so what's the use of getting angry at me?' He sat down and roared, pulled out his Bull Durham and rolled a cigarette (spilling it all over the place, as usual) and then we worked out our differences. There aren't many people who are big enough to laugh at themselves. I wouldn't have done that with most admirals."

Riley, then a commander, wanted to get back to the Pacific as soon as he could. On the day he reported to the bureau, Riley renewed his acquaintance with McCain and struck a deal. McCain agreed that when he got his own orders to return to the battle, he would get similar orders cut for Riley.[29]

10

DEPUTY CNO

On August 6, 1943, Rear Admiral John McCain was detached from duty as chief of the Bureau of Aeronautics, and on the same day he reported to Admiral King as Deputy Chief of Naval Operations (Air), taking five divisions from the bureau with him. The job of DCNO(Air) was not actually created until the Secretary of the Navy acted on August 18th. This allowed John Sidney to squeeze in seven days leave in New London with son Jack.

Simultaneously McCain was promoted to the rank of vice admiral, effective July 28, 1943. This was a temporary appointment to "continue in force until the end of the first session of the 78th Congress" in 1944. A new appointment would be issued upon Senate confirmation.

Ernie King had worked long and hard to create this new position. In May 1942 King had ordered a shake-up of the Navy Department to weaken the bureau system and centralize all procurement under his aegis. But King had not cleared the changes with his bosses, and President Roosevelt ordered King to rescind his orders for the reorganization.[1] A year later he tried again. This time he suggested that four new deputy chiefs of naval operations be created; one each for material, personnel, and aviation, plus a principal assistant to the vice CNO. Roosevelt disapproved the scheme once more as too complex and implying too much military control of the Navy Department.

Finally, in August 1943, the Secretary of the Navy, with Roosevelt's approval, created the post of Deputy Chief of Naval Operations (Air). The function of the post was "to correlate and coor-

113

dinate all military aspects including policy, plans, and logistics of naval aviation."

So King succeeded—at least in part—in shifting Bureau of Aeronautics functions under his own office. But, more importantly, he gave naval aviators a voice at a higher level than ever before in policy-making, strategic planning, and aviation logistics. Even so, the controversy was not ended. Some vocal aviators were still not satisfied. They wanted virtual autonomy for naval aviation. The dispute simmered for a year until King quashed the squabble with an order specifying that DCNO(Air) reported to the Vice Chief, not directly to King himself.

The Bureau of Aeronautics divisions transferred to CNO were Planning, Personnel, Training, and Flight; plus the Air Information Branch and Marine Corps Aviation offices. The shift was accomplished with a minimum of confusion and lost motion. The Bureau of Aeronautics then became a purely technical bureau responsible for aviation material, including the design, production, and repair of Navy and Marine Corps aircraft. The Bureau of Aeronautics carried out the plans and policies formulated by the DCNO(Air); thus Slew McCain kept a lot of his old job.[2]

Historians agree on the reasons that McCain got the new job. King could have recalled Towers to Washington, but he would have none of that. Aubrey Fitch was doing a good job in the South Pacific and should continue there. McCain was an aviator, experienced with the Bureau of Aeronautics, loyal to King, willing to fight when it was necessary, and stood ready in Washington. Furthermore, McCain had supported King, as expected, in urging that the operational units of naval aviation be moved from the technical Bureau of Aeronautics to King's Office of the Chief of Naval Operations.

So McCain got the job, and King personally wrote most of the press release announcing McCain's appointment.[3]

Evidently the new authority and responsibility didn't change the basic Slew McCain very much. He was still a much-storied character. Rather than use the intercom, McCain shocked his elderly secretary by shouting through the open doors, "Hey, woman! Get in here!"[4] But he was even-handed at work and at home. When he arrived home at day's end, he clapped his hands and, with a twinkle in his eyes,

Midshipman John Sidney
McCain, circa 1903.

Naval officers in New York City
with Mayor Fiorello LaGuardia,
circa 1934. A smiling McCain is
in the top row of officers, in
front of the man with the light-
colored homburg.

One of McCain's first ships, USS *Panay*, on which he served with young Ensign Chester Nimitz.

Commander John S. McCain, Executive Officer, USS *New Mexico*.

A plane from Coco Solo, Panama Canal Zone, circa 1937 (probably McCain in the front cockpit).

At age 52, Captain John S. McCain became Naval Aviator No. 4280.

Below, a scene aboard America's first purpose-built aircraft carrier, USS *Ranger*.

Rear Admiral John S. McCain, Chief, Bureau of Aeronautics.

This photo was taken by the famed Edward Steichen (1879–1973). Steichen served with the U.S. Expeditionary Forces in World War I and directed the Naval Photographic Institute in World War II.

Presentation of Distinguished Service Medal, circa 1942. Catherine McCain, Secretary of the Navy Frank Knox , McCain, Rear Admiral Richard S. Edwards, Mrs. McCain.

Slew McCain and Aubrey Fitch, September 1942: "I relieve you, Sir!"

Highline transfer between ships.

Planning conference with Major General Graves B. Erskine, USMC, commanding general, 3rd Marine Division, December 5, 1944.

John McCain receives the Navy Cross from William "Bull" Halsey,
November 1944.

Visit by Secretary of the Navy Frank Knox to Guadalcanal,
January 1943.

In this photo one can sense the strain of command that would lead to McCain's death immediately after the close of the war.

Below: Vice Admiral McCain visits Ensign D.E. Satterfield, wounded in action, and examines the bullet that went through his leg. (Hoover Institution)

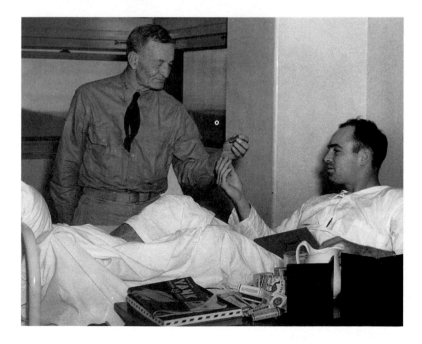

Above: Katori
class light cruiser
sunk off French
Indo-China,
January 12, 1945.

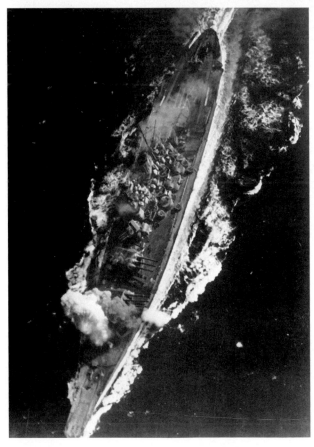

Direct hits on a
Yamato class bat-
tleship, Japanese
central force,
October 26, 1944.

Japanese aircraft burning on Batangas, Luzon, December 14, 1944.

A carrier strike on Heito airfield, Formosa, October 12, 1944.

A Consolidated PBY-5, probably McCain's personal plane.

Frank Knox, Chester Nimitz, John McCain, Adlai Stevenson, et al.,
in January 1943, probably Espiritu Santo.

"Jimmy" Thach demonstrates a flying technique to John McCain.
Probably June 1944 aboard USS *Lexington*.

Part of mighty Task Force 38. Task Group 38.4 is in the foreground,
August 1945.

Warabi POW camp ten miles north of Tokyo, August 25, 1945.
This is typical of the reception pilots of Task Force 38 received when
they flew over the camps in the Tokyo area.

Commander W.A. Sherrill, Vice Admiral McCain, Air Vice
Marshall Isitt (RNZAF), and Rear Admiral Wilder Baker on the flight
deck of the USS *Shangri La*, August 20, 1945.

Father and son on the USS *Proteus*, September 2, 1945, Tokyo Bay.

John McCain and Bill Halsey on the USS *Missouri*, September 2, 1945.

Vice Admiral John S. McCain coming aboard the USS *Missouri*, to witness the surrender. September 2, 1945.

Fleet Admiral Chester W. Nimitz signs the surrender documents for the United States. McCain is third from the left, looking slightly downward, in the first row of officers in the background.

Investiture in the Order of the British Empire, aboard HMS *Sheffield*.
British Consul General R.H. Hadow, Vice Admiral William Tennant,
and Mrs. John S. McCain, in July 1948.

Ceremony at the White House for the presentation of the Presidential
Unit Citation to the carrier task forces. Katherine McCain, Harry
Truman, Frances Mitscher, and Marc Mitscher, July 1946.

John Sidney McCain I, II, and III, at Coco Solo, Panama, 1936.

ordered "Women in the kitchen!"

McCain's first public exposure as DCNO(Air) occurred when he issued a statement to the press on August 30th. The occasion was the thirtieth official anniversary of American naval aviation. McCain's message was that twelve carriers had been built since the attack on Pearl Harbor and that "huge task forces, spearheaded by carrier-based aircraft, are poising for new pile-driver blows against the enemy."[5]

The increase in carrier strength was phenomenal. In the Pacific on December 7, 1941 there were just three: *Saratoga, Lexington,* and *Enterprise.* They were joined by *Yorktown* just as *Saratoga* withdrew after being torpedoed. After launching the April 1942 Doolittle raid on Tokyo, *Hornet* joined the Pacific carrier force. *Wasp* arrived (after ferrying British Spitfire fighter planes to Malta) in time for the Guadalcanal campaign, pushing the total to five. But by early 1943 after the battles of the Coral Sea, Midway, Eastern Solomons, and the Santa Cruz Islands only the *Saratoga* and the *Enterprise* were left. *Saratoga* had been torpedoed twice already. The *Enterprise* was in such bad shape that she had to return to the mainland for overhaul. With *Saratoga* left on her own, the slack was picked up by the HMS *Victorious* in March 1943. During this period even the ever-aggressive Halsey operated his two carriers defensively, keeping them close to New Caledonia and the New Hebrides.

When the *Victorious* was detached in June 1943 and arrived at Pearl Harbor, she found the new fleet carriers *Essex, Yorktown,* and *Lexington,* and the new light carriers *Independence, Belleau Wood,* and *Princeton,* all awaiting action.

McCain was straining against the leash, anxious to get back to the war and put some of this awesome power to good use against the Japanese.

A Proposal for Future Operations

The new title and command structure did not keep McCain at home for long. In October 1943 McCain flew to Pearl Harbor again with intermediate stops at Jackson, Greenwood, San Diego, Burbank, and San Francisco. While in Pearl Harbor, McCain grabbed a chance to promote the aviation point of view. In a memorandum entitled "Proposal for Future Operations" that he had developed in August,

McCain proposed a large carrier task force operation against the Japanese home islands in order to draw out and defeat the Japanese fleet.[6] He may well have envisioned digging out the roots of the Japanese Navy in the home islands and letting outposts such as Formosa and the Philippines wither on the vine.

McCain's idea was dismissed as premature and extravagant. John Towers had concerns that such a proposal was of no help to the credibility of the aviators.[7]

There are several reasons why McCain came out with such a radical but far-sighted proposal at this particular time. First, he believed in what he suggested. Second, he now was at the top of the heap for naval aviation and the prime spokesman for naval aviators. He surely felt that he had to step forward to represent an aviation point of view. Finally, he already was aware of the pressure to unify all the military air services. As he later observed, "It is beginning to look to me that the war after the war will be more bitter than the actual war."[8] So his idea to hit Japan hard with a large carrier force would stake out a stronger postwar position for naval aviation.

Beyond all that, John McCain had a personal stake in the promotion of carrier warfare. His fighting spirit had helped transform the South Pacific campaign into an iron fist that smashed the Japanese in the Solomons and set the tone for aggressive thrusts against the enemy throughout the Pacific. Now he had been a good soldier in Washington for a year and was ready to start his own campaign to get back to the war. His "Proposal" was a step along the way.

A Spokesman for the Aviators

McCain had another significant opportunity to speak out for the aviators. Admiral King, searching for ways to strengthen naval aviation, asked retired Admiral Harry E. Yarnell to return to active duty as an aviation advisor. Yarnell agreed, and straight away undertook a survey of naval aviators. The results were explosive. The aviators wanted carriers to be used on the offensive, not as defenders of amphibious assaults. They also wanted aviators on all major command staffs.[9]

After moving into his new job, McCain undertook his own survey, in parallel to Yarnell's, about the condition of aviation in the Navy. Admiral McCain reported to King in October 1943, giving King some of the best advice he would ever receive. Slew commented colorfully about his fellow aviators: "Without exception, the older naval aviators cannot be separated from the Navy . . . with a hammer and a chisel."

He went on to point out that naval aviators felt that they were not just specialists, but that they were well-rounded naval officers who could represent the Navy as a whole. Further, the aviators felt strongly that carrier task forces should be commanded by an aviator and that in mixed forces either the commander or the chief of staff should be an aviator. King implemented this recommendation in January 1944.

McCain also pushed hard for improved publicity efforts, stating that the Navy was losing friends in the press. Further, Slew recommended early promotions for younger aviators to give them seniority for commands and key assignments. He asked for nineteen more aviation flag officers. King approved nine. That was just the first step; more aviators were promoted as the war progressed, but there never were enough to match the rapid expansion of naval air power.[10]

Finally, as ever the advocate for naval aviation, when a proposal was made by the Vice Chief of Naval Operations, Vice Admiral Frederick J. Horne, to limit the number of aircraft carriers to be kept in commission after the war, McCain recommended that *none* be decommissioned.[11]

A Firsthand View

In January 1944 Admiral McCain flew to Los Angeles for an Army-Navy conference to discuss global war problems. There he was able to catch up on the latest scoop from the South Pacific from his old friend Bill Halsey.

McCain was next off to the Pacific himself for a firsthand view. He left Washington on February 1, 1944 and spent the next day in San Diego meeting with Towers. Jack Towers wanted to discuss logistics, a priority for him, but McCain focused on his scheme to send carriers against Japan. Towers went away unhappy. McCain went on to San Francisco and then to Pearl Harbor. He arrived on February 5, and for the next three days he inspected air bases in the Gilbert Islands. The Gilberts had been seized in bloody action in November 1943, the first act in the Central Pacific advance.[12]

What McCain saw on this trip was how the war had completely turned around in the Pacific. Under Halsey's command, Guadalcanal was secured and his South Pacific forces had moved northwestward through the Solomons, actions that McCain surely watched with great satisfaction. MacArthur's Southwest Pacific forces had moved north-westward through New Guinea toward the East Indies and the Philippines. For the carriers in the Central Pacific, much of 1943 was a quiet period of building forces and organizing for the major push westward. There had been no major carrier strikes from November 1942 until August 1943, when Rear Admiral Charles A. Pownall struck Marcus with Task Force 15 as a shakedown for the new carri-er forces.

In September 1943 movement started against the Gilbert Islands with a strike by Task Force 15 under Pownall's command. Rear Admiral Alfred E. Montgomery took Task Force 14 to strike Wake Island in October. In November, the landings on Bougainville were supported by Rear Admiral Frederick C. "Ted" Sherman's Task Force 38, followed by strikes on Rabaul by Sherman and Montgomery. Then the two joined Pownall when Task Force 50 struck the Gilberts again and supported the landings on Tarawa and Makin Island.

By January 1944 Rear Admiral Marc A. Mitscher had returned to the Pacific to take command of Task Force 58, the new designation for the fast carrier task force. Landings were made by the Marines on Kwajalein and other islands in the Marshall Islands in late January with air cover from Task Force 58. Kwajalein fell on February 4th and nearby Majuro became the U.S. Navy's advance fleet anchorage.

McCain had now been commanding a desk for more than a year. For McCain, or any aviation admiral, the fast carrier task force was the place to be, the force to command. Jack Towers was behind a desk in Pearl Harbor, John McCain was in Washington, and Ted Sherman was in the Pacific commanding a carrier task group. All wanted the job that Mitscher held.[13] But King trusted the command of the carri-er task forces to only three admirals—Halsey, Mitscher, and McCain.[14] Clearly McCain had the inside track if Mitscher was to be relieved for a rest. He was paying his dues in Washington, and doubt-less had worked out a deal with King to get back to the war as soon as his new office was working smoothly and Mitscher was ready for some time off. Now all McCain had to do was make it all happen.

Too Many Planes

Upon his return from the Pacific, McCain addressed the issue of, strange to say, too many Navy airplanes. By the end of 1943, the number of planes in the Navy's inventory had increased from 7,058 the year before to 16,691. By the end of 1944, the total was 34,071, closing in on the authorized level of 37,735. A policy was needed about retirement of old or outmoded airplanes as well as a program for maintenance and supply of the planes on hand. McCain recalled Rear Admiral Arthur W. Radford from the Pacific to become his deputy as an Assistant Chief of Naval Operations (Air). McCain was apologetic about calling Radford back so precipitously, but he explained that these problems needed quick and expert solutions. McCain was not one to waste time, so in April Radford assumed the chair of the first "Radford Committee."

The committee's recommendations (and those of the second Radford Committee in September) formed the basis for the Navy's Integrated Aeronautic Program. Under that program, the newest planes headed out for combat, some planes were junked on the spot, and some planes returned to the United States for reconditioning and use in training. Trained mechanics and adequate spare parts would be available when and where needed. Also, Radford gained some helpful management experience that would serve him well as he climbed the Navy's leadership ladder.[15]

The program was considered a great success. By mid-1945 some 11,000 planes were deployed in the Pacific, and new planes were arriving off Okinawa within three months of leaving the factory.[16]

Publicity

John McCain practiced what he preached about public and press relations. In a newspaper story in April 1944, Slew made statements that might have been drawn right from his October 1943 "extravagant" proposal to strike Japan with a large carrier force: "With 100 aircraft carriers the Navy could ruin the Japanese empire . . . I really believe that with a fleet of carriers that big it would be possible to destroy all

Japanese air forces at hand on the home islands, to [harass] and destroy a great part of her shipping, probably force her fleet to fight, and do sizable damage to her cities . . . We could then take our time in landing armies."

McCain went on to lay out his unshakable principle: "The carrier is now the heart of the task force. . . . Carriers can go wherever there is enough water to float them and so long as they have fuel oil. They can move thousands of planes, scores of mobile airfields, and enough bombs, torpedoes, and bullets."[17]

During the duty tour in Washington, McCain's wife, Katherine, garnered honors as well. On April 29, 1944, she sponsored the launching of the 27,000-ton *Essex*-class aircraft carrier *Bon Homme Richard* (CV-31) at the Brooklyn Navy Yard. As a remembrance she was presented with a silver-jacketed commemorative bottle nestled in a nice wooden box.

Sampson

During this period, McCain's aide, pilot, and general sidekick continued to be Lieutenant Commander William S. Sampson, who had flown Slew's PBY into Henderson Field in August 1942. When McCain needed his help, he summoned Sampson to his office with a whooping "Sam!"—ignoring the battery of buttons on his desk. Sometimes when McCain wasn't in his office, Sam searched for the admiral by following a trail of loose tobacco through the building.[18]

Sam and his wife Helen were great friends to Sidney and Kate. Their son was named John Sidney Sampson, a marvelous tribute. Their daughter, also named Helen, remained a close friend to Kate and Catherine long after Slew's death. She often visited Coronado and shared laughs at the McCain home. Daughter Helen reported that when she was a wee lass, John Sidney played a pretty good game of hide-and-seek in his Washington office.

Later in 1944, when her husband and his admiral were headed back to the war, Helen Sampson drove Slew's 1939 Chevrolet from Washington to the West Coast.

But, more importantly, it was Helen Sampson who made and repaired Slew's famous and fabulous good-luck combat cap.

Relief in Sight

McCain still had his mind set on getting back to the battle zone in the Pacific, and he was already making preparations. On a trip to Jacksonville in March 1944, McCain met with Commander John "Jimmy" Thach and told him that he, McCain, was slated for a combat command. He then asked Thach to come to work for him as his operations officer. Thach accepted, so McCain had orders cut for Thach to join Mitscher's task force staff in May on temporary duty. Thach would then re-join McCain when McCain had turned over the reins in Washington and reported to Pearl Harbor.[19]

So McCain got the ball rolling for a combat command and was well ahead of the game. But lots of details still had to be worked out. Decisions had already been made on the next sequence of campaigns: Hollandia, the Marianas, the Palaus, and the Philippines; but the command structure, and the use of the Fifth Fleet under Spruance and the Third Fleet under Halsey, remained unresolved.

A major step was taken in early May 1944 by King and Nimitz at one of their periodic meetings in San Francisco. The "two-platoon" system was proposed by Rear Admiral Charles Cooke and endorsed by King and Nimitz.[20] They confirmed the arrangement at a July meeting at Pearl Harbor.

Under the two-platoon system, Spruance and Mitscher would run the offensive in the Central Pacific for a period of months as the Fifth Fleet and Task Force 58. Then they would be relieved by Halsey and McCain, who would run the operations as the Third Fleet and Task Force 38. This was a unique approach to command. It was possible only because there was a Spruance and a Halsey available, plus a Mitscher and a McCain. Halsey was told about this arrangement at the May meeting, and that he would be relieved in the South Pacific in June and could then shift himself and his staff to Pearl Harbor to begin planning.[21]

The question of who would take John McCain's job in Washington was an issue, but not a big one. Aubrey Fitch, who had relieved McCain in the South Pacific in 1942, could repeat the performance in 1944 in Washington because things were winding down in the Solomons.[22]

Some thought may have been given to Mitscher's return to Washington when McCain went back to sea. In Washington Mitscher would work on building the Navy's case about the proposed unification of the armed services. But Forrestal was not in favor of bringing Mitscher home. He evidently feared that Mitscher would not be effective in Washington, nor would McCain be effective in the Pacific.[23]

Artemus Gates, the assistant secretary of the Navy for air, raised the only objection to the Fitch appointment, and this was a compliment to John McCain and the job he had done in Washington.[24] Gates was an old-time airman who had qualified as Naval Aviator number 65 during World War I. He was an experienced administrator and had solid political connections.[25] Gates was concerned about relations with Congress on regular issues such as budget and appropriations as well as the growing battle with the Army Air Forces about unification of the air services. Gates sent a note to Forrestal stating his opinion that relieving McCain would not be a good move. Gates had nothing against Fitch, but he felt that McCain knew the ropes in Washington and worked well with Congress. For example, Carl Vinson had presented McCain with a copy of his portrait inscribed, "To my esteemed friend Vice Admiral McCain." Gates was afraid that newcomer Fitch might not be able to fill McCain's shoes.[26]

But in the end, McCain joined Mitscher in the Pacific and Jake Fitch returned to Washington.

Coming Attractions

In May, Slew took a preview trip for his next duty. He wrote to his son Gordon on May 15th: "I am going west to witness as an observer some operations; thereafter will return to Washington for a short period, and have the promise of a sea command. . . . I feel I have a lot to learn in the fleet, and am glad that I am to be an observer merely for the first few weeks."

McCain departed Washington on May 22 and arrived in Pearl Harbor on the 24th. He checked in with CinCPac and was sent onward that same day. On May 26 McCain reported to Admiral Raymond Spruance, Commander of the Fifth Fleet, for 27 days of Temporary Additional Duty (TAD). During the same period, as planned, McCain's operations officer designee, Jimmy Thach, hustled out to the *Lexington* for TAD with Mitscher.[27]

Thus John Sidney McCain became a keenly interested observer of the controversial Battle of the Philippine Sea. He knew he would soon be on his way himself to a major command in the Pacific, and he knew he had lessons to learn. What he was to see reinforced his advocacy for the offensive use of fast carriers and explains his subsequent negative attitude about Spruance's conservative tactics that tied the fast carriers to the beachhead. His differences with Spruance, however, were always on a professional basis, never personal.[28]

While in Pearl Harbor, McCain had a chance to read and discuss a rough draft of the plan for forthcoming operations. He stated his criticisms, perhaps too harshly in view of his outsider status in the Central Pacific, but in the end he worked with Towers to effect some improvements in the types of aircraft assigned.[29]

From May 26 to June 21 McCain rode aboard Spruance's flagship USS *Indianapolis*. On May 26 *Indianapolis* left Pearl Harbor for Majuro, Kwajalein, and Eniwetok in the Marshall Islands. The *Indianapolis* reached Eniwetok on June 6. She moved among the lagoons so that Spruance could meet with the amphibious force commander Kelly Turner, Marine commander Holland M. Smith, carrier boss Mitscher, and others to discuss the upcoming invasion of Saipan. McCain was looking over Spruance's shoulder the whole time. He even tagged along with Spruance on his exercise walks about the deck of the flagship. Spruance wore his Hawaiian shorts while McCain went shirtless.[30]

On June 9, *Indianapolis* rendezvoused with Task Force 58, which had sortied from Majuro on the 6th. From June 11 through the 13th Task Force 58 aircraft struck Saipan, Tinian, Guam, Rota, and the Pagan Islands. On June 13 and 14 *Indianapolis* joined the pre-invasion bombardment group. Spruance and McCain got a close look at the target island.

On the 14th, Spruance received the alarming news that the Japanese fleet was on the move in the direction of the Marianas. The report led him to believe that there were two forces approaching, a fixed idea that influenced his decisions throughout the battle. He constantly feared an end-run by the enemy to strike the amphibious forces near the beachhead.

D-day on Saipan was June 15th. *Indianapolis* cruised just off the beaches while Spruance sent two of the four carrier task groups (William Keen Harrill and Jocko Clark) north to strike enemy aircraft at Iwo Jima and Chichi Jima. Although this split Spruance's forces, the northern group could be (and was) quickly recalled on June 16. Spruance ordered Mitscher to take the rest of Task Force 58 westward toward the estimated location of the enemy fleet, and sent the battleships to guard against a possible southern attack.

Also on the 16th, Spruance met with Turner on the *Rocky Mount* and heard about the heavy fighting ashore.[31] Then he ordered the bulk of the amphibious forces under Turner to head to a position 300 miles east of Saipan, out of danger if the enemy launched an air attack on the beachhead. Then, on June 17, Spruance rejoined Task Force 58 and issued his battle plan. He specified that Task Force 58 must give primary emphasis to covering the invasion forces on Saipan and not to seeking out and hitting the enemy fleet.

Task Force 58 left close air coverage of the beachhead to the escort carriers, while Alfred Montgomery's Task Group 58.2 and Blackjack Reeves' Task Group 58.3 moved westward and Clark's Task Group 58.1 and Harrill's Task Group 58.4 searched to the southwest. Clark wanted to outflank the enemy, but a reluctant Harrill refused. Both rejoined Task Force 58 on June 18.

On the 18th Vice Admiral Willis Lee's battleships moved ahead of Task Force 58, nearer to the suspected enemy position. Air cover for Lee was provided by Harrill's Task Group 58.4. The other three task groups followed behind, moving westward. That night Lee recommended against a night surface action, so Spruance reversed course to the east, thus missing any chance to hit the enemy fleet with his carrier planes. Although Mitscher recommended that they continue sailing west, Spruance still feared a two-pronged enemy attack and took the task force east, closer to Saipan.

On June 19th, Mitscher launched early searches and strikes against Guam. By mid-morning the Japanese planes from the on-coming enemy carriers swarmed toward the task force. *Indianapolis* and the other ships went to general quarters. What followed was the spectacular, one-sided "Marianas Turkey Shoot." Mitscher sent his bombers east to orbit near Guam and leave the decks clear for the fighters. The fighters launched and circled 100 miles west to intercept the incoming Japanese. They did, and the enemy lost an estimated 383 planes. Mitscher lost only twenty-five, and his carriers were not touched by the enemy.[32]

By the time the fighters had finished their work, the fleet was 50 miles off the Marianas. *Indianapolis* gunners shot down one enemy torpedo plane during the battle. At 4:30 p.m. Spruance told Mitscher to prepare to attack the next day. He also recalled Turner to Saipan. Mitscher sent Task Group 58.4 to cover Guam, and the other three task groups moved northwest. By then the enemy had itself reversed course to the west.

During the day of June 20th, Mitscher, now in tactical command, searched for the Japanese fleet. When contact was made at 3:40 p.m., the enemy was reported to be 220 miles to the northwest. Mitscher launched immediately. Although the enemy fleet was subsequently found to be farther away—270 miles—the attack was not called back. Contact was made at 6:40 p.m., with hits reported on enemy carriers and oilers. Then the attack force of bombers and fighters turned homeward.

The strike force arrived back over the task force in darkness and short of fuel. Jocko Clark saw their predicament and, following an advisory by Mitscher, turned on all his flagship's lights including the searchlights. The rest of the task force soon followed suit so the planes could find their way back to the carriers. Even so, many ditched in the sea, but most airmen were recovered.[33]

The planes were up again on June 21 for a stern chase, but with no luck. At 8:30 a.m. McCain transferred to the *Lexington* for TAD with Mitscher until the 24th. On the 23rd Spruance ordered most of Task Force 58 to Eniwetok. At Eniwetok, McCain was with Mitscher when Lieutenant Commander James D. "Jig Dog" Ramage, commanding officer of bombing squadron 10, visited to report that the strikes on June 20 had not been particularly productive. Mitscher agreed "It wasn't a great victory."[34]

From June 24 to the 26th McCain completed his observer duty with Rear Admiral John W. "Black Jack" Reeves, Jr., commanding Task Group 58.3. Then it was back to CinCPac on June 30 and home to Washington by July 6.

New Orders

On July 25, 1944, Slew finally received his orders: "When directed by the Chief of Naval Operations on or about 1 August 1944, you will regard yourself detached from duty involving flying as Deputy Chief of Naval Operations for Air . . . and upon arrival report to the Commander-in-Chief, Pacific Fleet, on 10 August 1944, for duty involving flying as a Carrier Task Force Commander."

He cleaned up his desk and was detached on August 1, 1944. As agreed earlier, Commander Herbert Riley also benefited by McCain's orders. He was detached from the bureau to take command of the carrier *Makassar Strait*.[35]

Lieutenant Commander Sam Sampson also received his orders. He was directed to report to San Diego to take command of a squadron of PB4Y "Privateer" four-engine patrol bombers. He told his family that he would always be indebted to John McCain for his leadership example of "Carry a soft stick." As a commander, Sampson led squadron VPB-106 from July 1944 through July 1945, operating from North Island and Camp Kearney in California, and from Kaneohe, Tinian, Iwo Jima, and Palawan in the Pacific.

11

THE FAST CARRIERS

On July 26, 1944, orders were issued to move the McCain's household goods from 1870 Wyoming Avenue, NW, to 625 A Avenue in Coronado. Packing was set for August 4th, collection on the 5th, and shipping scheduled on the 7th.

Sidney's and Kate's home at 625 A Avenue was one of three built in 1927. Two were on the street and one behind, all served by a single driveway. The three-home complex still exists, and is known locally as Herreshoff Court. Two of the homes have been given historic designation by the Coronado Historic Resource Commission. The homes were designed by Charles Herreshoff, a naval architect and boat builder.

The house in the rear was designed for the original "Gibson Girl." Artist Charles Gibson's popular drawings made this beauty an icon of the early 1900s. That popularity lasted into the 1940s, when the emergency radio transmitter used by ditched air crews was labeled the "Gibson Girl" due to its curvaceous shape.

The larger house on the street was occupied during the war by John Roosevelt, then in the Navy. Eleanor Roosevelt visited her son there, with presidential security across the drive at the McCain home.

Sidney bought the smaller house on the street in 1942. The McCain home was originally Herreshoff's residence and is full of nautical space-saving concepts. For example, there is a block-and-tackle device to raise and lower the stairs to the attic. The pull rope and securing cleat are hidden in a small cabinet at the top of the main staircase.

The Two-Platoon System

McCain was detached in Washington on August 1, 1944, and didn't waste much time getting back to the Pacific. He left Washington on August 3, spent the night in Greenwood, stopped in Glendale on August 4, and arrived at Alameda on the 5th. He flew on from there to Pearl Harbor and was checked in at CinCPac by John Towers on August 9.

Earlier, in June 1944, Halsey had been relieved of his South Pacific command and joined the Central Pacific campaign in his role as commander of the Third Fleet. Halsey and his staff remained in Pearl Harbor preparing to assume the fleet command and working on plans for the invasion of the western Carolines.

On August 5, while McCain was in transit to Pearl Harbor, the Fast Carrier Task Force under Mitscher's command was split into two commands: the First Fast Carrier Task Force under Mitscher, and the Second Fast Carrier Task Force commanded by McCain. This was a key to the two-platoon command system soon to be initiated.

Under the two-platoon system, Spruance and Mitscher would run the offensive in the Central Pacific for four to five months as the Fifth Fleet and Task Force 58. Then they would rotate out and be relieved by Halsey and McCain, who would take over operations for the next four to five months as the Third Fleet and Task Force 38. While one team conducted operations, the off-duty commanders and their staffs had time off for leave. Then, rested, they plunged into planning the next series of actions. When ready, the Third Fleet commanders, with plans in hand, relieved the Fifth Fleet commanders, who would be off on their own cycle of leave and planning. Then the rotation would be repeated.[1]

It worked out pretty well as intended. Halsey made plans for the Carolines and the Philippines and then went into action. Spruance made plans for Okinawa and then executed them. Later both worked on plans to strike Japan during their next rotation.[2] If only one staff had been available, the three- to five-month planning period would have been heel-to-toe with battle operations, and that might have stretched out the war by months, maybe more than a year.

While this scheme kept the commanders and their staffs fresh, the pressures on the whole fleet were still immense. The air groups—the pilots—were under the greatest pressure, and rotated in and out on a six-to-nine-month schedule (later reduced to six months). But the undamaged ships and most of their crews remained at sea. The Fifth Fleet became the Third Fleet, and vice-versa, but the ships were the same.

Although the two-platoon system speeded up the war effort, sadly the overflow of resources did not reach very far down the line. The ships and sailors had to get by with whatever rest and recreation they could carve out when the fleet found time to retire to one of the great fleet anchorages such as Eniwetok or Ulithi.

A side effect of the two-platoon system was that for a while the Japanese were fooled into thinking that there were two great fleets stalking them through the Pacific. A lot of Americans were fooled as well.[3]

Two Old Salts

Both fast carrier task force commanders were small, tough, and wiry; and both had wizened, weather-beaten faces. Many people confused the two because they looked alike and rotated in and out of the same job.

Both were unorthodox. Mitscher wore a long-billed cap and sat in his special chair on the flag bridge, facing the stern of the ship and overlooking the flight deck. He was physically gentle, personally cool, and spoke very, very softly.

McCain, on the other hand, was everywhere at once, trailing cigarette ashes all over the flag bridge. His boiling point was low and when he exploded, his staff scattered.[4]

McCain's trademark was his combat-area cap that combined the crown from a Marine fatigue cap with his admiral's hat brim and gold braid. The hat became a lucky charm for both McCain and his men. Halsey found the unorthodox headgear revolting, saying that it "was the most disreputable one I ever saw on an officer." But McCain, like most sailors, was superstitious. He would not part with his hat when in the combat zone. He never wore it elsewhere.

Everyone on McCain's flagship treasured this good luck symbol as well. Whenever the wind blew the hat from his head, the men scrambled to keep it from being blown overboard. McCain would grin broadly when it was handed back to him.[5]

Mitscher had entered the Naval Academy in 1904, just two years behind McCain. But in 1906, he resigned with a full load of demerits and a brush with a hazing scandal. However he obtained another appointment and graduated in 1910, four years behind his future fellow task force commander.[6] He was an early naval aviator (number 33 in 1916), and was pilot of the NC-1 in the famed 1919 trans-Atlantic flight. In contrast, McCain was a "latecomer" to naval aviation, winged as number 4280 in 1936. Mitscher made flag rank in 1942, a year and a half after McCain, and was promoted to vice admiral in March 1944, eight months behind McCain.

In late 1943, after fast carrier attacks by Task Force 50 on the Gilberts and Marshalls, Nimitz was seeking a more aggressive leader for the carrier force than the man he had, Rear Admiral Charles A. Pownall. After conferring with King, Mitscher was selected to relieve Pownall. King and Nimitz agreed that Mitscher was the best prospect for the job. He knew aviation in and out, he had a good record as the commander of aviation in the Solomons under Halsey, and—importantly—he was immediately available on the West Coast.

Task Group Commander

When McCain arrived at Pearl Harbor in early August, Jack Towers (at this time deputy to CinCPac Nimitz) informed McCain officially that Mitscher was remaining as commander of Task Force 38. Mitscher had not been at sea as long as Spruance, who was to be relieved by Halsey later in the month. McCain eventually would lead Task Force 38, but Mitscher wanted to stay in command of the fast carriers until the Philippines campaign was finished.[7]

McCain did not give up easily. He headed out to meet with Mitscher during one of Mitscher's rest periods. McCain aimed to persuade Mitscher to relinquish command of Task Force 58 right away.

Mitscher knew McCain was coming aboard, and probably knew McCain wanted him to rotate out of the task force command and go home for a rest. Mitscher was tired from his earlier campaign, but giving up his command was out of the question as far as he was concerned. McCain and Mitscher met privately in Mitscher's quarters. When the hour-long meeting was over and McCain left the *Lexington,* his face was grim. "Pete thought he still had plenty of work to do," McCain later told his son Jack. No more is known about exactly what transpired between the two admirals, but Mitscher kept command of Task Force 58 through October.[8]

With Mitscher remaining in command of the task force for an extra two months, McCain took over Rear Admiral J. J. "Jocko" Clark's Task Group 38.1 in a learning role. Clark stayed on for a while to coach Slew and his staff in their new jobs.[9]

It was noted by some historians that Admiral McCain was "understandably chagrined" when Mitscher did not soon follow Spruance back to Pearl Harbor.[10] But whether Slew was in fact chagrined is subject to question. Commander John S. "Jimmy" Thach related, "This was the way Admiral McCain wanted it." That attitude squared with McCain's earlier comments about having a lot to learn.[11]

As McCain moved into the new job, his first task was to assemble a staff. His preference was to keep Mitscher's staff, but Nimitz, Towers, and others disagreed. The rotation concept required that the off-duty staff remain intact to plan the next operations. Slew was ruffled, but he was generally reassured when his overall status as the future task force commander continued to be endorsed by his bosses.[12]

So McCain got busy working with Jimmy Thach, who had returned to Pearl Harbor from TAD with Mitscher's staff and had already interviewed and picked many of the future staff officers. McCain selected Rear Admiral Wilder Baker for the key post of chief of staff. Spruance had suggested to his own chief of staff, Carl Moore, that he take the job, but Moore objected rather violently to the idea because he felt that he would not be able to work well (or at all) with the competent but impulsive McCain. Moore stated "I haven't any influence on him. . . . I could tell that his ideas were screwball in many ways, and I wouldn't have agreed with him on practically anything he wanted to do."[13] His attitude reflected one side of the dichotomy of opinion about John Sidney McCain. Moore spent the remainder of the war in Washington.[14]

Rear Admiral Wilder Du Puy Baker was a vital member of Admiral McCain's staff. Although Baker was a grandfather, Slew McCain addressed him as "son" (McCain called everybody on the flag bridge "son").[15] Baker had been a cruiser commander, and for a short

time had commanded carrier Task Group 58.2 when Rear Admiral
Keen Harrill was taken ill.[16] As an experienced surface-warfare officer
he could relieve McCain of many routine duties such as refueling and
maneuvering the carrier formation. Baker was soft-spoken and smart.
He has been called the father of the Navy's modern antisubmarine
warfare techniques.[17] After the hostilities ended, McCain dedicated a
photo to Admiral Baker, "Who more than any other was responsible
for the precision and excellence of overall fleet operations."

Inasmuch as Jocko Clark was staying on to assist McCain, Towers
suggested that McCain also borrow members of Clark's staff to serve
in an advisory capacity.[18] This was done, and for the training period
Clark loaned McCain his operations officer (to work with "Jimmy"
Thach), his logistics and navigation officers, his assistant operations
officer, his flag secretary, and his fighter director. This arrangement
lasted for about two weeks until McCain and his staff became famil-
iar with task group operations.[19]

Commander John Smith Thach was a tremendous asset to
McCain. This talented officer was in Fighting Squadron 3 at North
Island (commanding the squadron in 1941) while McCain was commanding officer of the base, and when McCain flew his flag there as
patrol plane commander. But evidently they did not meet during this
period. It was at North Island that Thach developed the famous
"Thach Weave," a defensive fighter tactic that allowed the less maneu-
verable American F4F fighter to match and beat the nimble Japanese
Zero.

John S. McCain III noted about Jimmy Thach: "My grandfather
did give enormous responsibilities to his operations officer and had
always taken care to credit Thach with many of the innovations implemented by Task Force 38. When he hired Thach for the job, having
never met him prior to that, Thach had asked him why he had selected him. 'I've heard you're not a "yes" man,' my grandfather answered,
'and I don't want any yes man on my staff.'"[20]

McCain had selected Thach for the key job on his staff because he
felt, rightly so, that he could rely heavily on Thach for his up-to-date
air combat savvy. Thus McCain could leave the detailed planning in
competent hands and devote himself to the broader picture. Thach
stated, "I never did anything concerning policy or of great significance

without his approval," and McCain regularly backed Thach's operational decisions. McCain treated Thach like a member of his family.[21]

Jimmy Thach was a four-star admiral when he retired in 1967. His relief as Commander-in-Chief, U.S. Naval Forces, Europe, was none other than Admiral John Sidney McCain, Jr.

Reaction

It is interesting that there always seemed to be a reaction to John Sidney McCain. He had hundreds of friends, but not everyone understood or approved of his style, which occasionally was unorthodox, and a number of his peers seriously underestimated his abilities.

It was noted that the appointment of McCain to alternate the command of Task Force 38/58 with Mitscher caused something of a stir among the aviators. The early-day flyers felt a latecomer did not deserve the top carrier command.[22]

This comment about a "stir" seems to refer mainly to the senior officers, particularly those involved in the ongoing skirmish between air admirals and battleship admirals. This sort of reaction from the senior aviators is puzzling, because John McCain had been fighting so hard for them in Washington.

But if such a stir occurred, there was no evidence that it extended down through the ranks. One pilot's view of Slew McCain is provided by an absolutely wonderful story recorded by Harold Buell, a dive-bomber pilot on the *Hornet*. He related how the pilots were allowed to go ashore for recreation while Task Force 38 was at Eniwetok. After an afternoon at the junior officer's bar, they returned to the dock to catch a boat back to their ship. Evidently the pilots were not feeling much pain and a game of the old heave-ho started, launching newcomers into the water. As events unfolded:

A fresh group had just arrived, and we were up to the count of three on a small man, when I noticed that the person we were launching into space was Vice Admiral J.S. McCain. Shouting a warning, which was too late, I dove with a couple of others into the water to retrieve him . . . As we got hold of him and helped him to his feet, he was gasping and wheezing and said: "Get my hat, boys, get my hat." We retrieved the hat, got the admiral back up on the dock, and expressed our deepest regrets for our conduct.

What a great little guy he was. . . . He was a small man, almost fragile, and looked like a strong wind could blow him away. Dripping salt water, seaweed, and coral sand, he kept grinning as he shook hands with each of us while we continued making our apologies. He asked for a dry cigarette, lit up, and started telling us how good it was to be back with his "fighting men." With blue eyes twinkling from a wrinkled face, dominated by both a nose and ears of heroic proportions, McCain looked for all the world like a leprechaun.

Still in the spirit of the game, McCain called in his launch, flying his three-star flag, and delivered the wet and grimy pilots back to their ships. This created consternation on the part of the officers standing formal watch at the head of the gangway on each of the carriers.[23]

Carrier Tactics (II)

Carrier tactics had changed radically as the war progressed. In pre-war exercises, the job of the few carriers in the fleet was to support the battleships. The carriers were usually stationed to the side of the battleship line away from the enemy. They provided scouting and protection for the battle line against enemy bombers and submarines.

By the time of the Battle of Midway, in June 1942, the carrier task force had evolved. Now the carrier was at the center of the force surrounded by an antiaircraft screen of cruisers and destroyers. When two carrier task forces were together (as they were at Midway and Coral Sea) they operated far apart to avoid interference. Thus they forfeited the benefits of a mutually supportive combat air patrol to protect the carriers from enemy aircraft.

Heavy emphasis was placed on patrols and searches to locate the enemy force. Long-range, land-based patrol bombers and carrier-based scouts were used. One carrier might undertake the scouting duties while the other carrier had the fighters and bombers poised for a strike when the enemy was found.

The contact reports were critical. The location, size, composition, course, and speed of the enemy were all key pieces of information.

Enemy carriers remained the top priority. A key question was whether or not the enemy had spotted *our* carriers. Range to the enemy ships was also critical. The fighters and bombers had to carry enough fuel to fly to a sometimes vague location, conduct the strike, and fly home to a carrier that, in the meantime, had moved.

Further, the carrier always had to balance closing on the enemy against having to sail into the wind to conduct flight operations. At the Battle of the Philippine Sea, this factor had worked sharply against Spruance and Mitscher. To move closer to the enemy carriers, they had to sail on a westward course outward from Saipan. Then, to launch and recover aircraft, they had to reverse course into the prevailing winds and sail back toward Saipan, away from the enemy. The Japanese had a huge advantage in that conditions were reversed for them. They could continue on an eastward course into the wind, closing on the American fleet, launch and recover aircraft, and not lose ground as did the zigzagging Americans.

As more carriers became available in 1943, the larger fast carrier task force evolved. The fleet commander (four-star admirals Spruance or Halsey) directed the overall actions of the fleet in accordance with theater strategy. The fleet could include the carrier task force, the amphibious force, attached service groups, and special task units that might be formed to conduct, for example, a shore bombardment. When an amphibious operation was not in the offing, the fleet could be slimmed down to the carrier task force. This was often the case for Halsey's Third Fleet.

The fleet commander was not expected to take direct tactical command except in rare cases. That usually was left to the task force and task group commanders.

The fast carrier task force, commanded by a three-star vice admiral, typically consisted of three or four task groups. Each task group, commanded by a two-star rear admiral, could include three or four fleet and light carriers, a battleship or two, three or four cruisers, and a dozen-or-more destroyers. This was an awesome congregation of naval power. The task force commander controlled the course, speed, and formation of the task force (unless the task groups were operating independently), and gave orders to the task groups for operations such as refueling and launching missions. The task group commanders, in their turn, sent orders to the carrier commanding officers, who passed on the orders to the embarked air groups.[24]

The task force, whether 58 or 38, did not always act as a single unit. Task groups were often assigned separate targets some distance apart, at times vast distances. When this happened, the task group acted independently. Also the composition of each task group changed as ships moved in and out to repair battle damage or get a long-awaited overhaul.

As the Japanese fleet, particularly the carriers and carrier pilots, was whittled down at Coral Sea, Midway, Guadalcanal, and the Philippine Sea, the target priority shifted away from the enemy fleet to enemy land-based air. Land-based bombers, a powerful Imperial Navy component, had always been a particular threat to the carriers. Land-based carrier planes, in addition to striking from their home fields, could also shuttle to the carriers and then, refueled and rearmed, return to the attack. As was seen at the Battle of the Philippine Sea, carrier-based planes could shuttle to land bases as well.

The American fast carriers had the capability to stay out of range of this land-based threat unless tied to a beachhead or when attacking a stronghold like Formosa. The land-based air threat worsened significantly when the Japanese unleashed the deadly kamikazes. McCain always advocated wiping out the enemy air threat first. Others, including Halsey, still felt that the Japanese battleships should receive high priority attention as well.

By May 1944, the fast carrier task force had demonstrated that it could go anywhere it wanted, and had sufficient combat air power to seize and hold air superiority while there.

So carrier tactics evolved from the early carrier-versus-carrier battles of 1942 to a period of preserving carrier strength in early 1943. Then the Japanese carrier threat was virtually ended at the Battle of the Philippine Sea, when so many experienced Japanese carrier pilots were lost. The American fast carrier force could then shift their focus to supporting landings and attacking enemy air bases.

Important adjuncts to the fast carrier force were the escort carriers, which provided close air support to amphibious troops. This allowed the fast carriers to use their mobility to more aggressively pursue the enemy.

To Battle

Vice Admiral John McCain started off modestly. On August 18, 1944, while anchored at Eniwetok in the Marshall Islands, he hoisted his flag on the USS *Wasp* as commander, Task Group 58.1. McCain relieved Rear Admiral Jocko Clark, who remained in *Hornet* as an advisor while McCain and his staff worked into their jobs.

Halsey got a slap on the wrist for this particular act, it seems. Evidently he had ordered Clark's relief without clearing the command change with his boss, Nimitz. The change of command was not the problem—Clark was due to leave in any event—but Nimitz felt his prerogatives were being violated. Halsey apologized. Although he was bold and aggressive, Halsey was not arrogant.

Task Group 58.1 remained anchored at Eniwetok for a few more days. Then McCain took the force out for routine flight and gunnery training as his first exercise of command. They were back at the anchorage by August 23.

Halsey relieved Spruance on August 26. The Fifth Fleet became the Third Fleet, Task Force 58 became 38, and Task Group 58.1 became Task Group 38.1. McCain's group was composed of the carriers *Wasp, Hornet, Cowpens,* and *Belleau Wood*; the cruisers *Boston, Canberra,* and *Wichita*; and three destroyer divisions.

Task Force 38 included three other task groups. Task Group 38.2 was commanded by Rear Admiral Gerald F. Bogan and Task Group 38.3 was headed by Rear Admiral Frederick C. Sherman. Rear Admiral Ralph E. Davison was running Task Group 38.4. Task Force commander Marc A. Mitscher was riding in *Lexington,* which was a part of Ted Sherman's Task Group 38.3. The force remained at anchor in Eniwetok until it sortied on August 29 en route to the Palaus. Halsey had not yet joined up. He was in his flagship, *New Jersey,* making his way from Pearl Harbor to rendezvous with Task Force 38.

Sadly, on the next day, John McCain lost his assistant operations officer when Commander Gordon Cady crashed on *Belleau Wood* while attempting to land. He died from his injuries and was buried at sea on August 31, 1944. Admiral McCain sent condolences to Mrs. Cady, commenting that her husband had been specially selected for staff duty because of his excellent reputation and wide experience. He lauded Commander Cady's careful planning of air operations.

Before leaving Eniwetok, Admiral McCain produced his first operation order, labeled "OpOrder 1-44." It directed that "This force will . . . strike Palau, Palmas, Talud and Morotai; destroy Japanese aircraft, ships, aircraft facilities, and defenses in order to support the capture of Peleliu . . . Morotai . . . and Yap. . . . In case the opportunity for the destruction of the Japanese fleet is presented, or can be created, such destruction will become the primary task." This tactical principle, "The opportunity for the destruction of the Japanese fleet" issued by McCain in August is virtually the same as that issued by Nimitz to Halsey in September in the operation plan for the invasion of Leyte, and often cited in analyses of the Battle of Leyte Gulf.

While Davison took his Task Group 38.4 north to hit Iwo Jima and Chichi Jima, the other three task groups moved on to the Palaus. McCain operated Task Group 38.1 independently during the day for intensive ship and air group exercises. Then he rejoined the task force at night. On September 2, Task Group 38.1 refueled at sea in preparation for the invasion.

McCain's group reached its launching point, 150 miles southeast of Palau, on September 6. As part of the overall Task Force 38 attack, McCain's air groups conducted sweeps and strikes for the next two days, including the first use of napalm by carrier planes. Even with overwhelming air support, the Marines ashore had a hard time of it. The Japanese were well dug-in on Peleliu, and Marine losses were high.

All three task groups fueled and then withdrew on the evening of September 8 to make a high-speed run westward to Mindanao. There, on the 9th and from fifty miles off the coast, all three groups launched strikes against airfields and shipping. Targets quickly became scarce, but a 46-ship convoy was destroyed. Task Group 38.1 delivered a 200-mile strike and probably sank five medium cargo ships and five smaller vessels at anchor on the north side of Mindanao.

The three task groups withdrew 300 miles to the east on September 10 for fueling and to receive replacement pilots and planes. Halsey, after meeting with Vice Admiral Thomas Kinkaid (commander of MacArthur's Seventh Fleet) at Manus, caught up with Task Force 38 on September 11. Davison, with Task Group 38.4, returned from his mission to the north and took station to cover the Palaus.

The other three task groups, including McCain, were back in action on September 12 to strike the Negros and Cebu. This action was described as a field day for the flyers of Task Force 38, who shot down 173 enemy aircraft and destroyed 305 on the ground.[25]

On that day Ensign T. C. Tillar, a fighter pilot from *Hornet* in McCain's group, was forced down just off the coast of Leyte. On shore he was told by the friendly islanders that there were no Japanese on Leyte. Tillar was rescued before dark by scout planes and passed his observations on to Admiral Clark. The findings were forwarded immediately to McCain, Mitscher, and Halsey. This information, combined with the weak resistance encountered by Task Force 38, suggested to Halsey that the projected invasion of Leyte could be advanced. Why not invade right away instead of waiting until December, as planned? Halsey made the recommendation, and the answer came back immediately. The Leyte operation would be undertaken with a target date of October 20.[26]

Late on the evening of September 13, Task Group 38.1 was detached from Task Force 38. McCain proceeded independently to support the landings on Morotai. Along the way his planes conducted sweeps over Mindanao and the Celebes. On the 15th, Slew set up shop about 50 miles north of Morotai and for two days sent out a strong combat air patrol. The landings were unopposed, so McCain was relieved on September 16.

Kinkaid sent: "CTG 38.1 has been relieved. Will not require your further services. Thank you for your excellent assistance and cooperation. Good luck and best wishes."

McCain then took the task group eastward to a fueling rendezvous. On September 17 the light carrier *Monterey* relieved *Belleau Wood*, which shifted to Task Group 38.4. John Sidney wrote to Kate on September 17, "My gang did right well in the fighting . . ."

McCain's task group rejoined the main body on September 18 for strikes on the 21st against airfields and shipping around Manila, and to hit airfields, military facilities, and shipping in the central Philippines. The weather was not favorable, but targets were plentiful. Planes from *Wasp* and *Hornet* left Manila Bay strewn with burning ships and oil slicks.[27] Continuous strikes were launched throughout the day.

Up to this point air opposition was almost nonexistent. Now land-based enemy planes began to probe the fleet. A weak attack was launched by the Japanese on the morning of September 22. The *Hornet* and *Monterey* were strafed with minor damage but with two fatalities. Three of the six attackers were downed and two were damaged by antiaircraft fire.

After refueling and picking up more replacement pilots and planes from the escort carriers on September 23, Task Force 38 made a high-speed run to a point about 60 miles east of the San Bernardino Strait. From there continuous raids were conducted for two days against Coron Bay (on Palawan), Negros, Cebu, and Panay. There was no aerial opposition. McCain's pilots reported six vessels sunk (including a transport and a destroyer-escort), three probably sunk, and twenty damaged.

McCain then took Task Group 38.1 independently to Manus in the Admiralty Islands for provisioning. They arrived on September 28.

After his first period commanding fast carriers in action, McCain and his staff had a number of recommendations for future operations. Following up on his thoughts about fighter-bombers from his tour in Washington, McCain made a particularly strong plea for replacing all two-seat dive-bombers with single-seat Hellcats and Corsair fighters. The fighters could be armed with 500- or 1000-pound bombs. McCain claimed they performed better as dive-bombers than the two-seat SB2Cs. After dropping the bombs, the Hellcats and Corsairs reverted to their role as high-performance fighters. The fighters could also carry and be highly successful with air-to-ground rockets. His thinking was also influenced by the increasing need for fighters as defenders of the task force as operations worked into the Philippines, where large numbers of land-based enemy planes were expected to be encountered.

He had made some progress in his quest when, in July, Admiral King approved an increase in the number of fighters on the *Essex*-class carriers from thirty-six to fifty-four by replacing part of the SB2C complement. But McCain wanted even more fighters.[28]

McCain's report also praised the work of the night fighters. He recommended that night fighters operate from specialized aircraft carriers. This would avoid conflicts and delays caused by shuffling day fighters and night fighters when both were working from the same flight deck. One additional recommendation was to increase the number of destroyers attached to a task group from ten to fourteen. (He later upped this to eighteen.)

By the end of September Mitscher decided that McCain and his staff knew the ropes of task group operation well enough for Jocko Clark to be detached from his advisory role. Clark was ordered back to Pearl Harbor and on to thirty days leave Stateside.[29]

McCain felt even stronger about his learning period. He included in a memo to Mitscher on September 25: "Am ready and willing to relieve you which please communicate to Halsey if in your opinion appropriate and in accord with his desires. Have had a great time, thanks in part at least, to your assignment of targets."

The Service Force

The refueling and replenishment pattern during September 1944 was fairly typical of fast carrier operations. Periodically the task force found time to retire to one of the large forward bases for rest, repairs, replacement pilots, new planes, more ammunition, and other stores. These bases spread westward as the Central Pacific offensive advanced through the islands. Initially the large lagoons at Majuro, Kwajalein, and Eniwetok in the Marshall Islands served the fleet. Next were Manus in the Admiralties and Saipan in the Marianas. Ulithi fell with no opposition on September 23, and its huge lagoon became the major fleet anchorage. At these anchorages, the service force repair, cargo, refrigerator, ammunition, and hospital ships, plus the tankers, awaited the return of the fleet as well as the occasional individual ship returning from battle.

But far beyond these periodic rests, the fleet required a near-constant mobile source of supplies. Task Force 38 needed fuel every four to seven days. The service force met this need. They were an underrated and under-praised part of the Pacific victory. Progress in the war would have been slowed or stopped without a steady supply of bombs, pilots, and planes. The at-sea service force task groups and task units were a secret weapon—a sophisticated logistical supply system that allowed the carrier task forces to stay at sea for months at a time.

The at-sea replenishment groups were under the tactical command
of the fleet and were designated as separate task groups, for example
Task Group 30.8. A group might include a dozen oilers, a couple of
tugs, and escorting destroyers and destroyer-escorts. Two escort carriers might be along as well. One CVE furnished air cover for the service group, while the other CVE carried replacement planes and pilots.

A service group, as it approached the task force, split into separate
units to match up with the individual units of the task force.
Replenishment proceeded with each pair operating together, but independently of the other pairs.

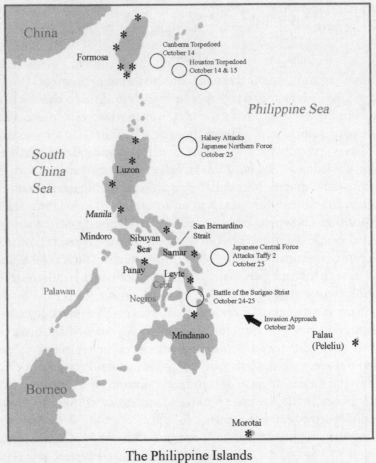

China

Formosa

Canberra Torpedoed
October 14

Houston Torpedoed
October 14 & 15

Philippine Sea

South
China
Sea

Luzon

Halsey Attacks
Japanese Northern Force
October 25

Manila

Mindoro

Sibuyan
Sea

San Bernardino
Strait

Samar

Japanese Central Force
Attacks Taffy 2
October 25

Panay

Leyte

Cebu

Negros

Battle of the Surigao Striat
October 24-25

Palawan

Invasion Approach
October 20

Mindanao

Palau
(Peleliu)

Borneo

Morotai

The Philippine Islands
Target Areas = *

12

THE PHILIPPINES CAMPAIGN

McCain took Task Group 38.1 out of Manus on October 2, 1944, for the opening air action of the campaign to reoccupy the Philippines. The group remained essentially as before with the *Wasp, Hornet, Cowpens,* and *Monterey* forming the carrier unit. As usual, McCain ordered flight and gunnery exercises while en route to the rendezvous point. Heavy weather encountered along the way resulted in the loss of five planes on *Cowpens* and one man on *Wasp.*

Halsey's plans called for the Third Fleet to hit hard at Okinawa and Formosa before the landings in the Philippines got underway. This would cut off enemy air support at its source. Then he was to hit Luzon and the central Philippines.

McCain's task group rendezvoused with the rest of the task force On October 7, some 375 miles west of Saipan. Nimitz had loaned Halsey's amphibious ships to MacArthur, so the Third Fleet and Task Force 38 were one and the same. The force refueled on October 8 and commenced a high-speed run to Okinawa on the 9th.

Task Force 38 struck the Ryukyus on October 10, concentrating on Okinawa. No air opposition was encountered by McCain's planes over the targets. At least twenty enemy aircraft were reported demolished on the ground and seventeen vessels were sunk by Task Group 38.1. Overall, Task Force 38 launched a total of 1,396 sorties, and destroyed about one hundred planes and many ships. The cost was twenty-one American aircraft.[1]

The task force refueled on October 11, and McCain launched a fighter sweep against northern Luzon that netted fifteen Japanese aircraft destroyed on the ground. Merchant shipping was also hit.

Navy Cross

There was little or no opposition to the strikes against the Ryukyus and Luzon on the 10th and the 11th; but when the task force hit Formosa on October 12, the enemy was waiting.

All through the night of October 11–12, the entire task force was shadowed by enemy snoopers that kept track of the fleet's course and speed. All ships were warned to expect an attack at dawn. Bombers and torpedo planes were kept below on the hangar decks while fighters on the flight decks waited to launch. But the enemy did not appear, and Task Force 38 commenced the launch of a fighter sweep and four bombing strikes against targets on Formosa and the Pescadores in the Formosa Strait. A total of 1,378 sorties were flown by planes from the four task groups of Task Force 38, and about two hundred enemy planes were destroyed. No Japanese fighters rose to oppose the third wave of American planes. Forty-eight Task Force 38 planes were lost.[2]

That day McCain's task group put 325 planes over the targets. Nine planes were lost in combat. This was the price for destroying a reported 13 enemy planes in the air, 68 planes on the ground, and various other ground targets.

After nightfall, fourteen Japanese planes came out to attack McCain's task group. All were destroyed—ten by night fighters and four by antiaircraft fire. McCain ordered evasive emergency turns and made smoke to confuse the attackers.

The next morning, October 13, Task Force 38 continued the attack on Formosa. Planes from McCain's carriers encountered no air opposition but antiaircraft fire was intense at Heito Airfield. Again, enemy planes were destroyed on the ground and shipping was hit. Two of McCain's planes were lost in combat, plus one operational crash. Three strikes had been launched by the Task Group 38.1 on October 13, but the fourth strike was cancelled when the task group ran out of daylight.

The night of the 13th was a different matter for McCain's ships. All that afternoon more and more bogeys—unidentified aircraft— appeared on the task group's radar screens. After the third strike was recovered at 4:52 p.m., *Wasp, Hornet,* and *Cowpens* each readied sixteen fighters for immediate launching. At 6:23 p.m., the screening cruiser *Wichita* spotted low-flying torpedo planes headed toward the carrier formation. There was no radar warning. McCain immediately ordered Task Group 38.1 into an emergency turn to port that presented the carrier's sterns to the oncoming torpedo planes and lessened the chance of torpedo hits. Six of the ten attackers were shot down by antiaircraft fire. One penetrated the screen and tried to line up on *Wasp*, but the emergency turn threw him off. The attacker then shifted to *Hornet* as his target, but his torpedo struck the cruiser *Canberra* instead.

One enemy plane crashed close on the starboard bow of *Wasp*, McCain's flagship. Its wingtip damaged a radio antenna and fire from the burning plane seared the paint work.

McCain ordered the destroyer *Conner* to stand by the stricken *Canberra*. When *Canberra* reported both engine rooms and one boiler room flooded, McCain ordered *Wichita* to take her in tow. McCain informed Mitscher that he intended to stay with the crippled cruiser, then lying about ninety miles off the Formosan coast. Mitscher augmented McCain's protective cover by ordering the other three task groups to attack Formosa and Luzon the next day to suppress Japanese attempts to launch strikes against the damaged cruiser.

On October 14, although operating alone to protect the towing group, McCain also launched sweeps and a fighter and bomber strike against Formosa to discourage enemy attacks. As soon as the planes were recovered, he made ready to defend the towing group. He positioned his carriers east of the towing group where the enemy was expected to appear. The Japanese kept snoopers near the group all day, and nineteen were shot down.

At dusk, right on schedule, the enemy returned. They attacked, as before, from the east so the ships were silhouetted against the setting sun and the attacking torpedo bombers were hard to see in the gathering dusk. Nevertheless, gunners on the screening ships and the carriers knocked down ten attackers.

The cruiser *Houston*, which had reported in that afternoon to augment McCain's escort screen, caught a torpedo that left her powerless. Her skipper reported that *Houston* was breaking up and he was abandoning ship. He soon reversed his decision and the cruiser *Boston* was given the assignment to tow *Houston* to safer waters. Again, McCain positioned Task Group 38.1 between the crippled ship and the expected direction of any enemy attack.

And they came. For the next three hours bogeys were almost always overhead. McCain once again ordered emergency turns and high speeds, and the ships of Task Group 38.1 avoided any further damage.

October 15 became the third day of independent operation by McCain's Task Group 38.1. McCain sent *Cowpens* and four destroyers to cover the cripples. Halsey had decided not only to try to save the damaged cruisers by towing them to Ulithi, but also to use them as bait to try to lure the Japanese fleet into a trap. Although enemy planes kept up their attacks on the slow formation, and even managed to get another torpedo into *Houston,* the Japanese fleet refused to take the bait. The cripples eventually made their way to Ulithi and back to the United States for repair

Task Group 38.1 was under constant attack on October 15. Eleven raids were launched against the ships. An estimated 80 planes attacked, of which 52 were reported shot down by McCain's combat air patrol. Only two of the task group's fighters were lost.

Over the three days of action, Task Group 38.1 had been attacked by 191 enemy planes. The group's combat air patrol shot down 76 enemy planes (plus 11 probables), and 19 were knocked down by the ship's gunners. McCain's losses were five planes in combat and two to operational accidents.

Thach observed about the action: "They left McCain up there to protect them [the crippled cruisers] and get them out . . . just one task group . . . where [the enemy] could hit us from all angles, and they did their best."[3]

For this action Halsey awarded Slew the Navy Cross on November 30, 1944. The Citation reads:

For gallantry, intrepidity and outstanding achievement in the line of his profession, while in command of Task Group 38.1 during the period 13-15 October 1944. Covering the withdrawal of the torpedoed *Canberra* and *Houston*, Vice Admiral McCain interposed his task group between the crippled ships

and the major enemy air threat and by his skillful and courageous handling of his forces broke up repeated heavy enemy
air attacks and contributed in great measure to the ultimate
successful salvaging of the two damaged cruisers. His conduct
throughout this trying and critical period was in keeping with
the highest traditions of the United States Naval Service.

Jimmy Thach received a Silver Star medal for planning the air
operations.

The carrier strikes in October virtually ended the Japanese air
threat in a conventional sense. The enemy carrier-borne aircraft threat
had been effectively ended in June at the Battle of the Philippine Sea
when the corps of experienced Japanese pilots was decimated. Now, in
October, the Japanese had foreseen the attack on Formosa and liter-
ally put all their eggs in one land-based basket. But, against the
Americans, the enemy land-based fighters proved to be little more
than eggs thrown at a stone wall.[4] Now all that was left for the
Japanese were the kamikazes.

Leyte Gulf

After reshuffling ships to provide an escort for the crippled cruisers,
McCain's Task Group 38.1 consisted of the carriers *Wasp, Hornet,*
and *Monterey*; cruisers *Chester, Salt Lake City, Pensacola, San Diego,*
and *Oakland*; and a dozen screening destroyers. Although the ubiqui-
tous screening destroyers are easy to overlook individually (because
there were so many of them), their role cannot be dismissed. In addition to pinging for submarines and attacking underwater contacts, the
tin cans were the first ships encountered by attacking planes. The antiaircraft fire of the destroyers could break up enemy formations before
the planes could penetrate the formation to where the cruisers and carriers were positioned. Further, the destroyer war diaries are replete
with heroic rescues of downed airmen and assistance to stricken ships
like *Houston*.

On October 16 McCain rendezvoused with Task Group 38.2 and
the service group for fueling. The Japanese had finally ended their
attacks, so the 17th was a quiet day for a change. Slew took time to
drop a letter to an old friend, Captain George Carver of the Navy

Medical Corps. He made a plea: "I am running out of the stomach powder and am in a bad spot. Please airmail me at once six tins separately to insure that I get some of them. . . . Please mark 'Urgent' and 'Important.' Thereafter please send me two a month. . . . If the airmail costs you anything, will give you two for one. Expedite."

Maybe a titanic three-day air battle is not good for a sensitive tummy! But Slew went on to comment, "It's a helluva good war out here."

John Sidney also received reassuring word from home about his two sons, Jack and Gordon (perhaps about their health and Jack's submarine duty), and scrawled a reply:

> Now that my two fine boys are laid by, can go Jap hunting with an undivided mind.
> Was in the thick of the Formosa fighting and got plenty scared.

One can easily imagine Slew McCain during this period, sitting in his chair on the flag bridge or pouring over maps with his staff in flag plot. He had to be elated to be back in the war. He had lobbied long and hard to get out of Washington, and he proved himself as a battle commander at Morotai and off Formosa. Also, he had to be extremely pleased with the hard blows struck against the enemy by the men and planes of his Task Group 38.1, even as he was saddened by his losses. Clearly he was impatient to take command the whole task force, the job he had been promised. But he still had to wait on Mitscher's decision.

At the end of the day on October 17, Task Group 38.1 started a high speed run to the Philippines. On the morning of October 18 two fighter sweeps and a bomb strike were launched against the enemy at Manila Bay. Considerable damage was done to adjacent airfields but no enemy shipping was struck due to unfavorable weather. Thirty enemy planes were destroyed in the air (five by one pilot), plus thirty on the ground. Three of McCain's planes did not return. The next day, 191 of the task group's aircraft again struck Manila Bay and the Clark Field area. No aerial opposition was encountered, but four planes were lost to ground fire. During the night McCain steamed south to help cover Army landings on Leyte on October 20.

From off of Leyte, Task Group 38.1 sent a 20-plane fighter sweep against airfields on Mindanao and 124 planes in two bomber strikes against trenches and mortar areas near the beachhead. Air superiority was established by task group planes over the beachhead and the invasion proceeded without opposition from the air. The task group refueled on October 21 and stood by to continue air support, but no requests were received for sweeps or strikes.

On October 22 Task Group 38.1 circled in an area about 240 miles out, ready to provide air support to the invasion. The light carrier *Cowpens* was back in the fold after covering the crippled cruisers during their escape, and that afternoon the *Hancock* and her escorts reported to McCain. That brought Task Group 38.1 up to five carriers, making it the most powerful group in Task Force 38. Near midnight, Halsey initiated a rotation plan that sent McCain and his group off to Ulithi for rest, refueling, and reprovisioning. Davison was to get ready to go the next day, and the other task groups would follow along in turn. The men were tired. Many had not set foot on shore for ten months.[5] So when the famous Battle of the Leyte Gulf started, McCain's Task Group 38.1 was moving away on an easterly course.

In essence, the Japanese attempted to disrupt MacArthur's invasion of Leyte Island by sending a powerful force of battleships, cruisers, and destroyers from the east—the Center and Southern Forces—and a decoy group of carriers from the north—the Northern Force. Defending were Kinkaid's Seventh Fleet and Halsey's Third, now essentially Task Force 38 inasmuch as the amphibious force was on loan to Kinkaid.

Kinkaid's assets were mainly transports, cargo ships, six old battleships, cruisers, and destroyers; plus eighteen escort carriers screened by destroyers and destroyer escorts. The CVEs were commanded by Rear Admiral Tommy Sprague, and were split into three task units code-named Taffy 1, Taffy 2, and Taffy 3.

Halsey's Third Fleet was awesome. McCain (Task Group 38.1) had five carriers, six cruisers, and fourteen destroyers. Bogan (Task Group 38.2) had three carriers, two fast battleships, three cruisers, and sixteen destroyers. Sherman's force (Task Group 38.3) included four carriers, two battleships, four cruisers, and thirteen destroyers; and Davison's group (Task Group 38.4) had four carriers, two battleships, two cruisers, and fifteen destroyers.

To counter the invasion and inflict a major defeat on the Americans, Japanese Vice Admiral Takeo Kurita moved his ships, the Center Force, out of Singapore. Kurita commanded four battleships, seven cruisers, and several destroyers. Along with him was Vice Admiral Shoji Nishimura's group of two battleships, a cruiser, and destroyers. They joined with Vice Admiral Kiyohide Shima's force of three cruisers bound from Japan to form the Southern Force.

The last piece of the puzzle was the decoy Northern Force of Vice Admiral Jisaburo Ozawa, composed of four carriers. But they were without many planes—only 166 embarked. Ozawa also had two battleships, three cruisers, and eight destroyers. This force sortied from Japan to lure the American carrier fleet north away from covering the invasion. If successful, this would allow Kurita's Center Force to move in and strike a deadly blow.

The Center Force approached through the Sibuyan Sea, heading for the San Bernardino Strait. Once through, it planned to turn south to the beachhead on the east coast of Leyte.

The first contact was on October 23, when American submarines attacked the Center Force off Palawan. Two of Kurita's cruisers were sunk and another was seriously damaged. As the threat became known, Halsey stationed Sherman to the north at a point east of Luzon, Bogan covered the San Bernardino Strait, and Davison covered the Surigao Strait. When the Center and Southern enemy forces were spotted by search planes, Halsey ordered the carriers to attack.

McCain's Task Group 38.1 had been steaming uneventfully eastward at 16 knots toward Ulithi. Training flights were undertaken on October 23. On the morning of the 24th, four destroyers were detached and the cruiser *Boston* and five destroyers reported for duty. A strike against Yap had been planned for the morning, but those plans were cancelled when a message was received at 9:46 a.m. from Halsey: "Reverse course. . . . Launch search to north and northwest at dawn 25 October." This would place McCain in position to search the very area where Ozawa's carriers were approaching, exactly where Halsey suspected the enemy carriers to be. McCain came about and increased speed to 21 knots, later to 25 knots.

Meanwhile, nearer Leyte, Davison hit the Southern Force without much effect and then shifted northward to support Bogan, who had taken on the Center Force in the Sibuyan Sea.

Sherman was under heavy Japanese air attack from Luzon and from the few planes Ozawa had left on his carriers. More than 150 Japanese planes attacked in three waves. They suffered enormous losses, but a few broke through. Sherman lost the light carrier *Princeton* to enemy air.

Evening out the score, Task Force 38 planes sunk the Japanese super battleship *Musashi* in the Center Force. At about 2 p.m. Kurita turned the Center Force westward in apparent retreat.

Halsey still hadn't seen any carriers, but they were still thought to be the primary threat. Finally, Sherman's search planes found the Northern Force late in the afternoon. After considerable discussion about the remaining capabilities of the Center Force, Halsey concluded that they could be handled by Kinkaid. Halsey decided to go north after the carriers. He ordered the three task groups to join together and took off after Ozawa's Northern Force.

Both Bogan (Task Group 38.2) and Vice Admiral Willis Lee (commanding the battleships) tried or considered trying to question the wisdom of the move northward. Bogan was rebuffed and Lee dropped the idea, feeling that Halsey was not easily approachable.[6]

To the south, Nishimura's Southern Force moved into the Surigao Strait. It was met late on the night of October 24 by Rear Admiral Jesse Oldendorf's bombardment group. The PT boats, destroyers, cruisers, and battleships of Oldendorf's force scored a stunning victory; Nishimura's force was almost totally destroyed. Only one cruiser and four destroyers escaped from the battle and the follow-on attacks as Oldendorf and planes from the escort carriers gave pursuit.

Meanwhile, McCain refueled his task group on the morning of October 25. Halsey ordered McCain to report any positive search results immediately. Further north, Mitscher's planes from Task Force 38 had sighted the carriers of the Northern Force and were pressing the attack. The Japanese were sitting ducks. By afternoon Task Force 38 planes had sunk three of the four carriers. The last, damaged and abandoned, was sunk by cruiser gunfire.

While Mitscher's planes struck the Northern Force, the Japanese Center Force under Admiral Kurita had reversed course back to the east and slipped through the San Bernardino Strait and southward to directly attack the escort carriers.

McCain received a message from Halsey at 7:24 a.m. on October 25 requesting search results. One minute later he intercepted a message from Kinkaid to Halsey stating that Taffy 3 was under fire from enemy battleships and cruisers. McCain terminated refueling and readied for a strike to the north to assist the rest of the task force in its attack on the Northern Force.

But at 9:40 a.m. McCain overheard another message from Kinkaid that four battleships and eight cruisers were attacking the Taffys. That decided the issue for him. Five minutes later McCain changed course to the southwest at 30 knots to take Task Group 38.1 to the aid of the embattled escort carriers. He sent out search planes and directed that a strike be launched at 10:30 a.m.

Life magazine commented about McCain's initiative: "It is significant that he so quickly appreciated the gravity of the situation and the duty of the Third Fleet to remedy it."[7]

Finally, at one minute after 10 a.m., Halsey confirmed John McCain's action by ordering Task Group 38.1 to strike the enemy battleships and cruisers off Leyte and Samar. The first strike was off by 11:02 a.m., followed by a second at 12:55 p.m. Because of the distance to the target, it was necessary for the planes of the second strike to carry wing tanks and bombs instead of torpedoes, which were a better weapon against the enemy surface ships.

Thach had tried by radio to find out if the airfield at Tacloban, Leyte, could take his planes after their attack. The strike planes could have carried heavier and more lethal loads if they could refuel ashore. But Thach never received an answer, so he had to assume that the field was not yet secure.

The Taffys and their screening destroyers were fighting heroically. Planes from the CVEs pressed the attack on Kurita's ships even though some had no ammunition. The destroyers and destroyer escorts laid smoke screens and made fierce torpedo attacks. Three of these vessels were lost and three were damaged.

McCain was moving his task group west, to Leyte, as fast as he could, not only to relieve the escort carriers as soon as possible but to shorten the range his planes had to deal with in making their attack.

The wind was at his back, from the east, so McCain and Thach worked out an unorthodox maneuver. McCain ordered the carriers to increase speed to 33 knots. They moved ahead of the rest of the task force, reversed course into the wind, launched planes, and reversed course again to catch up with the formation.[8]

When McCain's first strike approached Kurita's attacking Center Force, the enemy ships turned and began a high-speed retreat back through the San Bernardino Straits. McCain speculated that the fierce and desperate attacks from the CVEs and their escort destroyers, plus the threat represented by the waves of attacking Task Group 38.1 planes, forced a decision by the Japanese to withdraw. And this appears to be pretty much the case, although Kurita may also have been thinking about attacking an American carrier group to the north.

McCain reported fourteen bomb hits on the four battleships, twelve hits on four of the five cruisers sighted, and one hit on each of four destroyers. The Japanese did not confirm this amount of damage. Even though damage claims were often exaggerated in the fog of battle, in this case McCain had some photographic evidence.

Nine of McCain's planes from the first strike were shot down or missing.

All the returning planes of the first strike were low on gasoline. Several landed in the water and eight planes of the second strike managed to land after all at Tacloban, which was already full of planes from the damaged CVEs.

One can speculate about what might have happened if Halsey had not sent McCain to Ulithi, or had called him back sooner. Was there any chance that Halsey might have left McCain's Task Group 38.1 to protect the San Bernardino Straits? If Halsey had done so, the many critical reviews of Halsey's decision to go north seeking the enemy carriers might have been forestalled. But Halsey believed in the principle of the concentration of forces. When he recalled McCain, he ordered him to search to the north for the carriers rather than head south to protect the invasion fleet. So the presence of McCain's task group probably would have made little or no difference in Halsey's plans and the final outcome.[9]

Later on, McCain described his part in the fracas to the press: "The escort carriers put up a big fight, one of the biggest fights I've ever seen. I don't claim credit. The southern Jap unit [was] hit at Surigao Strait on the 24th. Admiral Halsey discovered the enemy's northern carrier forces on the 25th. I went down to Leyte at 10:30 the morning of the 25th, a half hour before the Jap fleet turned around. It turned around for at least two reasons. Our escort carriers fought so furiously the Japs assumed that they were a larger force. Also because we sent in carrier groups to help out. The point is I don't claim credit by any means."

To this statement, Commander Jimmy Thach added "The Admiral is modest."

Although the battle ended with the decision by the enemy to retreat, the sum total was that the invasion was saved and the battered Japanese fleet was never again a factor in the Pacific War. But this action saw the arrival of the new, devastating Japanese weapon—the kamikaze. As Kurita broke off his surface attack on the escort carriers, Japanese land-based suicide planes discovered these same targets. The escort carriers *Santee* and *Suwanee* were damaged by direct hits, and *St. Lo* was sunk.[10]

On October 26 Halsey ordered Slew's Task Group 38.1 and Bogan's Task Group 38.2 to rendezvous and launch further strikes against the retreating Center Force. McCain told his air groups to "Listen for contacts from the searchers and kick the hell out of those ships."

McCain's carriers sent out three strikes. The pilots reported lots of hits, but only one cruiser and a seaplane tender were sunk for sure. Twelve enemy planes were shot down and fifteen were reportedly destroyed on the ground. McCain's losses were eight planes to anti-aircraft fire and one in an operational accident.

Although McCain's Task Group 38.1 was only on the periphery of the great Battle of Leyte Gulf, it acted valiantly when called upon. McCain had at least rung the bell on the closing round.

On October 27 McCain's Task Group 38.1 refueled. Task Group 38.3 took up the task of fighter cover for the gulf. Then, on October 28, Task Groups 38.2 and 38.4 took over the job at Leyte to provide support to Kinkaid's ships and U.S. Army ground forces. McCain's Task Group 38.1 and Sherman's Task Group 38.3 withdrew to Ulithi to rearm, provision, and refuel. By the early morning of October 29, both groups were safely at anchor.

It was in this time period that Halsey witnessed his first kamikaze attack.[11] On October 29 a plane crashed into the carrier *Intrepid*, leaving ten dead and six wounded. The next day suicide planes hit the *Franklin* and *Belleau Wood*, destroying 45 planes, killing 148 men, and wounding 70.

Action Report

McCain's action report for the period October 2 to October 29 described attacks against Okinawa, Formosa, northern Luzon, Leyte, and the Japanese fleet. The report cited 1,694 sorties flown over enemy targets and listed 133 enemy aircraft shot down, 19 destroyed by antiaircraft fire from the ships, and 283 planes destroyed on the ground. Twelve enemy ships and fourteen small craft were sunk. Among the many damaged were four battleships and five cruisers.

Losses suffered by Task Group 38.1 were 44 planes lost in combat and 12 lost to operational accidents. The cruisers *Canberra* and *Houston* were cited as extensively damaged.

Operational accidents were a regular part of the scene. Sometimes operational losses exceeded the number of planes lost in combat. Planes ran out of fuel, collided with each other, suffered mechanical failure, and crashed on takeoff or landing.

McCain's comments and recommendations noted that the enemy had made good use of twilight torpedo attacks, and suggested that stationing picket destroyers to the east of the task group, plus dusk anti-snooper flights, might be the solution to stopping that type of attack. The report also emphasized that the Japanese were skillful at evading radar. This evasion capability, combined with the fanatical new suicide attacks, formed the most threatening problem yet faced.

Hot Water

Slew McCain's impulsive nature got him into some hot water about this time. He sent an intemperate message to King, Nimitz, Halsey, Spruance, and Mitscher, condemning his long-time nemesis, the Curtis two-seater SB2C Helldiver dive-bomber. McCain thus had not only stepped on some Navy toes, but he was up against the politically powerful Curtis-Wright company.[12]

Nimitz reacted by chewing out McCain, and he asked Halsey to talk to McCain and let him know if Slew was ready to relieve Mitscher. Halsey replied that McCain had used poor judgment but should still take command of Task Force 38. Nimitz agreed.

Ernest King may have intervened on McCain's behalf as well. McCain thanked King in December 1944 for his good wishes and vote of confidence.[13]

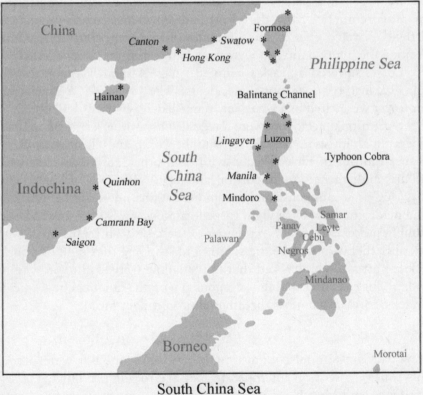

South China Sea
Target Areas = ✳

13

SLEW TAKES OVER

Captain Arleigh Burke, Marc Mitscher's chief of staff, and other members of the task force staff all harbored concerns about Mitscher's well-being. He was quieter than usual, and less energetic. He had been at sea for ten months and his platoon partner, Spruance, had gone home in August. There were even rumors that Mitscher had suffered a heart attack at sea on top of two earlier attacks on Guadalcanal. Burke had often looked over at Task Group 38.1, where McCain had repeatedly demonstrated that he could effectively run his end of the show. McCain's learning period was over.[1]

Thach, in his oral history, described working with Mitscher during the learning period: "Of course, working under Mitscher, we broke our necks to be sure that we did everything exactly as it was planned. We didn't try to go off on our own in any way, and we got some particular 'Well dones' from the task force commander. . . . I know that Arleigh Burke wrote them, but nevertheless Mitscher did send them."[2]

Change of Command (II)

When Task Groups 38.1 and 38.3 withdrew to Ulithi to pick up replacement air groups, U.S. Army ground troops were firmly entrenched on Leyte. The invasion of the Philippines had been successful and Mitscher was ready to go home.

Vice Admiral John McCain relieved Vice Admiral Marc Mitscher as Commander, Task Force 38, at Ulithi on October 30, 1944. The two commanders sat at a table covered with a green cloth in the flag quarters of the carrier flagship. "Well, John," said Admiral Mitscher, "are you ready to take over?" "Yes, Pete," McCain told him, "I am."[3]

Mitscher left on well-deserved leave with plans to return and relieve McCain in January 1945 in accordance with the two-platoon system. Rear Admiral Alfred E. Montgomery relieved McCain as commander of Task Group 38.1 on October 31 and hoisted his flag in *Hornet*. McCain remained aboard *Wasp*. Slew McCain had finally grasped the brass ring.

As a task group commander John McCain had had Mitscher between himself and Bill Halsey, and had been concerned with meeting Mitscher's requirements while he directed the operations of three to five carriers. Now he was directly under the command of his friend Bill Halsey and was responsible for directing and coordinating the operations of up to sixteen carriers organized in three to four task groups.

Thach clarified the way McCain, the tactical commander, worked with Halsey, the fleet commander: "The tactical commander, when he puts out a signal or a dispatch for an operation, includes the fleet commander as one of the information addressees. In other words, he informs the fleet commander what he's planning, which direction he's going to go, and so forth. There's a continual exchange all the time between them." Thach observed further about their personal relationship: "[Halsey and McCain had a] marvelous rapport. I have photographs of them when they didn't know they were being taken, and they were just wonderful close friends. Halsey would kid McCain and McCain would come right back at him sometimes, and they'd laugh about it. They were very friendly and very cordial, and every time I went over, there was no inkling that there was not perfectly wonderful rapport between Halsey and McCain."[4]

Not only had the command ascension changed McCain's immediate world, but two big external factors came into play at this point in the war. First was the inability of the Army Air Force to provide air cover to the Leyte invasion. Halsey and McCain, now teamed for the first time, planned and hoped to move next against the Japanese home islands and Tokyo itself. But heavy rains on Leyte hampered air coverage by the Army land-based fighters. The Army planned to take responsibility for the air coverage assignment on October 27, but

Tacloban air base was too crowded and the rains wiped out any hopes of building new airfields. As it turned out, the Third Fleet and Task Force 38 remained involved in the Philippines through the end of the year.

The second factor, and a far more important problem, was the growing impact of the kamikaze suicide planes. On October 29 and 30, *Franklin and Belleau Wood* in Davison's group and *Intrepid* in Bogan's group all were hit. *Franklin* and *Belleau Wood*, whose losses totaled 45 planes and 216 casualties, headed back to Ulithi for repairs by the omnipresent repair ships and tenders. On November 1 a destroyer was sunk and four or five others were damaged.

Luzon and Leyte

Bogan's Task Group 38.2 and Davison's Task Group 38.4 had remained in the Philippines when McCain and Sherman withdrew to Ulithi. They struck the Visayas (the central group of islands in the Philippine archipelago) and Luzon, and provided air cover over Leyte. Davison, with his heavy losses, then made it back to Ulithi to replace exhausted pilots and to resupply. Task Group 38.4 was temporarily disbanded and its undamaged ships distributed to the remaining three groups.

McCain's Task Force 38, now reorganized into the three task groups, sortied from Ulithi, refueled on November 3, and arrived off Luzon on November 5. The increased size of each task group, provided by the change from four groups to three, concentrated the protective antiaircraft fire to counter the kamikazes.

McCain ordered Task Force 38 bombers and fighters to be launched against airfields and shipping from Luzon to Mindoro and struck shipping in Manila Bay. Ground targets included oil stores, rail lines, and docks. On November 5, Sherman's flagship *Lexington* took a kamikaze in her island structure. Ten died and 132 were injured.

Task Force 38 hit Japanese airfields and shipping again on November 6. A total of 439 enemy planes were reported destroyed and a cruiser sunk.

Inasmuch as *Wasp* was to withdraw to Guam to rotate air groups, McCain elected to stay with his flagship and delegated tactical command of Task Force 38 to the ever-able Ted Sherman for the next few days, until the 13th. During one of many changes of carrier air groups, McCain was invited to award medals to the air group that was being relieved. There were lots of awards. McCain came back shaking his head, "I never realized they were so young. What a pleasure to pin medals on the gunners and radiomen! Why, they are so young they haven't been shaving but a few years! They're not long from their mother's arms. You know, one of the scariest things is to be in the back seat of a dive bomber on its dive, sitting there looking backward! Hats-off to the kids!"

On November 11, Task Force 38 (still in Sherman's hands) searched, found, and destroyed a large transport convoy approaching Ormoc Bay on Leyte Island. At least twenty-five enemy planes were reported destroyed, but nine American planes were lost.

Nimitz continued to press MacArthur to release the carriers for strikes against Japan, but the enemy was making strong efforts to reinforce Leyte. The pipeline of enemy planes from Formosa and Luzon was still working, although the pilots were not well trained. So the fast carriers remained and Halsey ordered continuing attacks against shipping and airfields. Lieutenant Commander William N. Leonard served as assistant operations officer on McCain's staff. His oral history provides a nice insight about this period:

General MacArthur was agitating to have TF38/3rd Fleet operate offshore in continuing support even though he had all of Seventh Fleet and a slew of CVEs dedicated to his mission. . . . Our problem with MacArthur centered on his need for air support, which the Army Air Force was supposed to bring to Leyte by a certain date. Bad weather and other things delayed Army self-sufficiency, so the fallback was to retain the fast CVs on the scene.

McCain and his ops officer, Captain Jimmy Thach, wrote fervent dispatches to Halsey to free the CVs and, incidentally, illuminate Army air's failure to keep on schedule. Halsey was with us and reverberated up to Nimitz . . . We did our duty as Mac requested.[5]

After refueling, Task Force 38 resumed strikes against shipping on

November 13 and 14, and McCain resumed tactical command on the 14th. Thirteen Japanese ships were sunk (a light cruiser, five destroyers and seven transports) and more than eighty enemy planes were destroyed. The price was twenty-five U.S. Navy aircraft. On November 17 McCain shifted his flag, by high-line transfer at sea, from *Wasp* to *Hancock*.

There was further action on November 19, when more than a hundred enemy planes were scored on the ground. Thirteen American planes were lost in that action. Task Force 38 then withdrew again to refuel, conduct training exercises and, as Halsey put it, "Give the Japanese time to bring in more targets."[6]

McCain took two groups of Task Force 38, Sherman's and Bogan's, to attack Luzon on November 25 and 26. In this heavy action 170 tons of bombs, 25 torpedoes, and 227 aerial rockets were loosed. Thirty-one enemy ships were sunk or damaged and 119 enemy planes were damaged or destroyed. Thirteen American planes were lost in combat and to accidents.

Task Force 38 ran into strong opposition from enemy planes. Kamikazes scored hits on *Hancock*, *Intrepid* (hit twice), *Cabot,* and *Essex*. A bomber that attacked *Wasp*, McCain's flagship, was knocked down by antiaircraft fire close to the ship. Parts of the plane, including a wing and a piece of the fuselage, fell on the flight deck.

This kind of hammering was totally unsatisfactory to McCain and Halsey. As long as the carriers were tied to the beachhead, they were highly vulnerable to suicide attack. Starting on October 29 kamikazes had cost the Third Fleet 328 men, about 90 aircraft, and three carriers damaged severely enough to require shipyard repairs.

Halsey ordered all of Task Force 38 to withdraw to Ulithi to repair damage and rest the crews. Air cover over Leyte was left to the Army and in the competent hands of newly arrived Marine night fighters.

Thach later elaborated about the kamikazes: "This was a weapon, for all practical purposes, far ahead of its time. It was actually a guided missile before we had any such things as guided missiles. It was guided by a human brain, human eyes, and hands and, even better than a guided missile, it could look, digest information, change course, avoid damage, and get to the target. So we had to do something about this."[7]

New Tactics

Task Force 38 was to stay at Ulithi through December 10. Ships were refueled and repaired. All hands were able to catch a little rest and recreation. Mog Mog Island, the location of a thatched-hut recreation center, provided a swimming beach and sports fields, plus two bottles of beer for each enlisted man. The officers had a little more—a bar with scotch and bourbon.

McCain, sometimes with members of his staff, visited the battleship *New Jersey* to confer with Halsey. Since Slew usually scattered tobacco wherever he went, Halsey had a steward's mate follow him with a brush and dustpan.

"What the hell's *this* for?" demanded Slew.

"So you won't dirty up my clean ship," replied Halsey, "that's what!"[8]

The main item on the agenda was to get a start on devising new methods to deal with the kamikaze suicide planes. Thach suggested that it might be smart to emulate a sporting tactic. He designed a training exercise labeled "Moose Trap." McCain's implementing letter stated, "The most successful football teams obtain the formations and trick plays used by their opponents and duplicate them against the first team in practice until a satisfactory defense is perfected. Exercise Moose Trap is designed to do just that."

In a Moose Trap exercise, one or two carrier squadrons simulated a kamikaze attack so that the new defensive measures could be evaluated. McCain directed the task group commanders to conduct these exercises independently and report results. McCain planned to drill the whole task force as soon as possible to test the new defenses against the Japanese kamikaze threat.

McCain's report stated: "As never before, the offensive air strength of the fast carriers has had to be spread to cover the enemy in his large island systems and land mass dispersions. At the same time the force has found it necessary to concentrate its defense to a degree never before considered necessary. Before the innovation of suicide attacks by the enemy, destruction of 80 or 90 percent of his attackers was considered an eminent success. Now 100 percent destruction of the attackers is necessary to preserve the safety of the task force."

Continuing, McCain pointed out, "These new offensive and defensive requirements inherently conflict, and making the correct compromise is the continual task of the force commander." Further, "The two cardinal principles which have evolved are: (1) to defend the force with adequate patrols, (2) blanket the threatening enemy air opposition day and night with the most air power available."

Picking up on the second principle, the new tactics grew from a pressing need to protect the invasion fleet from enemy airpower based on Luzon as the fleet moved through the Philippines archipelago. McCain figured the only way to do the job was to concentrate the fighters above the Japanese airfields to suppress the new menace at its source. He asked Wilder Baker and Jimmy Thach to work out the details. Thach figured that it would take six hundred fighters to cover the one hundred enemy airfields on Luzon. Slew gave him all he had—five hundred and ninety.

Jimmy Thach devised a concept he called the "three-strike system." The Moose Trap training exercises were intended to set up better defenses against the suicide planes. The three-strike system was an offensive tactic using a revised schedule of launching carrier plane strikes. The usual practice was to send off a deck-load of planes on a mission—about half of the air group—and follow up with the second group when the first returned. Instead, by sending the planes off in three groups, the time of coverage was extended so that planes could be kept over the enemy fields nearly the whole day. In practice, the time between the departing and arriving strikes was on the order of ten minutes. This enticed the enemy aircraft to try to takeoff. Thus the enemy planes moving onto the runway became targets for the next "three-strike" attack.[9]

The three-strike blanket system was more popularly called the "Big Blue Blanket." Once in a while it was called the "McCain Lid," although McCain probably would have been just as happy to see it called the "Thach Lid."

The "Big Blue Blanket," or BBB, left short gaps between strikes and another short gap between dusk and dark. In January 1945 the *Enterprise* and *Independence* joined Task Force 38 under the command of Slew's former chief of staff, Matt Gardner, now a rear admiral. They were both night fighter carriers. Designated as Task Group

38.5, they operated only at night and helped close the gap between the daylight BBB strikes and darkness.[10]

A number of other ideas were implemented. One with particular appeal to McCain was the increase of the number of fighters on the large carriers from fifty-four to seventy-two. Like the earlier increase in fighter strength, approved in July, the gain was balanced by a reduction in dive-bombers (nine fewer) and torpedo bombers (three fewer). This left the plane complement of the large carriers at seventy-two fighters, fifteen dive-bombers, and fifteen torpedo bombers. Inasmuch as the modified Hellcat and Corsair fighters could carry 2,000 pounds of bombs each, they were dual-purpose planes—first bombers, then fighters. This measure actually increased the striking power of each carrier.[11]

Further, McCain reduced his number of task groups from four to three. Thus his antiaircraft fire and combat air patrols were more concentrated.[12] McCain loved to run outside on the bridge when the task force was under attack. He often returned to flag plot in wonder at the intensity of the antiaircraft fire. A passing comment was made in flag plot that Task Force 38 could put up the most concentrated antiaircraft fire in history, second only to the island fortress of Malta in the Mediterranean Sea.

Another successful anti-kamikaze tactic was the use of outlying picket destroyers. McCain stationed radar picket destroyers (labeled "Tomcats" and "Watchdogs" by McCain) fifty or sixty miles out from the task force in the most likely direction of an enemy attack. U.S. aircraft returning from a strike were required to make a turn around the picket so that the destroyer's own combat air patrol could pick off any suicide planes that tried to sneak in with the returning formation.[13] Jocko Clark had come up with the initial version of the picket destroyer concept, and McCain greatly expanded this idea.[14]

Yet another scheme expanded the combat air patrol. Enemy torpedo planes had been very successful at sneaking in at dusk and attacking ships silhouetted against the setting sun. "Jack Patrols" (named after Jimmy Thach's son Jack) patrolled out at dusk in the direction of the enemy at a low altitude. If anything was spotted, the Jack Patrol shot them down or broke up the formation before the enemy could press an assault. The Japanese were surprised by this tactic. They expected the carrier planes to be aboard for the night, or on high altitude patrol.[15]

All of these new tactics are examples of the work by the fine talent present on McCain's staff. All evidence points to McCain being, appropriately for a senior commander, an effective leader and delegator. He asked a lot from his staff and they responded. Although McCain is often dismissed as lacking aviation experience, he brought to the table his earlier thinking about carrier design and tactics as well as his experience with land-based air warfare. His staff included smart young pilots and others who added to the mix their experience in the early carrier battles. They had seen firsthand all the successes, mistakes, and new tactics that Slew missed while he was in Washington. Pulled together by McCain, they produced some outstanding work.

Mindoro

Task Force 38 departed Ulithi on December 1 as part of the support of MacArthur's invasion of Mindoro. But they returned almost immediately when they got the word that the invasion had been postponed ten days. This allowed more time to work on the new tactics.

McCain also found time to drop a line to his sister, Katie Lou. He had run into one of her former students who had an interesting story to relate. McCain told Katie: "While walking the deck yesterday, a pilot named Brady introduced himself. He had a number of very nice things to say about you, and in the course of the conversation I discovered the following: He is a pilot of a torpedo plane with the rank of lieutenant. On the morning of October the 26th, my forces hit the retreating Japanese fleet and harried them throughout the Sibuyan Sea. He took part in an attack on a Japanese cruiser, hitting the cruiser with a torpedo. The cruiser was sunk that morning. However his plane was hit by antiaircraft and disabled, so he landed close to the northern coast of Panay, and he and his men took to a rubber boat. Shortly after landing, a Philippine boat came out and picked them up. He was fed chicken and rice, fish and rice, and wine and liquor, and was toured throughout parts of the southern islands. The Filipinos had not seen Americans for three years, so they were given a thoroughly royal time with receptions, dances, etc. They got through the underground to our forces on Leyte, and by means and by methods not unknown, but not stated, to Tacloban on Leyte, from which place he returned to his ship on the 28th day of November." Quite an adventure!

Halsey held his final briefing for his commanders on December 10 in an informal setting. At the flag officer recreation area on Asor Island, he assembled his admirals and, after a swim and cocktails, detailed his plans. Then his cook and mess boys served up a buffet.[16]

Task Force 38 finally left Ulithi on December 11 to return to action. Direct tactical support for the Mindoro operation was to be provided by Army land-based planes on Leyte and the Seventh Fleet's escort carriers. Halsey's strategic support would come in the form of the Big Blue Blanket laid round-the-clock over the Luzon airfields by Task Force 38 planes.

As before, Task Force 38 was organized in three task groups: Task Group 38.1 under Montgomery with *Yorktown, Wasp, Cowpens*, and *Monterey*; Task Group 38.2 commanded by Gerry Bogan with *Lexington, Hancock* (McCain's flagship), *Hornet, Cabot*, and *Independence*; and Task Group 38.3 under Ted Sherman with *Essex, Ticonderoga, Langley*, and *San Jacinto*. Each group included, of course, escort battleships, cruisers, and destroyers. Rear Admiral Jocko Clark was back in the Pacific, riding along as a standby in *Hornet*. Davison, now without a task group, had left earlier for Pearl Harbor, but he would be back.

Halsey's flagship, the battleship *New Jersey*, was riding with Task Group 38.2. Halsey's plans were to strike Luzon on December 14, 15, and 16 to suppress air attacks against the Seventh Fleet as the invasion force approached Mindoro. Then he planned refueling on the 17th, with strikes again on December 19, 20, and 21.[17]

Flag Plot

As the fleet put to sea, flag plot got busy. This nerve center was the heart of McCain's operation. Flag plot was a compartment on an upper level of the carrier's island structure, usually just below the ship's bridge from which the ship's captain ran his part of the show. The central feature of flag plot was the large chart table. Maps were laid out on the chart table for plotting enemy and friendly positions and formation courses and speeds. Thus the chart table was the focus of tactical planning.

Flag plot was full of radios, radarscopes, clocks, and various dials and gauges. The walls were covered with maps and status boards displaying information about the current operations. There were always a staff duty officer and staff enlisted personnel on watch in flag plot when the task force was at sea.

Right outside flag plot was the flag bridge. There the task force commander and his staff could observe flight deck operations and eyeball the surrounding fleet.[18]

Another important feature of flag plot was the long leather transom—a couch. This was a favorite seat for both McCain and Mitscher. Wilder Baker, McCain's chief of staff, spent long hours in flag plot when action was pending or the task force was in range of enemy land-based planes. He often slept on the transom so he would be immediately available. When things settled down, he took time to go below for a shower and some well-deserved rest in his cabin.

The cigarette stories are all true. Slew arrived in flag plot each morning in freshly pressed khakis. He took a seat on the transom and the message board was handed to him for his review. Sometimes his teeth were out or he might take them out and put them in his shirt pocket. He might unbutton one cuff and pull up the sleeve, followed by the other sleeve. Then he pulled a bag of Bull Durham out of his shirt pocket and dumped tobacco into a cigarette paper. The tobacco fell all over the messages and the front of his shirt and pants as well.

When faced with the transfer from *Wasp* to *Hancock* he ordered the radioman to call ahead and find out if the *Hancock's* small stores had any Bull Durham and, if not, to order some.

Wilder Baker's son, Wilder Baker Jr., relates a story about a time when McCain picked up Admiral Baker in Washington to start a trip back to the Pacific. Wilder Jr. was invited along for the ride to the airfield and sat next to McCain in the back seat of the sedan. McCain asked him "Do you want to see a trick?" Then he proceeded to fish out tobacco and paper, roll a cigarette, and light it—all with one hand. It's not clear if he spilled any tobacco this time.

Slew's relationships with his staff were never complicated by protocol. For example, conferences with his operations officer, Thach, were often prefaced with a shrill "Hey, Jimmy!" or "Get Jimmy up here!" If McCain was tickled about something he let go with his cackle of a laugh, slap his thigh with his hand or with his hat, or toss his hat to the deck in merriment.

McCain loved his sailors, and they loved him. McCain always kept his flag mess open and manned so that the staff watch officer could provide coffee and sometimes fresh juice for the crew on watch in flag plot.

The sailors never had a bad word to say about "their" admiral. The ship's crew felt that McCain treated them like his sons. Once in a while, he dropped by the signal bridge to visit and have a cup of coffee. He was a sound sleeper, but his orders to the night messenger were to "Always come right in and shake me."

McCain was well known for his fast exercise walks—more like runs. Correspondents noted that a half-hour interview usually turned into a mile walk back-and-forth across the bridge.[19] He also took his exercise along the flight deck. During these walks he always had a cheery "hello" for anyone close by. One time an aviation ordnanceman was loading ammunition on the wings of a fighter plane. With a load in his arms he swung around and knocked fast-moving Admiral McCain right off the flight deck into the catwalk alongside. He was mortified, and deathly afraid the admiral's Marine orderly was going to shoot him on the spot!

When the force was under air attack, McCain's staff saw to it that he donned his helmet, lifejacket, and clothing designed to protect against flash burns. This was garb he did not like very much. Slew would grumble and toss it aside. Then his aides would have to rush back to put it on him again.

Flag officers are welcomed aboard a ship with side-boys (two ranks of saluting sailors) and a bos'n's pipe (a shrill pipe used to signal special events and drills). One time McCain was being piped aboard but the bos'n made an error. He piped "sweepers man your brooms" instead of the admiral's trill. Afterward McCain got on the ship's loudspeaker system and told the crew "That's the first time I've ever been swept aboard!"

Spreading the Blanket

The task force refueled on December 13 and then commenced a high-speed run toward Luzon. The refueling group consisted of twelve oilers, two escort carriers, four destroyers, and eight destroyer escorts.[20]

McCain's team implemented the Big Blue Blanket plan on December 14, 1944, from a point about 90 miles off the east coast of northern Luzon. By day fighter patrols kept the airfields under continuous observation, and by night the night fighters harassed any attempts to get planes in the air under the cover of darkness.

On the first day, 40 enemy aircraft were reported shot down, 139 were destroyed on the ground, and 54 were damaged on the ground. The Japanese air fleet on Luzon was rendered impotent; no attacks were launched from Luzon against the Mindoro invasion forces. In addition, nine ships were sunk and several others damaged. Losses were ten planes in combat and sixteen in accidents.

The second day, December 15, brought more strikes in which 123 tons of bombs were dropped and more than 1,000 rockets fired. Fifty-four enemy aircraft were destroyed, all but seven on the ground, and sixty-one were damaged. More shipping was hit. Six planes were lost to enemy fire and three to accidents. McCain reported to Halsey that no undamaged shipping remained in Manila Harbor.

Bogan was running short of fighters to attack the land targets. In the absence of enemy air attacks, McCain granted permission for Bogan to send two divisions of the combat air patrol (who normally protected the carriers from enemy air attacks) against the land targets. Also McCain told his task group commanders to give dual priority to fighter planes covering the enemy airfields and those patrolling the skies above the task force. The commanders were not to launch any bombers that required a fighter escort unless the first and second priorities had been met.

During the deployment of the Big Blue Blanket, photo reconnaissance flights were regularly undertaken to help assess the effectiveness of the new tactics. Thacher "Stretch" Longstreth was an intelligence officer on McCain's staff, and later a prominent civic and political figure in Philadelphia. He describes how he compared morning and evening photo images and determined that Task Force 38 planes had destroyed more than 320 aircraft on the ground at thirty-two enemy airfields. Nimitz was skeptical about these totals, and took McCain to task for inflating the figures. Slew hit the ceiling and asked

Longstreth, "Son, they're trying to get me. Where'd you get those figures?" So Stretch pulled his stuff together, and the next day McCain, Thach, and Longstreth went to the *New Jersey* to see Halsey. They presented the highly accurate photographic evidence, prompting Halsey to comment, "Gee, this is great stuff." Needless to say, Longstreth's reputation with McCain was solid from then on, and the Big Blue Blanket was a proven success.[21]

The Army landed on Mindoro on December 15. The landings were a complete success. On December 16 the enemy managed to launch an eleven plane attack against the task force. First strike planes from *Lexington* and *Hancock* along their way to hit the airfields met the enemy, and they splashed all eleven. On this third day of the Big Blue Blanket coverage, 15 enemy planes were shot down, 22 were destroyed on the ground, and 46 were damaged. Nine vessels were sunk, and a train and a railroad bridge were destroyed. Seven American planes were lost in combat plus seven due to operational incidents.

So far, the Big Blue Blanket was an unqualified success. No attacks were launched against the invasion fleet from Luzon. Halsey ordered McCain to take Task Force 38 eastward at the end of the day to rendezvous with the refueling group, and he sent congratulations: "To you and [your] force well done on a brilliantly planned and executed operation."

14

HEAVY HITS

Late on the evening of December 16, 1944, McCain ordered Task Force 38 southeastward. The force contacted the fueling group early on the 17th. Halsey had selected a refueling area about 300 miles off the Philippine island of Samar. This was far enough out to reduce the chances of being spotted by a land-based snooper, but close enough to enable the fleet to make its strike commitments over the next several days. McCain changed course to expedite the rendezvous. Fueling started at about 10:25 a.m. with the task groups operating independently, each with its own fueling group.

This refueling was important. The fuel replenishment on December 13 had been little more than a topping-off because the force was just out of Ulithi. Now some of the destroyers, after three days of high-speed sailing during flight operations, were running low.

The December Typhoon—Cobra

The seas were heavy and the winds brisk. Poor weather had been anticipated and, in fact, the overcast was considered desirable to help hide the fleet from air observation. The destroyers ran into heavy going as they steered parallel to the fueling ships at a speed of eight knots. Constrained by mooring lines and large fuel hoses, they had extreme problems steering. Lines parted and hoses snapped. Seeing this, Halsey ordered the fueling discontinued and picked a new, hopefully calmer rendezvous to the northwest for the next morning.

A tropical storm had been spotted to the southeast but its location was vague. It was hoped that it would follow the normal pattern and veer to the northeast. Still guessing about the storm, Halsey and his staff picked yet another location to the south. Following Halsey's plan, McCain steered the task force westward through the night, then south.

The storm location had still not been pinned down. Bogan and Montgomery felt they had a fix on the storm, but Sherman later said he did not. Probably all of them, including McCain, thought that Halsey and his staff had better information. Bogan suggested to McCain that southward was the safe direction to go, but he did not give any estimated location for the storm center.

Although many of the admirals and ship captains scattered throughout the fleet felt they had adequate warning of a serious storm, not much, if any, of this information was passed on to Halsey's staff. As it turned out, Halsey didn't have better data.

Once again Halsey and his staff picked an alternative fuel rendezvous, this time further to the north. The service group was spotted shortly after midnight and the fleet turned to the northwest—directly ahead of and moving in the same direction as the storm—but they didn't know that at the time.

Around four in the morning Halsey queried McCain: "Give me your estimate on the weather situation."

McCain replied: "Present indications small probability of using fueling units. Hope to fuel [destroyers] from large carriers."

McCain has been criticized for not sending a storm position at that time, but instead he cut to the core issue of refueling the small vessels. Destroyers could be and frequently were refueled from larger ships such as carriers and battleships.

Halsey then cancelled the latest rendezvous and ordered the fleet to a southerly course. Bogan, McCain, and Commander George F. Kosko (Halsey's aerologist) all developed storm locations, but these were spread out widely to the east of the fleet. McCain changed course to the northeast in a desperate attempt to fuel the destroyers. Then at 8:00 a.m. he halted all fueling attempts and, in accordance with Halsey's desires, turned the task force south to try to escape the worsening weather.

It was too late. All the twisting and turning in the attempt to refuel took place right in the storm's path and simply delayed the fleet's escape. Ships began to take independent action. Aircraft broke loose on *Monterey's* hangar deck and in the ensuing melee other planes were set afire. Heroic efforts eventually saved the ship.

Halsey ordered the force to take the most comfortable course they could find. McCain immediately tried a variety of courses to help the ships ride easier, but to no avail. Ships were spread all over the ocean. Winds were up to more than 60 knots with gusts much higher. Fire broke out on *Cape Esperance* and *Cowpens*. *San Jacinto* reported planes loose on the hangar deck. Throughout the day Halsey and McCain directed cruisers, destroyers, and tugs to stand by to help the stricken ships.

To the north, near the center of the storm, the destroyers *Spence*, *Monaghan*, and *Hull* of the service group capsized and sank with nearly all hands. They were already top-heavy with equipment such as radar added during overhaul and now they were short of fuel in the hull, a low-slung weight that typically acted as ballast.

Shortly after noon the storm center was about 42 miles due north of the flagship. Winds were 68 knots and visibility was 100 yards.

At 3:20 p.m. Halsey stated that he expected to be able to move south at 6:00 p.m. to search for a new fueling area. McCain gave the orders, and the task force was able to make the course change by 8:00 p.m. Task Force 38 joined with the tankers at 7:15 a.m. on December 19. The task groups were directed to operate independently to take on fuel. The waters and wind were comparatively calm. During the fueling, McCain went aboard *New Jersey* to confer with Halsey.

The search for survivors officially began at about noon on the 19th with a 360-degree, 250-mile air reconnaissance. When fueling was completed at 7:17 p.m., McCain gave orders for the task force to move northward for a surface search that Halsey described as "the most exhaustive search in naval history." The commanding officer, four officers, and thirty-six enlisted men from the capsized *Hull* were picked up by a destroyer right on the path the storm had followed.

Early the next morning, December 20, five survivors from the capsized *Spence* were recovered by an escort carrier, again close to the storm's path.

Nearly 800 men and 186 planes were lost to the storm, which was code-named "Cobra."

The task force continued to regroup. On the evening of December

20 it was back in business, although as badly battered as if it had fought a major battle.[1] Halsey issued his night orders and McCain took Task Force 38 on a high-speed run to Luzon to launch strikes. But heavy weather was still around. Following several course changes, the scheduled strikes for December 21 were cancelled.

Halsey turned the fleet back to the search area. Six survivors from *Monaghan* were found by a destroyer, and the search was kept up after dark. If the picket destroyers thought that they heard a whistle signal from a floating survivor or spotted the warning lights on life preservers, chief of staff Baker ordered a search of the area. McCain told his ships to use their searchlights if necessary, a highly unusual tactic in a combat area.

The task groups refueled on December 22 and withdrew to Ulithi. The battered fleet was ready for rest and repairs. The ships were at anchor by the morning of December 24. Replenishment, refueling, rearmament, rest, recreation—and questions—were the agenda through December 29.

Nimitz ordered a court of inquiry into why the fleet had been caught by Typhoon Cobra. The court was headed by Vice Admiral "Genial John" Hoover, commander of the land-based planes in the Central Pacific. The court called all the commanders and their senior staff to testify. McCain was asked only ten questions. He stated that he did not appreciate the rapid pace of the storm, and that he was giving priority to the commitment for the task force to strike Luzon. Admiral Baker commented that McCain and his task group commanders had been asked only once by Halsey and his staff about their estimates of the weather. Baker felt the task force did not have timely warning about a severe storm. The task group commanders gave their opinions as well.[2]

The verdict was that Halsey must bear the blame, but his errors "were errors of judgment stemming from a commendable desire to meet military requirements." King added, "resulting from insufficient information." The final result was a letter from Nimitz to the fleet with advice for dealing with severe storms.[3]

One error in judgment by Halsey, in hindsight, was to persist in fueling efforts in face of the worsening weather. But as he received information about the storm, initially thought to be well to the east of the fleet, Halsey continually shifted the fueling rendezvous areas westward to what he and his staff thought would be calmer waters. By the time Halsey realized that he was in a typhoon, it was too late. McCain, of course, followed Halsey's orders.

Another error in judgment, again in hindsight, was Halsey's failure to seek information and advice from his subordinate commanders. Further, it was an error on the part of the commanders, including McCain, to not press their judgments on to Halsey and his staff.

That settled, the war awaited. Halsey had received an okay from Nimitz to strike the soft underbelly of the enemy. With this strategic guidance from Nimitz and Halsey, McCain prepared plans to cover MacArthur's landings at Lingayen Gulf on Luzon and then launch a sortie into the South China Sea.

Due to a non-combat injury suffered by Rear Admiral Alfred E. Montgomery, Rear Admiral Arthur W. Radford (who had worked for McCain in Washington) took command of Task Group 38.1. Also, two squadrons of Marine fighters, each with 18 F4U Corsair fighters, were assigned to *Essex* to fill out McCain's requirement for more fighters.

On the morning of December 30 the three task groups sortied independently to a late-afternoon rendezvous. Then McCain (riding in *Hancock)* took over tactical command. Radford (in *Yorktown*) commanded Task Group 38.1, Bogan (in *Lexington*) remained as commander of Task Group 38.2, and Sherman (in *Essex*) continued to run Task Group 38.3. The task force conducted training exercises on December 31 and moved onward to a fueling rendezvous scheduled for January 1.

Thus started what McCain characterized as one of the most successful cruises of the Pacific war.

South China Sea

The Third Fleet—slimmed down to just Task Force 38—consisted of seven heavy and four light carriers organized in three task groups, one heavy and one light carrier organized in a night group, and a replenishment group with one hunter-killer and seven escort carriers. This force struck Formosa and the Ryukyu Islands on January 3 and 4. Formosa remained an important target because it was the staging base for Japanese air units operating in the northern Philippines. Although there were weather delays on January 3, nearly a thousand sorties were flown over numerous targets. Bombs dropped totaled 275 tons and more than 1,100 air-to-ground rockets were fired. Thirty enemy planes were reported shot down and 81 were destroyed on the ground. Another 205 were damaged. American losses were 32 planes.

On January 5, Matt Gardner's night fighter task group, with carriers *Enterprise* and *Independence,* joined the task force and formed Task Group 38.5

The Big Blue Blanket was spread again over Luzon on January 6 and 7. The weather was still poor, but nevertheless more than 200 enemy planes were destroyed or damaged. On January 8 and 9 Task Force 38 again attacked Formosa and the Ryukyus, destroying or damaging 108 Japanese aircraft. Most were on the ground, as was expected, because the Big Blue Blanket was designed to hit the enemy before he could take to the air.

Then Task Force 38 advanced through the Luzon Strait into the South China Sea. They passed nervously through the Balintang Channel with land in sight all around. To the north was Formosa with its fearsome land-based fighters and bombers.

From positions in the South China Sea, the pilots and planes of Task Force 38 hit the Indochina coast on January 12, achieving absolute tactical surprise. Targets included Saigon, Camranh Bay, and Quinhon harbor. Halsey hoped to sink two battleships that had escaped him at Leyte Gulf, but they had long since fled to safer waters.

Task Force 38 approached the targets in two groups. Ted Sherman was leading Task Groups 38.1 and 38.3 while Gerry Bogan was leading Task Groups 38.2 and 38.5. They all rejoined by 7:00 a.m. on the 12th, and McCain resumed tactical command. At 7:30 a.m. Halsey dropped the green flag and McCain directed all groups to launch strikes on schedule.

It was a busy day. A total of 984 sorties were flown, with 245 tons of bombs dropped, 71 torpedoes launched, and 1,082 rockets fired. Losses were sixteen planes in combat and seven in operations.

The payoff was tremendous. Forty enemy ships were sunk and 22 were damaged. Five cargo vessels and five or six convoy escorts were entirely destroyed. A cruiser was sunk. Another group of four destroyers and six cargo ships were sunk, and seven cargo ships and a patrol boat were beached. Yet another convoy of three destroyers, an oiler, and six cargo ships was wiped out. Fourteen enemy planes were reported shot down, and 153 were destroyed or damaged on the ground. McCain figured that the total tonnage sunk or damaged approached 200,000 tons, possibly a new high for a single day's work.

Halsey then turned the fleet back to the north, where it encountered heavy weather. McCain, possibly thinking about the horrific losses from Typhoon Cobra, recommended that the fleet reverse course and cancel the strikes on January 15. Halsey took a careful look and remained determined to carry out the operations against Formosa and China.[4]

The pilots and crews persisted in the face of the bad weather and, with guts and skill, kept flying combat patrols and air strikes through squalls and overcast. On January 15 and 16 strikes were made against Canton, Formosa, Hong Kong, Swatow, the Pescadores, and Hainan.

Of the first sixteen days of January, eight had been devoted to air strikes. This was a grueling pace for the air crews under the heavy weather conditions.

McCain evidently considered that the strikes on the China coast were not up to Task Force 38 standards even though 392 tons of bombs were dropped and 1,578 rockets were fired. A total of 86 enemy planes were reported destroyed or damaged, but 64 American planes and 41 men were lost. The results at Hong Kong were particularly disappointing. Although ground installations were heavily damaged, only a fraction of the shipping in the harbor was sunk. McCain was not happy, and he wanted answers.

His analysis pointed out that on January 12 Task Force 38 planes had secured nearly a 100 percent kill-rate against convoys in the open seas. Then the same pilots and planes failed in closed waters at Hong Kong. There was no loss of fighting spirit. Instead torpedoes were gallantly dropped close in to the targets. But this aggressive attack led to the torpedoes getting stuck in the mud of the shallow harbor.

Further, the dive bombers had to attack through heavy and accurate antiaircraft fire. Inasmuch as shore installations had been hit first, the pilots' visibility was sharply limited by smoke from the burning targets.

McCain recommended more dive-bomber training in forward areas and better direction of the attacking planes in the target area. He also urged acceleration of the replacement of SB2C Helldiver dive-bombers with F4U Corsair fighter-bombers, citing the 25 percent better dive-bombing accuracy of the F4U, the better storage characteristics (three F4Us could be parked in the space of two SB2Cs), and the higher productivity of the F4Us (six strikes in a typical day for the F4U as compared to four for the SB2C). McCain closed his report with "I wish to assure Commander, Third Fleet, that if we were to attack Hong Kong again under precisely the same conditions with the same forces and dispositions on both sides, and knowing what we know now, we would sink every ship in the harbor inside of six hours and burn the waterfront too."

Following Halsey's direction, McCain took the task force out of the South China Sea on January 20 through the Balintang Channel between Luzon and Formosa. The enemy made sporadic attempts to hit the fleet from the air.

On January 21 the carrier air groups hit Formosa again. Halsey had made shipping the top target priority. As always, Formosa was a beehive of Japanese air activity. Strikes against the island were launched by Task Force 38 at 6:50 a.m. As the day wore on the enemy persisted in their attacks on the American fleet. Around noon they began to have success. First *Langley* was hit by a bomb that penetrated to the second deck. Then *Ticonderoga* was hit by a kamikaze, and later hit again. An hour later the picket destroyer *Maddox* was hit by a suicide plane. To make matters worse, one of *Hancock's* torpedo planes returned with its full bomb load. The plane opened its bomb-bay doors as directed by the deck crew, and a bomb came loose. The result was a chain-reaction explosion that did major damage. Twelve officers and 96 enlisted men died in the disaster.

In view of the ferocity of the enemy air attacks, McCain requested and Halsey granted permission to give top target priority to attacks against the enemy airfields instead of against shipping. With that done, only two further enemy air attacks were attempted on January 21, and those were after dark.

A special task group was formed around the damaged *Ticonderoga* and *Maddox*. They were unfit to continue in action and departed under this escort for Ulithi.

The strikes continued into January 22. At the close of business, Task Force 38 withdrew to a fueling rendezvous.

In the two days of attacks, McCain's task force had flown 1,415 sorties against enemy targets, dropped 421 tons of bombs, and shot off 2,129 rockets. Forty-one Japanese planes were shot down and 392 were damaged in the air and on the ground. Six oilers and seven cargo ships were sunk, three oilers were damaged, and two destroyers were damaged.

This period saw the initiation of Marine pilots into Task Force 38 carrier operations. They were being assigned to carrier duty to bolster fighter strength against the kamikazes. The Marines had a rough start to their tour as they re-learned carrier landing techniques. Although they had received the same training as the Navy pilots, the Marines were out of practice. When Task Force 38 entered the Balintang Channel on the 20th, the enemy attempted an attack, giving the Marines on combat air patrol an opportunity to show what they could do. In the space of two hours, they shot down eight penetrating kamikazes, just over half of the total of fifteen bagged for the day by Task Force 38. First Lieutenant William McGill shot down got three of these planes in less than three minutes. McCain responded with a message reading: "Three cheers for the Leathernecks!" It made the *Essex* Marines feel more like they were really a part of the team.[5] John McCain still held a deep reverence for the Marines, dating from his Guadalcanal days.

Rotating Out

On the morning of January 23 McCain gathered in the night fighters of Gardner's Task Group 38.5 and joined with the fueling group. At 3:30 p.m. on January 23 the colors on *Hancock* were lowered to half-mast. Funeral services were held for the officers and enlisted men who had perished in the bomb accident on the 21st.

McCain formed a new Task Group, 38.6, consisting of his flagship *Hancock,* Halsey's flagship *New Jersey,* the light carrier *Langley,* and seven escorts. He left Ted Sherman as tactical commander of the remainder of Task Force 38 and departed for Ulithi. The new task group was at anchor by 4:10 p.m. on January 25.

By now, per the two-platoon system, it was time to alternate the command staffs. As of midnight on January 26, 1945, Vice Admiral John S. McCain was officially relieved by Vice Admiral Marc A. Mitscher. Halsey was relieved by Spruance and the Third Fleet became, with a salute and a handshake, the Fifth Fleet. Halsey's farewell message to the Third Fleet lauded his men: "I am so proud of you that no words can express my feelings. This has been a hard operation. At times you have been driven almost beyond endurance but only because the stakes were high, the enemy was as weary as you were, and the lives of many Americans could be spared in later offensives if we did our work well now. We have driven the enemy off the sea and back to his inner defenses. Superlatively well done!"[6]

The score for Slew McCain's Task Force 38 between October 30, 1944, and January 26, 1945, included 101 warships sunk or damaged, 298 merchant ships and 298 small craft sunk, for a shipping total of 697. The estimated total tonnage sunk was 1,163,500. Also, 357 aircraft were destroyed in the air over targets, 107 were destroyed in the air above the task force, and 21 were knocked down by antiaircraft fire. On the ground the total number of aircraft destroyed was 1,172, plus 971 damaged on the ground, and 310 probably destroyed on the ground. Planes probably destroyed in the air totaled 24.

McCain's combat losses for the period were 203 planes, 155 pilots, and 96 aircrewmen. Additionally 180 planes, 43 pilots, and 9 aircrewmen were lost in operational incidents.

McCain left Ulithi on January 27 for Pearl Harbor. The staff transferred from *Hancock* to *Ticonderoga* on the 28th to start their trip homeward.

John Sidney McCain was awarded his second Distinguished Service Medal for his "gallant command" of fast carriers during his first rotation through command of the fast carrier task force. The citation praised his "indomitable courage" as he "led his units aggressively and with brilliant tactical control in extremely hazardous attacks."

15

FINAL BLOWS

John McCain, as soon as he was relieved by Marc "Pete" Mitscher on January 26, wrote himself a set of orders (from Commander, Second Carrier Task Force, to Vice Admiral John S. McCain) to report to Nimitz for temporary additional duty. It was not unusual for an admiral to write himself orders this way to initiate a sequence of events.

McCain spent the period from February 1 to February 8 in Pearl Harbor. While there, he had the pleasure of a reunion with Commander William Sampson, his former aide and pilot. Sam took Sidney for the admiral's first flight in a PB4Y Privateer patrol plane from Sampson's squadron.[1]

Nimitz sent McCain onward with further TAD orders to report to CominCh—Admiral King—in Washington. Then, as directed by King, McCain was to proceed to other places as might be necessary.

All this paperwork served to get McCain to Washington (via Kansas City and Toledo, where he was forced down by bad weather) with selected members of his staff to discuss the Pacific War. Jimmy Thach spoke about the Washington phase of the rest break: "During one of these periods ashore, Admiral McCain went back to Washington, D.C, and he took me with him. We went to see Admiral Ernie King, who was CominCh, and it was a very pleasant visit. I didn't think Admiral McCain would take me into Admiral King's office with him but he did, and I was very pleased that he would do that. I thought they'd probably want to talk about something that only they were cleared to discuss. But they had a good conversation. Admiral King had a great admiration for Admiral McCain. I knew—

and, of course, Admiral McCain knew—that there were other officers who wanted very much to have that prize job of Commander, Fast Carrier Task Force. Mitscher and McCain were alternating, and there was a lot of talk started such as, 'Wasn't it about time somebody else had a chance to do that?' . . . Admiral King indicated, not directly, but by what he said concerning the future plans, that he wasn't about to relieve Admiral McCain. It was a very cordial visit."[2]

Thach wasn't kidding about other admirals lining up to take Slew McCain's job. Ted Sherman, probably McCain's most able task group commander, always felt that he should have been selected for the job in the first place. And aspirant Jack Towers was described in the press as morosely watching the war from an administrative position.[3]

Vice Admiral John McCain left Washington on February 22 to return to San Diego via Greenwood, Mississippi. John Sidney had an overnighter in Greenwood with his kin, and was checked in at North Island Naval Air Station by Rear Admiral Alfred E. Montgomery, who had relieved McCain as task group commander in October. Montgomery was now wearing the hat of Commander, Fleet Air, West Coast. Then John Sidney began a 30 day leave with Kate at their home in Coronado. He was interrupted once to star in a press conference at the Hotel Del Coronado.

Also, the Navy Department formally announced the award of the gold star to McCain in lieu of a second Distinguished Service Medal. McCain was cited for his services as commander of the carrier task group from September 1 to October 30, 1944, and as commander of the Second Fast Carrier Task Force from November 1 to January 26, 1945. Achievements cited included the difficult and urgent task of providing support for the landings in the Philippines and leading his units aggressively and with brilliant tactical control in extremely hazardous attacks. The medal was presented by Admiral Royal E. Ingersoll (Deputy Commander-in-Chief of the U.S. Fleet and Commander, Western Sea Frontier) on March 23, 1945, at the Federal Office Building in San Francisco.

During this period Jimmy Thach, who started the war as a lieutenant, was promoted to captain. John McCain pinned the eagles on Thach's collar with the comment that Thach's job ought to be an admiral's.[4]

Back to the War

John McCain's leave was completed on April 1, and he departed by air on April 3 for Pearl Harbor to report back to Nimitz. His staff left for Pearl on March 27 via ship, and they reassembled on Ford Island for the balance of the month for operational planning.

While the staff officers worked on operations plans, some of the enlisted staffers were not terribly busy on Ford Island. On one occasion they were sitting on a rail fence outside of the bunker offices when chief of staff Wilder Baker arrived in his staff car. They jumped to attention with the greeting, "Good Morning, Admiral," but to a man they forgot to salute. Baker passed them by, and with his hand on the door, half-turned and said, "Men, I must remind you when you're on the beach you'll have to learn how to salute!"

Later, on a more somber note, Admiral Baker called the staff together and said he had bad news. The Commander-in-Chief, Franklin Roosevelt, had died on April 12. As Baker read the dispatch, a tear rolled down his cheek.

On May 9 most of the staff officers and enlisted men departed for Ulithi on the cruiser *Duluth*. McCain followed by air on May 16. On May 17, at Ulithi, Vice Admiral John McCain hoisted his flag aboard the carrier USS *Shangri La*, CV-38.

Shangri La departed for Okinawa on May 24. At sea on May 27 Mitscher and some of this staff came aboard for a day of conferences. At midnight on May 28, Halsey relieved Spruance, the Fifth Fleet became the Third Fleet, and all the other unit numbers changed once more.

On the morning of May 28th, McCain visited the battleship *Missouri* for a conference with Halsey. At 3:00 p.m. he relieved Pete Mitscher as Commander, Task Force 38, and resumed tactical command. The carrier *Shangri La* remained his flagship until the end.

The commanders and carriers of Task Force 38 were set: Task Group 38.1 was commanded by Rear Admiral Jocko Clark with *Hornet, Bennington, Belleau Wood,* and *San Jacinto*. Task Group 38.3 was led by Rear Admiral Ted Sherman with *Essex, Randolph, Bataan,* and *Monterey*. Task Group 38.4 operated under the command of Rear Admiral Arthur W. Radford with *Yorktown, Shangri La, Ticonderoga,* and *Independence*.

The next day, before Mitscher and his staff left for Guam aboard *Randolph*, Mitscher visited Halsey aboard the *Missouri*. Halsey was shocked at Pete Mitscher's appearance. Mitscher had to be helped up the ship's ladder. He was gaunt; he weighed less than a hundred pounds. Before Mitscher took his final departure, Halsey sent him a farewell dispatch expressing the sentiment of the whole Third Fleet: "It is with the very deepest regret that we watch a great fighting man shove off. I and my staff and the fleet send all luck to you and your magnificent staff."[5]

There seems to be no question that command takes its toll, particularly one as demanding as commanding a fast carrier task force in heavy battle. It ultimately took its toll on John McCain as well.

This change of command, from Fifth Fleet to Third Fleet, was not just a routine change as a part of the two-platoon rotation. Halsey and McCain were rested, experienced, and ready. But a command change in the midst of a campaign—in this case Okinawa—was unprecedented. Nevertheless Spruance and Mitscher had been under unrelenting pressure. Their ships and men had been hit heavily by the deadliest weapon Japan had left to offer: the kamikazes. After staff consultations and with King's approval, Nimitz decided to go ahead with the rotation. When Halsey took over, he did so with the intention of freeing the fleet from its defensive tasks of covering the invasion and to launch offensive strikes against Japan and its airfields.[6]

Battle Update

During the four-month Spruance/Mitscher rotation, Task Force 58 had made the first American attack on Japan since the 1942 Doolittle raid. Then, on February 19, 1945, Iwo Jima was invaded by the Marines. Task Force 58 provided cover for the landings, and then moved back to attack Japan again. This was followed by more strikes on Okinawa. Iwo Jima was secured by March 16.

Mitscher hit Japan again on March 18. The enemy was waiting. Task Force 58 suffered heavy losses from the kamikazes and from aggressive Japanese fighters and bombers.

Mitscher withdrew to reorganize, and Task Force 58 was joined by the Royal Navy's four-carrier Task Force 57 until the end of May.

The Army and Marine landings on Okinawa followed on April 1, 1945. Heavy suicide attacks by the Japanese lasted to the end of the campaign. Mitscher demonstrated the power of the fast carriers by sinking the Japanese super-battleship *Yamato* as she had tried to sail for Okinawa on her own version of a suicide mission.

But the kamikazes had continued to strike with deadly efficiency. In February the venerable *Saratoga* was hit by six suicide planes and withdrew to the United States for repairs, never to fight again. March was a bad month. *Wasp* and *Franklin* were damaged (*Franklin* by conventional bombing), and both had to return to Stateside shipyards. *Randolph* was knocked out for eighteen days. *Enterprise, Intrepid,* and the new *Yorktown* all had scrapes.

April wasn't any better. *Hancock* and *Intrepid* were benched, and *Enterprise* slightly damaged. That was followed in May by severe damage to *Bunker Hill* and *Enterprise*. Both were sent Stateside. Marc Mitscher had to move his flag from *Bunker Hill* to *Enterprise* to *Randolph*, all in four days' time. The cruiser *Indianapolis* and four escort carriers were also hit hard, with one of the latter sunk.

By the time Halsey and Slew arrived again on the scene, the Army and Marines were finding heavy going on Okinawa. Kamikazes had sunk 26 ships and damaged 133.

Task Force 38

At first things were quiet on the new rotation. Weather was poor over Okinawa and no enemy air opposition was encountered. Halsey sent Sherman's Task Group 38.3 to Leyte for rest and replenishment as part of the regular rotation plan. San Pedro Bay on Leyte had replaced Ulithi as the forward base.

McCain assigned the job of OTC temporarily to Radford and sent Radford's Task Group 38.4 to launch strikes against Okinawa. Clark's Task Group 38.1 was sent southward for replenishment. The task groups continued to operate independently through June 1.

McCain resumed tactical command on that day. For the next 48 hours Clark maintained the air patrol over Okinawa while Radford sent a fighter sweep against airfields on Kyushu. Weather was still poor. Ground operations on Okinawa were brought to a halt by heavy rainstorms.[7]

Typhoon Reprise—Viper

One of the final blows that affected John McCain's life was not by or against the enemy. It was of nature's making—another typhoon. Just as in the case of the first typhoon, encountered in December, lack of efficacious communications compounded the problems of maneuvering two carrier task groups and a service group away from harm. It was Halsey's bad luck to get nailed by a major storm again, and McCain's bad luck that tactical command had reverted back to him as the carrier fleet maneuvered to avoid the typhoon.

Early on the morning of June 4, McCain recommended to Halsey that, due to the storm conditions, the fleet should withdraw from the Okinawa area. Halsey agreed, so the planes were recalled and the fleet (which was just Radford's Task Group 38.4 at this point) headed to the southeast. McCain suggested due east, but Halsey postponed any decision until he had more information. The storm had actually split. Halsey's staff had the storm located to the west, whereas the worst half was to the south.

Meanwhile, Clark's Task Group 38.1 had completed refueling and replenishment. About 8:00 p.m. in the evening the two task groups and the refueling group rendezvoused, with McCain in tactical command. Halsey and McCain discussed various course changes to dodge the storm. McCain wanted to keep moving eastward and recommended that they should increase speed to escape the heavy weather. This, in fact, would have carried the fleet clear. Halsey finally made a judgment call and directed McCain to turn the fleet to the northwest, to course 300 degrees.[8] McCain's reaction was, "What the hell is Halsey doing, trying to intercept another typhoon?"

This small, tight and vicious storm was coming on like a raging bull, and Halsey was like a blindfolded matador. He could hear the bull charging but he couldn't see it. He knew the animal could swerve right or left, and he had to decide which way he should move to escape the charge.

McCain ordered the course change to 300 degrees as Halsey wanted, but later, with Halsey's concurrence, he came to due north. McCain and Halsey were in Radford's Task Group 38.4, the northernmost group. Clark's Task Group 38.1 was sixteen miles south. The service group of oilers, cargo ships, and escort carriers under the command of Rear Admiral Donald B. Beary was another eighteen miles further south. Those distances made all the difference.

Radford zigzagged northward for the next five hours and suffered insignificant damage.

Admiral Beary, on the far south, directed his ships to proceed independently to the northwest, in search of easier riding. They went right back toward the center of the storm and were hammered pretty well. But only four of the service ships—two escort carriers, a destroyer escort, and a tanker—suffered severe damage.[9]

Clark, in the middle, had the toughest time of all. He reduced speed to stay with a damaged destroyer but remained on the fleet course. Then, at 4:20 a.m. he told McCain that he could steer clear of the storm center on course 120 degrees and asked, "Please advise." McCain, who did not have the storm center on his radar, checked with Halsey, who signaled that Clark was to maintain his position. McCain felt that the formation he was riding with (Task Group 38.4) was getting clear of the storm and had nothing to gain from changing course. Finally, at 4:40 a.m., McCain told Clark that he was remaining on course 000 degrees and for Clark to use his own judgment. Clark maneuvered in an effort to find a course his ships could hold. He ended up circling around to a southerly course, all the time in the middle of the storm.[10]

Damage was pretty bad. The cruiser *Pittsburgh* lost her bow, which floated away; it was later retrieved and towed to Guam. Fast carriers *Hornet* and *Bennington*, two escort carriers, and three cruisers also suffered major damage. Twenty-six other ships reported minor damage. Six men were lost and 146 aircraft were destroyed or damaged.

Task Force 38 regrouped on June 6. Task Groups 38.4 and 38.1 rendezvoused, and Clark came aboard *Shangri La* to confer with McCain. In Clark's opinion, McCain's personal loyalty to Halsey kept him from saying anything about whether or not Clark could have avoided the eye of the storm had he been released twenty minutes earlier. Then McCain and Clark went aboard *Missouri* to meet with Halsey. As a result of that meeting, Clark felt that Halsey was fully aware of where the blame lay for running the fleet into the storm.[11]

The task force was back in business on June 6 providing air cover for the ground troops on Okinawa. Two groups of enemy planes were intercepted and ground-support strikes were launched.

The front edges of *Hornet's* flight deck were severely bent down by the fierce storm. Jocko Clark tried to launch aircraft over *Hornet's* damaged bow, but the first Corsair spun-in due to extreme turbulence created by the distorted deck. The pilot was saved. Clark met his commitments by having *Hornet* launch planes over her stern while going 18 knots full astern. She continued that wonderfully innovative tactic for two days.[12]

Support for troops on Okinawa was undertaken again on June 7th. Then on June 8 a 200-plane concentrated glide bombing and strafing strike was made on the Kanoya airfield on southern Kyushu. Damage to enemy planes on the ground was extensive. The next day the Daito Islands were hit by surface and air bombardments. McCain used this action to test the accuracy and effectiveness of napalm. Clark's planes dropped the napalm on heavily protected shore emplacements and incinerated 75 to 90 percent of the targets.

Action was winding down on Okinawa, so Task Force 38 withdrew to Leyte Gulf and anchored in San Pedro Harbor on June 13.

Rest, recreation, repairs, and replenishment were necessary for the tired men and ships in anticipation for the forthcoming pre-invasion strikes against Japan. But the fleet had hardly arrived before Halsey, McCain, Clark, and Beary were called before a court of inquiry, set to convene on June 15 aboard the *New Mexico*. The court was convened, of course, to find out just what had happened during the typhoon, now named Typhoon Viper. Vice Admiral John H. "Genial John" Hoover presided over the court, as he had for Cobra.[13]

Right off the bat Halsey took a swipe at the weather service: "Had I any knowledge beforehand of the track of this typhoon such as I now possess, it would have been the easiest matter in the world to have employed [the knowledge] way ahead of the storm. I was without such knowledge."[14]

In the end, the court held that Halsey bore the primary blame for the damage. The court's opinion was that the main cause was Halsey's change of course from 110 degrees to 300 degrees early on the morning of June 5. McCain had to shoulder the secondary blame. This was for McCain's twenty-minute delay in granting Clark permission to change from course 000 degrees to 120 degrees. Clark and Beary also caught some blame because their ships were damaged, and the commanders always have the ultimate responsibility.[15]

The court recommended that letters be sent to Halsey and McCain pointing out errors. Further, the court felt that serious consideration should be given to assigning Halsey and McCain to other duties.

Some historians have indicated that Secretary Forrestal was now ready to retire Halsey. Admiral King agreed with the court that Halsey (and thus McCain) had botched the operation, particularly inasmuch as they had been through a typhoon before. Nevertheless, King was not ready to retire or publicly reprimand "Bull" Halsey, who had become a national hero. Calling Halsey home would depress American morale and boost the enemy's. Forrestal went along. On top of that, Halsey was still penciled in to run the Third Fleet during the invasion of Japan.[16]

McCain, on the other hand, was more vulnerable. He did not enjoy such public adulation. Further, McCain and Mitscher both were tired, maybe ill, and in need of a rest. Both had qualified replacements in the wings, rarin' to lead the fast carriers. Nimitz was already thinking about bringing McCain home.

McCain closed out the month of June with an action report which emphasized that adequate time must be allowed for proper planning of operations. He contrasted the strikes on June 2 and 3 against southern Kyushu to the strike against the Kanoya airfield on June 8. For the earlier strikes, because of short notice, only a superficial briefing for the pilots was possible. Against Kanoya, the pilots had time to thoroughly study the details of the target and the plan of attack. McCain did not want to place his pilots at risk unless they completely understood and had assimilated the mission. McCain also had some pointed comments about improving the weather-reporting system.

Striking Japan

Although he was going to end up being made the goat for the Typhoon Viper fiasco, Slew McCain wasn't finished yet, or gone yet, not by anyone's reckoning.

The Third Fleet and Task Force 38 left Leyte on July 1, 1945, for the most protracted period of naval attacks on the Japanese homeland undertaken by the carrier force. Now that organized fighting had ended on Okinawa, the fast carriers were free to concentrate on the big prize.

McCain's force was still deployed in three task groups, part of the Task Force 38 tactics to concentrate firepower and foil the kamikazes. Task Group 38.1, commanded by Rear Admiral Tommy Sprague, included *Bennington, Hancock, Lexington, Belleau Wood,* and *San Jacinto,* plus three battleships, seven cruisers, and twenty destroyers. Task Group 38.3, commanded by tough and feisty Rear Admiral Gerry Bogan, included *Randolph, Essex, Ticonderoga, Monterey* and *Bataan,* as well as three battleships, six cruisers, and eighteen destroyers. Rear Admiral Arthur Radford commanded Task Group 38.4 which included *Yorktown, Shangri La* (McCain's flagship), *Bon Homme Richard* (sponsored at its launching by Kate McCain), *Independence, Cowpens,* and later *Wasp;* three battleships, four cruisers, and twenty-two destroyers. One of Radford's battleships was Halsey's flagship, *Missouri.*

On the way north from the Philippines, McCain's flagship, *Shangri La,* was the scene of a unique ceremony. John L. Sullivan was sworn in as Assistant Secretary of the Navy for Air. Sullivan's trip had started in Washington on June 1 with stops at Pearl Harbor, Eniwetok, Guam, Ulithi, the Admiralty Islands, Peleliu, and Manila. Sullivan was greeted upon his arrival on Leyte by a host of flag officers including Halsey and McCain. He was escorted to *Shangri La* and from there witnessed the sortie of Task Force 38 from San Pedro Harbor. He was reported to be at a loss for words to try to describe the mighty task force as it moved to sea, the greatest striking power of any naval force in history. Sullivan's report also lauded the service group that drew alongside to deliver fuel, bombs, food, and that most important item—mail from home.

With a Marine guard of honor and the crew at attention, Admiral McCain introduced Aubrey Fitch (who had followed McCain as Deputy CNO in Washington), who administered the oath of office. The ceremony ended with a seventeen-gun salute from the five-inch antiaircraft battery. Before starting his homeward trip, Sullivan toured *Shangri La,* visited other ships, and had a game or two of cribbage with Slew.

Dignitaries aside, the trip north was occupied with training and replenishment. Then, on July 9, the force started its high-speed run toward Japan to launch strikes against Tokyo the next morning. Tactical surprise was complete. The weather was perfect. Strikes were launched throughout the day on a 210-mile front, concentrating on enemy aircraft and airfields. More than a thousand sorties were flown over the targets, and more than one hundred Japanese airplanes were destroyed on the ground.

Task Force 38 withdrew on July 11 and refueled from Don Beary's service group on the 12th. The strikes planned for July 13 were cancelled due to poor weather, but Task Force 38 was back in action on the 14th and 15th. Shipping and aircraft were hit on Hokkaido and northern Honshu. Adverse weather interfered again, so attention was shifted from airfields to shipping, plus rail lines and other ground installations.

On July 14, a special task unit was formed with the battleships *Massachusetts, Indiana,* and *South Dakota,* plus two cruisers and nine destroyers to conduct a shore bombardment of the steel plant at Kamaishi on Honshu. Throughout July such special units were regularly formed to hit shipping along the coast or bombard shore targets. In fact, Halsey had asked McCain to find some "battleship jobs." The *Missouri* herself got into the action on July 15 as part of the bombardment of the steel works at Muroran, Hokkaido. *Missouri* fired at ranges up to 18 miles. The target area was saturated.[17]

McCain's assistant operations officer, Bill Leonard, gave his slant (perhaps unkindly) on the surface bombardments: "There was clamoring by the surface people to get a whack at action, and we had the spectacle of battleships shelling furniture and bicycle factories while Task Force 38 provided air cover! Intelligence could not find any significant strategic targets within range of the 16-inchers, and none of the objectives merited an air strike. Some wag on the staff referred to this effort as a make-work project for the black shoes."[18]

The Japanese were getting hammered pretty well, but McCain got a shock himself. On July 15, now that the war in Europe was over, he received word from the Navy Department that when the Third Fleet returned to Eniwetok in mid-August, a month hence, he would be relieved as Commander, Task Force 38, by John Towers.[19] Word was that McCain was to report to Washington to serve as Deputy Director of the Veteran's Administration under General Omar Bradley.

This quickly became public knowledge. News releases from the Navy Department in mid-July described the "Big Stir Up." Mitscher was scheduled to become Deputy CNO for Air, Rear Admiral Ted Sherman was to take Mitscher's place commanding Task Force 58, and Towers was to relieve McCain as commander of Task Force 38. These were among twenty-nine flag-officer reassignments that were being made, it was reported, to bring officers with combat experience ashore to plan and direct the final phases of the war. No new assignment was announced for McCain, and Secretary Forrestal declined to comment on the VA job. McCain's orders simply directed him to report to the Secretary of the Navy.

McCain may have felt that this new non-Navy job was a result of his shouldering the blame for Typhoon Viper. But the shakeup had been in the works for some time, though the typhoon may have tipped the balance.

The war wasn't waiting. The task force refueled on July 16 and launched strikes against Tokyo the next day. Bad weather prevented all but the first two air strikes from reaching their target. Instead, a night shore bombardment was carried out under the cover of *Bon Homme Richard's* night fighters.

On July 18, Task Force 38, with British Task Force 37 in company, hit Tokyo and the surrounding area, as well as the Yokosuka naval base. The British carriers added 29 ships to the Third Fleet's 105. Weather was not good, but the Japanese battleship *Nagato* was hit and one cruiser and two destroyers were sunk. The fleet then pulled back to refuel and take on stores.

This service group operation on July 21 and 22 was described in McCain's action report as the largest refueling, replenishment, and rearming operation ever undertaken at sea. The service group delivered nearly 380,000 barrels of oil, more than 6,000 tons of ammunition, 99 aircraft, more than 400 men, and tons upon tons of provisions to the fighting ships. It was also at this time that Halsey first heard that an atomic bomb would be dropped on Japan.[20]

On July 24, the two task forces were back in action for two days of continuous day and night strikes against a variety of targets until bad weather again interfered. Airfields and aircraft were hit on western Honshu, Shikoku, and northern Kyushu. Naval and merchant shipping was struck in the Inland Sea. Nagoya and Osaka were hit. Kure was a ripe target. Twenty-two warships were damaged or sunk. Carrier planes working over the airfields nabbed 18 planes in the air and 129 on the ground. The enemy had the planes gassed and ready to hit the fleet, so these strikes were particularly timely. Four enemy torpedo planes tried to attack the fleet and were shot down, three by the British.

After refueling on July 26 and 27, the carrier forces struck again on July 28 at Japanese naval shipping at Kure and in the Inland Sea, plus the usual airfields and aircraft. The weather was good and the results were devastating. The battleship *Haruna* was driven aground by dive bombers.

The fleet was back again on July 30. That day, 258 enemy planes were put out of action, many at Nagoya. Merchant shipping also suffered heavy damage.

McCain had some doubts about this kind of target selection. He felt that hitting ships and shipping was all a waste of time. He never gave up on his belief that his planes should be attacking airfields and aircraft factories, but he kept his mouth shut and did not complain until he prepared his operations report.[21] He probably didn't realize that Nimitz, from afar, still considered the Japanese naval surface forces a threat to the pending invasion and wanted them eliminated.[22]

For the next few days McCain and Halsey were stymied by bad weather. On August 1, British Task Force 37 and McCain's Task Force 38 separated for refueling and headed south to sidestep a typhoon. Replenishment continued until the afternoon of August 3, when air training exercises were undertaken. On the evening of August 4 Nimitz ordered Halsey to take the fleet north. B-29s of the Twentieth Air Force were ready to drop the atomic bombs.[23]

Weather caused cancellation of strikes scheduled for August 5, so training was resumed on the 6th. The task force refueled on August 7, but weather delayed it again on August 8.

Finally, on August 9 and 10 the carrier air groups hit northern Honshu again. The fleet had been given orders to stay north of 37 degrees North latitude, keeping them well clear of the atomic bomb drops on Hiroshima on August 6 and Nagasaki on August 9. Unfortunately this meant that the Big Blue Blanket could not be extended far enough south to cover airfields in the Tokyo area. A suicide plane got aloft, slipped out of Honshu, and dove in on a picket destroyer to score the only kamikaze hit on a Task Force 38 ship during the entire operation. The destroyer, *Borie,* withdrew under her own power. Other enemy attackers tried, but failed, to score on the carriers. One kamikaze narrowly missed *Wasp.* Seven enemy aircraft were shot down over the task force.

In his oral history, Thach discussed this period: "In the last two months of the war when we were roaming up and down the Japanese coast, where there were many [enemy] aircraft . . . we shot down 130 airplanes attempting to get to the carriers. They did hit some destroyer pickets, but the last two months of the war not one carrier was hit by a kamikaze or anything else."[24]

Admiral Halsey broke the tension of battle a little on August 9, McCain's 61st birthday. Harold Stassen (Halsey's flag secretary and assistant chief of staff) called from the *Missouri* on the radio: "Is Blackhawk [McCain] there?" He was, so Halsey stepped up and sang "Happy Birthday" to Slew on the radio.[25]

Later that evening the Task Force 38 staff filed into flag plot with ties on. The steward's mates brought in a large birthday cake and sat it on the chart table. Slew said, "Well, gentlemen, I want to say I appreciate this. I'm surprised. But you'll have to excuse me. I've had a big day. Carry on." There was applause and Slew ordered, "Take this cake down and share it with the radio shack boys and the signal bridge gang."

The strikes of August 10 made for a record day. They put 255 enemy planes out of action, bringing the two-day total to 588. These planes otherwise were scheduled to be part of a crash mission to the Marianas. Forty-four Japanese vessels were sunk, but the main damage was to the enemy airfields. Some pilots were able to make as many as a dozen passes over an airfield. No attacks were attempted by the enemy against the task force, but word of a surrender offer by the Japanese caused greater alertness against enemy surprise attacks.

With rumors afoot that the Japanese were willing to surrender, Halsey decided to stay off the coast of Japan and hit the enemy again before the end. He growled, "Have we got enough fuel to turn around and hit the bastards once more before they quit?"[26]

The Final Days

After refueling on August 11, and cruising east of Honshu on the 12th, strikes against Tokyo were ordered for August 13. Halsey had planned to strike on August 12, but he told McCain to hold up for twenty-four hours because of adverse weather.

Also on the 12th, the British force split up; some of the carriers and escorts headed for Manus and the remainder (one carrier and thirteen other ships) joined Task Force 38 as Task Group 38.5.[27]

Halsey still had reservations about hitting the Japanese now that the surrender seemed imminent. He told McCain to cancel strikes on August 13, then he reversed himself and gave the go-ahead.[28]

Nimitz also weighed in early on August 13 with a message to cancel the strike. Then he, too, reversed himself, and Halsey told McCain to "Follow original schedule of strikes."[29]

Task Force 38 aircraft were launched within an hour, and a grand total of 424 enemy planes were put out of action. No airborne opposition was encountered at the targets, but the Japanese attempted attacks on the fleet throughout the day. None were successful, and twenty-one enemy planes were reported shot down near the task force.

McCain remained convinced that the Japanese were hoarding planes and fuel for a final battle. In fact the Japanese Navy was capable of launching 5,000 aircraft and the Japanese Army had 3,300. One clue of an impending attack was if planes burned when they were hit on the ground. If so, they were fueled and ready to go. If there were no "flamers," the enemy was in a conservation mode.

The Japanese also were masters of dispersion and camouflage. McCain and his staff had seen this in the Philippines and Formosa, and were seeing it again in Japan.

McCain warned his task force: "Keep alert for tricks and banzai attacks. The war is not over yet. The Nips may be playing their national game of judo, waiting until we are close and unwary." While fueling on August 14, Slew told his pilots, "We cannot afford to relax. Now is the time to pour it on."

The strike on August 15 against Tokyo was already underway

when Nimitz signaled "Suspend air attack operations."[30] The second
strike force was still on its way to the target. These planes jettisoned
their bombs and headed back to their carriers. The first strike had
already encountered forty-five enemy planes over targets and had shot
down twenty-six.

The Japanese did not cut things off quite so quickly. When the Big
Blue Blanket was lifted in the morning the Japanese sent out a steady
stream of attack planes until about mid-afternoon. Eight enemy planes
were shot down trying to break into the task force formation.

McCain issued sharp orders after the morning strikes returned. "I
want wartime vigilance maintained until we're sure the Japanese plan
no further attacks." McCain queried Halsey as to what his ships
should do if attacked, and received the famous answer: "Investigate
and shoot down all snoopers, not vindictively, but in a friendly sort of
way."[31]

The last carrier campaign, launched July 1, had produced some
big numbers: 10,678 target sorties and 12,878 combat patrol sorties
flown; 4,619 tons of bombs dropped; 22,036 rockets fired; 136 aircraft destroyed or damaged in the air; 2,272 aircraft destroyed or
damaged on the ground; 31 warships sunk and 73 damaged; 55 merchant ships sunk and 105 damaged; and 117 airfields attacked.

Japanese warships sunk included two battleships, four cruisers, six
submarines, seven destroyers, and twelve other types. Damaged were
two battleships, five cruisers, six carriers, fifteen submarines, thirty-
two destroyers and destroyer escorts, and thirteen other types.

Destroyed or extensively damaged were aircraft hangars, rail lines,
docks, factories, warehouses, bridges, and antiaircraft positions.

The cost was 174 American planes lost in combat and 133 lost
operationally. Pilot and aircrew losses totaled 197.

Cooling Down

The war was ended, but Task Force 38 had to remain vigilant. The
carriers withdrew to "Area McCain" and maintained normal wartime
patrols.[32]

Things were quiet for the fleet, and McCain was quiet as well. As
Jimmy Thach put it, "When we got word of the cease-fire, I realized
that Admiral McCain wasn't feeling very well physically. He went to

his sea cabin, and he didn't pop out frequently into the flag plot and enter into things as much as he had. I missed him, and I'd go in there and talk to him and tell him what I wanted to do. I thought we should get a photograph of all of our ships as close together as they could get . . . so I went in to recommend to Admiral McCain that we do this. This was one of the times when I realized he just wasn't feeling well at all, and he said, 'Okay, good idea. Just go ahead and do it; no problem. Do whatever you want to.'"

Thach continued "'Admiral, you don't feel very well, do you?' He said, 'Well, this surrender has come as kind of a shock to all of us. I feel lost. I don't know what to do. I know how to fight, but now I don't know whether I know how to relax or not. I am in an awful letdown. I do feel bad.' He didn't look too well, either."[33]

With McCain's approval, the fleet drew together on August 16 and 17 for some spectacular photography. The planes of the task force conducted a mass fly-over on August 22, again producing wonderful pictures and providing a rehearsal for the surrender ceremonies.

McCain commented about this period: "The lines of strain have disappeared from the pilots' faces. They are laughing now all the time which is as it should be. Their main job now is to bomb prisoner-of-war camps with food, cigarettes, liquor, reading material, and medical supplies. They go low—a few hundred feet—over our cheering, waving, and gesticulating countrymen."

Accolades

On August 16, Carl Vinson sent the following message: "Now that victory is ours I wish to express my admiration of your work as one of the greatest air commanders of the war. The officers and men under your command have performed in an outstanding manner in striking at the heart of the enemy and thus dealing him a mortal blow. We of the House Naval Affairs Committee are well aware of the great part played by your air arm in fearlessly pressing home the attack. We salute you."

Tommy Sprague sent his boss a nice message from Task Group 38.1: "It was a carrier war. I know you must find great satisfaction in having command of the carriers at the finish of this show. It has not only been an honor to serve under your command but it has been fun besides. All hands at the north end of the line join me in god-speed and good luck."

Another honor of a sort, and a particularly appropriate one, occurred earlier on Wednesday, August 29, 1945, while McCain was still off the coast of Japan and just a few days before his death. The Del Mar Turf Club in California dedicated the day's racing card to the heroic admirals. The second race was "The Vice-Admiral John S. McCain."

Carrier Tactics (III)

After the last strike, wayward planes were recovered, and Task Force 38 withdrew to the southeast to await further orders. Now, McCain and his staff had time to reflect on what they had learned and how their knowledge might be applied in the future. McCain knew it was his last chance to make his points. He laid it on the line in his usual assertive manner. In his earlier action report for May 28 through July 1, 1945, McCain had concluded: "Employment of fast carriers in direct ground support for protracted periods is undesirable. It is wasteful of force, and it fails to exploit the fast carrier assets of mobility, surprise, and concentration. It invites damage to the fast carriers through continued operation in restricted waters. Finally, it diverts the fast carriers from profitable targets which only they can reach."

McCain's action report for the next period, July 2 through August 15, 1945, concluded that the "Tomcat" and "Watchdog" advanced radar picket system developed around Task Force 38 (as one of the means to trap the kamikazes on their way to the fleet) was an outstanding success. Further, McCain got in his licks about targeting the remnants of the Japanese Navy rather than concentrating on aircraft and airfields. But he made the issue one of timing, not of choice. He argued strongly that destroying the enemy air capability should come first. Then the ships could be handled with little problem. Destroying enemy air would remove the kamikaze threat.

McCain maintained his stance that the air complement on carriers should be 90 percent fighters and fighter-bombers. Without that, he observed, he did not believe that the fast carrier could achieve its optimum striking power.

He also emphasized the importance of aerial reconnaissance photography, the importance of on-the-spot use of weather information by the tactical commander, the need for a carrier-based amphibian rescue plane, and the need for forward-area base facilities for air groups.

A bit startling (and far-seeing) was McCain's proposal for the future use of carriers. The carrier's new mission would be the mid-ocean interception of enemy long-range, land-based, planes carrying atomic bombs. McCain suggested that the carriers carry long-range, high-altitude interceptor aircraft and be outfitted with improved radar.

McCain and his staff felt that confusing notions about offense and defense on the part of the carrier commanders resulted from the Spruance doctrine of keeping the carriers in a vulnerable position close to the landing force off Okinawa. McCain's approach would have been to hit the Japanese airfields and factories early and often. Thus the kamikazes would have been taken out of play before they had a chance to strike at the invasion fleet.

Spreading the Big Blue Blanket over the home islands—using the fast carriers offensively—was the McCain style and might have significantly reduced the tragic level of casualties off Okinawa. The moment Okinawa was invaded, McCain pointed out, all available air forces—the carriers, escort carriers, the marines, the army air forces—should have been thrown against Japanese airfields and aircraft factories with the overriding purpose of destroying the Japanese air effort. McCain felt it could have been done in less than a month and perhaps in two weeks. That it could be done was shown absolutely by the results the fast carrier task force produced once it went on the offensive. McCain's opinion was that had such offensive strikes been undertaken, the casualties to ships and personnel at Okinawa might have been cut to a minimum.[34]

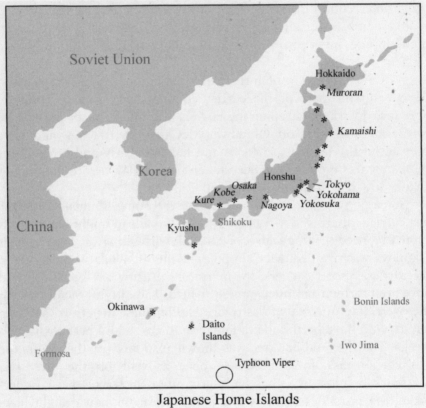

Japanese Home Islands

Target Areas = ✱

16

COMMAND PERFORMANCE

The war was over, and the record book about to be closed. Can we judge how well Slew McCain and his contemporaries did their jobs?

As anyone who has filled out fitness reports on fellow officers can testify, rating performance can be an intimidating process. In the case of John McCain, we are looking up at one of the Navy's highest ranking officers and back sixty years in time. In addition, measurement of command performance can have many dimensions.

One dimension is the military record. John Sidney McCain had a Navy Cross and, in the end, three Distinguished Service Medals. These do not come lightly. Under his command, Task Force 38 had record-breaking days destroying enemy planes and ships as well as conducting a record at-sea underway replenishment. John McCain fought long and hard in the South Pacific (and later in Washington) to get support for the Marines on Guadalcanal. Were there blemishes? Sure. The Savo Island battle in 1942, Typhoon Cobra in 1944, and Typhoon Viper in 1945 each brought criticism, some severe.

Another dimension, not to be overlooked, is the spotlight of publicity. John McCain was an outgoing personality—with his salty, weather-beaten looks he was a favorite of the press. Media correspondents with him in the Pacific loved his colorful and friendly style. He got a share of media attention all right, but Bill Halsey got the headlines. Halsey was a national hero.

Even another dimension is command performance as viewed by those up and down the chain of command. Sometimes these views were expressly stated, other times they were only implied.

Halsey and Spruance

Halsey was the dominant figure in McCain's most significant command period. To get a complete picture of Bill Halsey at this time, and thus inferences about McCain, one also has to take a look at Ray Spruance. He was Halsey's opposite in the two- platoon system. Spruance helps to define Halsey, and Halsey helps define McCain.

The styles of Halsey and Spruance contrasted sharply. Spruance was deliberate and cautious.[1] He was a meticulous planner, or to put it more precisely, he required meticulous planning from his staff. His advance plans were detailed and timely, easy to understand, and his operations nearly always turned out as planned.[2] Probably one of the few times when this was not the case was at Saipan. King was not reassured by reading Spruance's plan for the invasion. Spruance had no comprehensive plan for meeting the enemy should the Japanese fleet appear. Spruance and Mitscher preferred, not unreasonably, to wait until the situation developed before deciding on a course of action.[3]

Spruance was a brilliant strategist and coordinator. He could grasp the overall picture of operations where others (such as the carrier admirals) might be focused on just their part of the venture. He successfully commanded the complex amphibious operations against the Gilberts, the Marshalls, the Marianas, Iwo Jima, and Okinawa. He rarely assumed tactical command of the carrier task force. He preferred to give general directions for the deployment of the fleet and leave the details to Mitscher and the other commanders.

Spruance tried to foresee everything. He did not treat risks lightly. Nimitz trusted him implicitly. If there was a weakness, it was Spruance's reluctance to free the fast carriers from the task of covering the amphibious landings. Spruance, with a strategic perspective, placed priority on successfully defeating the enemy ashore and occupying enemy territory. So, rather than aggressively attacking the enemy air threat at its source, Spruance's plans kept the fast carriers tied to the invasion beaches.[4] There, they could only wait for the enemy to come to them. And the enemy did, with terrible consequences at Okinawa where the kamikazes wreaked havoc.[5]

Halsey, on the other hand, was a bold commander who specialized in imaginative improvisations.[6] Although he was a great combat leader, he rarely followed an established plan. Some commanders dreaded working under him. But his admirers pointed out that if *they* never knew what he was going to do next, his operations must completely bewilder the *enemy*.[7] Historian Clark Reynolds wrote, "He had daring and was unafraid to take risks, but he was also sloppy in his procedures." McCain was branded by the same iron. Reynolds continued, "Rather than issuing meticulous operations plans, [Halsey] operated by dispatch. This being the case, he lost valuable time in sending communications and his carrier admirals never quite knew his plans."[8]

Although Halsey inspired his men like no other, some officers felt that Halsey's command style was more suitable to the early days of the war, when carrier forces were smaller and tasks simpler. Now operations of the Third Fleet were too complex for his casual methods.[9]

Spruance's partisans were likely to brand Halsey's command procedures as sloppy and reckless. Admirers of Halsey called Spruance's style overcautious and inflexible.[10]

Mick Carney, Halsey's chief of staff, disagreed with those who branded Halsey careless and sloppy. While Halsey gave the appearance of quick decisions, his constant aim was to keep the enemy in the dark by avoiding fixed patterns of objectives and tactics. Such methods resulted in tactical surprise. Carney, who saw the man from as close as anybody, noted, "Halsey gave the appearance of precipitous action, but he had a strange intuition. I've had instances in which I have prepared a proposal for him and that I had worked out with the appropriate people there on the staff. . . . I'd take it up and submit it to him. Well, we'd argue about it and he would say . . . this didn't quite ring a bell. . . . On two or three occasions he said to me, 'I cannot fault your reasoning on this business . . . it's convincing, but I just have the feeling it's not right. We'll do it my way.' In each of these instances, his intuition was correct."[11]

Jimmy Thach agreed with Carney: "Halsey was wonderful as a fleet commander—the best, as far as I'm concerned—I experienced it under both Spruance and Halsey. . . . The business about having to turn on the lights during the battle of the Philippine Sea would never have happened if Halsey had been there, because Halsey had a better appreciation of the fact that you should run toward the enemy when you're going to have to run into the wind away from him the next day . . ."[12]

Halsey, the aggressive aviator, undoubtedly took tactical command of the fast carrier task force more than non-aviator Spruance ever considered doing. He had tactical command at Leyte Gulf on his run north to seek the enemy carriers. Mitscher was little more than a passenger in his own task force. Halsey stated, "[I] would have been a fifth wheel if I exercised no control or command over elements of my fleet. I always did this, and in doing it never felt I was bypassing any junior echelon in the command. . . . I always felt free to assume tactical command, if I thought the conditions warranted it."[13]

It was this very aggressiveness that gave Halsey the ability to recharge the spirit and morale of fighting men. He did this in the South Pacific, turning a downtrodden, dispirited force into a cheering bunch of eager kids.[14] He probably did much of the same for the fast carrier forces.

Regarding Halsey and Spruance, it seems to be often overlooked that they were close friends despite their sharply contrasting personalities. They and their families had been friends since destroyer days in 1920. Further, they greatly respected one another. After all, Halsey picked Spruance as his successor when he was forced by health to withdraw from his command just before the battle of Midway. Halsey noted, "Admiral Raymond Spruance has consistently displayed outstanding ability combined with excellent judgment and quiet courage."[15]

Spruance admired Halsey's leadership and fighting spirit. He wrote to his wife, "Bill Halsey is a grand man to be with. He is a splendid seaman and will smack them hard every time he gets a chance."[16]

John McCain

John McCain, as ordained by the chain of command, usually walked in Bill Halsey's shadow. Halsey set the course and McCain, following his plans, gave the orders. Often the criticisms directed at Halsey spilled over onto McCain. For example, Gerry Bogan, who ran Task Group 38.2 under both Mitscher and McCain, commented unflatteringly: "Pete Mitscher, in my opinion, was a consummate master of naval air power, and, when he ran Task Force 58 or 38, it was a professional outfit, doing a professional job, in a professional way. When

McCain ran it, it was a goddamn circus. He'd come up with one crazy idea after another. One night we changed the bomb load on the planes three times for morning strikes."[17]

Thach gave an entirely different perspective on what was happening, indicating that the "circus" might well have been the results of Halsey's orders, not McCain's:

Also, there were things that came from Halsey that you would prefer that he'd done it a little differently. If they were serious enough, McCain wrote out a long message describing why, and often Halsey would change once he understood what was on our minds. . . . Sometimes Halsey would want to change the target . . . maybe the night before we had planned to send 1,000 airplanes in, and if you change a significant number of airplanes from one target to another, it affects everything else. You might uncover a field that you were going to cover.

Admiral McCain and I went over one time to Admiral Halsey's flagship to describe what had been happening, that if he wanted to re-designate the priority of targets, please do it early, don't wait until the last few hours because the pilots have to start getting briefed about where they're going in the morning, and if he changes it at midnight this just causes one heck of a problem. We went over to explain that to him. He understood and told his staff, "Now, look, we'll do no more of this last minute changing. We can handle a late change, for example, if there's something like the sudden appearance of a threat. Of course, we're flexible; but just because some intelligence tells you that there may be a better target than one of the many that you're hitting, don't do a change too late because it hurts the pilots. They have to stay up longer and get up sooner and so on." So he didn't do it anymore. We had disagreements with him; this was one of them, but he changed.[18]

Commander Noel Gayler was an operations officer on McCain's staff, one of the experienced fighter pilots so important to forming Task Force 38's tactics. Gayler observed that McCain was a man of distinct courage, not only in battle but in standing up to Halsey when it was necessary. On one occasion McCain and several staff members, including Gayler, visited Halsey to suggest that the heavily armored and armed battleships should be placed in the formation so that the kamikazes would encounter the battleship first rather than the outlying thin-skinned destroyers, which were being hit hard. Halsey did not agree, and the discussion moved right along into an argument. Halsey won, but not for the lack of McCain's trying.

Thach continued in his oral history, "[McCain was] far easier than Mitscher to work with. He often said, 'I like to talk to the people who are actually doing it. For instance, if I want to learn how to tie a bowline on a bight, I'll go to the bos'n's mate, not my chief of staff.' He liked to talk to the pilots who returned from strikes. I was delighted with this because I would pick the ones that had the most significant experiences and bring them up in droves to the flag bridge and go into the admiral's cabin. He'd sit around and give them a cup of coffee and listen to them say what they saw and what they did. Then he always said, 'Do you think we're doing the right thing?'. . . they loved it, terrific. Something new to them, and this was good. He was a very human individual, very modest and thinking of his own experience and knowledge. He never quit learning."[19]

It has been stated that McCain never held tactical command of the task force in any crucial situation.[20] Thach disagreed: "This is not at all true . . . McCain had tactical command *all* the time. The fleet commander had overall command, but we gave the tactical orders to the task force. There was no better commander that I have ever known than John Sidney McCain"[21]

Marc Mitscher

Pete Mitscher was identified as a "superb practitioner" of carrier warfare and the leader of carrier aviation. He commanded the fast carrier task force for fourteen months as contrasted to John McCain's six months. His leadership inspired devotion and personal loyalty. Nimitz called him most experienced and most able.

But even Mitscher had his share of problems. As the Midway battle unfolded, when Mitscher commanded *Hornet,* Spruance's opinion of Mitscher deteriorated. Spruance was disturbed by Mitscher's disobedience of his orders about bomb loads, that bombers from *Hornet* completely missed the enemy on one day, and by Mitscher's inaccurate reporting. Nevertheless by February 1944, when Mitscher had returned to the Pacific to command the carriers under Spruance in the raid on Truk, he favorably impressed Spruance. By mid-year Spruance completely trusted him.[22] He left the tactical operations of the carriers to his technical expert, Mitscher.[23]

Both Spruance and Mitscher were aloof by nature. Early on they clashed sharply about how best to use the fast carriers, but no bitterness lingered between them.[24]

It might be concluded that Mitscher's reluctance to step into the tactical situation was not much help to Halsey during the Battle of Leyte Gulf. ("If he wants my advice, he'll ask for it.")[25] But Halsey's style did not encourage unsolicited input. Furthermore, Mitscher may have suffered a heart attack about this time and thus was not performing up to his usual level.[26]

Jimmy Thach and Jimmy Flatley were the operations officers for, respectively, McCain and Mitscher. These two had been very close throughout their Navy lives and worked well together. So when one discovered something new he immediately passed it on to the other. When McCain relieved Mitscher, Thach carefully studied all of Mitscher's reports and incorporated any changes in his own task force instructions. Differences between the two were small, although Mitscher wasn't very quick to pick up on new and untried ideas. Thach thought Mitscher didn't adopt anti-kamikaze tactics like the "Moose Trap" exercises. Mitscher's ships, tied to a limited operating area around the Okinawa beachhead, may have suffered for that.[27]

But it's easy to see why Mitscher was called the "pilot's admiral." He had long aviation experience. He understood the pilots' minds and needs.[28] John McCain paid Marc Mitscher the highest compliment when, after his orientation period as a task group commander, McCain described Mitscher as "The best skipper I ever had!"[30]

John Towers

Military leaders always seem to be targets for criticism and McCain got his share. But one aspect of criticism that seems particularly puzzling is the animosity against John McCain on the part of classmate John Towers. Jack Towers was Naval Aviator number 3. His concepts

for the application of naval aviation in the Pacific—moving aviators
into command positions and operating the carrier task force as the
prime weapon against Japan—were right on the money, even though
his perspective may have been too narrow for Nimitz or Spruance.[30]
Towers was a gifted administrator and a logistics specialist.

McCain relieved Towers as chief of the Bureau of Aeronautics and
Towers relieved McCain as Commander of Task Force 38. In between,
Towers was commander of aircraft in the Pacific (ComAirPac) and
then deputy commander of the Pacific Fleet.

Towers' biography is littered with negative comments about John
McCain. Towers was unhappy that McCain was to become chief of
the Bureau of Aeronautics in 1942. He felt that McCain lacked experience in the procurement process.[31] But Towers was wrong. In 1944,
when McCain was heading back to the Pacific, his loss in Washington
was lamented by Artemus Gates (assistant secretary of the Navy for
air) because McCain "had learned his way around and was effective
before Congress."[32]

But beyond his concerns about how McCain would perform in
Washington, Towers was reported to have considered Slew a schemer
who wrangled his way back into the war—not that Towers wasn't a
pretty good schemer himself.

There could be many reasons for Towers' opinions. Slew McCain
was a very likable and popular person, where Towers was shy and
could be stiff. In his zeal to promote naval aviation, Towers alienated
King, Nimitz, Spruance, and probably others. As a strident advocate
for naval aviation, Towers became notorious for his feuds with senior
surface officers.[33] Spruance came to loathe him.[34] After the Battle of
the Philippine Sea, where the Japanese carriers escaped, Towers
pressed Nimitz to fire Spruance.

Towers felt strongly that "early-bird" aviators should have priority in getting carrier commands. McCain, of course, joined the fraternity late in his career and still landed the plum command. The term
"JCL"—"Johnny Come Lately"—appears frequently in Towers' biography, and was used to describe John McCain.[35] Towers felt that being
"air-minded" was no substitute for long-term experience in naval aviation. Even though McCain shared Towers' opinions about how naval
air power should be used, Towers undoubtedly saw McCain as a car-

petbagger who came to the prize Pacific air command after Towers had spent years slogging away at solving administrative and logistics problems.[36]

This conflict between surface and aviation—between battleship admirals and aviation admirals—sometimes seemed to be as intense as the war against the enemy. It just kept popping up, and maybe rightly so. The Navy was undergoing a momentous change as carriers became the principal offensive weapon of the Pacific War. McCain seemed to have been caught right in the middle. He was a flyer, but a recent one. He wore the wings but also had solid experience in ships. Actually, he was just what was needed at the time, a surface-experienced commander who was a naval aviator with a deep understanding of carrier warfare. King knew that, so maybe that's one reason McCain shared the best job in naval aviation.

But perhaps the root source of Towers' negativity was that McCain was a "King man" and had obtained the task force command with King's backing. Towers and King were at odds, to put it mildly. Further, Thomas Buell (King's biographer) suggests that Nimitz came to despise Towers, and it was Nimitz, not King, who kept Towers from a combat command.[37]

Ernest King

Inasmuch as John McCain was a "King man," Fleet Admiral Ernest J. King cannot be overlooked when trying to appreciate McCain.

First of all, King was categorized as brilliant, caustic, arrogant, and tactless. He was described as imperious and supremely confident in his own abilities. Also it was said he drank too much (although he abstained during the war, showing his will power and control), and that he chased skirts.[38]

But he truly was the "Master of Sea Power." It was largely through his tenacity when dealing with national and international leaders that sufficient attention and resources were allocated to the Pacific Theater. He made it all happen there against the Japanese.

So how did McCain become a "King man?" King was up the chain of command when Slew was at Coco Solo and when he commanded the *Ranger*. King loved fleet exercises and evidently McCain did very well in those training operations.

An interesting perspective on the relationship between King and McCain is the large amount of correspondence between McCain and Frog Low, who served under King in several posts. Most notably, Low was chief of staff to King in King's role as commander of the Tenth Fleet. In effect, Low directed the Battle of the Atlantic. Thomas Buell characterized his role as "A nautical chess game between [German submarine admiral] Doenitz and Low."[39] The idea for launching Army bombers from an aircraft carrier, thus enabling the Doolittle Tokyo raid, has been attributed to Low.

The salutations in the Low/McCain correspondence were "Dear Skipper" from Low to McCain and "Dear Frog" from McCain to Low. Their close friendship began when Low served under McCain in the Bureau of Navigation in 1935. McCain appears to have sometimes worked through Low when dealing with the forbidding King. For example, McCain asked Frog to convey a thought to Admiral King but warned, "Lay off if he is crabby."

The biography *Fleet Admiral King* mentions Slew in only three places. Buell covers much more in *Master of Sea Power*. Does this mean they were not very close? Roberta McCain, the admiral's daughter-in-law, feels that King personally liked McCain very much.

King appreciated a fighting spirit, and Slew McCain had plenty of that. King appreciated competence and loyalty, and McCain obliged. King may not have appreciated McCain's intelligence (Slew could hide that under a "country boy" attitude), but loyalty was a King demand and a McCain family tenet.

King considered many factors in selecting and promoting leaders. These included seniority, qualifications, experience, reputation, age, and availability. So it is not too difficult to understand why he selected and promoted McCain. McCain was senior, had demonstrated his competence many times, and he was a fighter!

Chester Nimitz

Nimitz also cannot be overlooked as an influence on McCain's career. Although King had the ruling hand, Nimitz and King conferred regularly about flag officer assignments. The two of them gave the orders that sent McCain to the South Pacific, back to Washington, to the fast carrier task force, and, in the end, heading back to Washington again.

Looking back, it is hard to imagine anyone else commanding the Pacific Fleet and the Pacific Ocean Areas. The image of Nimitz is deeply ingrained in our minds. He eased into control after Pearl Harbor, ordered the early carrier strikes, and implemented the South Pacific strategy. He grasped the overall picture of the Pacific war, built up the fleet, and started them on the path through the Central Pacific to the coasts of Japan.

It is said that Ernie King felt that Nimitz was too willing to compromise and that he took bad advice, but King never remotely considered replacing Nimitz and, in the end, recommended him for his relief as Chief of Naval Operations.[40] Spruance observed about Nimitz, "His personality, character, and ability are those that any young man could emulate and make no mistake."[41]

Ted Sherman

Frederick C. "Ted" Sherman also can't be left out of the equation. From late 1942 onward, he led fast carrier forces. Like McCain, Sherman was a "latecomer" to aviation. He was a loyal follower and friend of Halsey, which put him in the same camp as McCain. Sherman always felt that he deserved McCain's job running the fast carrier task force and felt that he "came within an ace of relieving him [Mitscher] instead of McCain."[42]

Sherman was a superb tactician and loved a good fight. In 1943 Sherman and his staff devised the techniques for handling a multi-carrier task group. These tactics were then battle-tested and adopted.[43] Sherman continued to advocate five- and six-carrier formations throughout the war.[44]

But Sherman also had an explosive personality and was very independent-minded. He could create consternation by maneuvering his task group without regard to task force orders and without signals to others. Also, he could be outspoken and obnoxious. Towers evidently did not like Sherman's bombastic personality[45] Further, Sherman admitted that he chose carriers because they were the fast track to promotion. He did not claim any special commitment to naval aviation, an attitude that clearly did not endear him to Towers.[46]

Both Sherman and Towers came to the command of fast carrier task forces at the same time, after hostilities had ceased.

Seniority and Merit

Two attributes—seniority and merit—drove the system of promotion and duty assignment. Seniority was set right off the bat. When a midshipman left the Naval Academy, his class standing established his starting seniority.

Officers standing higher in their class might reach the zone for promotion a year or two earlier than their lower standing classmates. For example Fletcher and Towers, from the upper half of the class of 1906, achieved flag rank in 1939. Fitch and McCain from the lower half had to wait until 1940 and 1941, respectively.

Here's the way McCain's world stacked up (key fellow officers are shown on boldface):

Admiral	Class	Standing	Flag Rank	Winged
Top Command				
King	1901	4/167	1933	1927
Nimitz	1905	7/114	1938	Non-aviator
Fleet Command				
Halsey	1904	43/62	1938	1935
Spruance	1907	25/209	1939	Non-aviator
Task Force Command				
Noyes	1906	15/116	1939	1937
Fletcher	1906	26/116	1939	Non-aviator
Towers	1906	31/116	1939	1913
Fitch	1906	110/116	1940	1929
McCain	1906	80/116	1941	1936
Sherman	1910	24/131	1942	1936
Pownall	1910	81/131	1942	1927
Mitscher	1910	108/131	1942	1916
Murray	1911	147/193	1942	1915
Montgomery	1912	29/156	1942	1922
Ramsey	1912	125/156	1942	1917
Radford	1916	59/117	1943	1920

Merit came into the system through the fitness report, where the commanding officer rated a junior officer on his performance annually or at a change of duty. Seniority determined *when* an officer was considered for promotion (by a closed selection board), but merit determined *if* an officer would be promoted. McCain's travails in attaining flag rank illustrate the situation. At a point about mid-career, an officer either had to be promoted on merit or leave. The fittest survived.

The effect of seniority is clear. Seniority started with class standing, but class standing was not a particularly good predictor of ultimate performance. Seniority counted heavily after officers "made their number" in flag rank.

The effect of merit is also clear. Merit made flag rank possible in the first place. Nimitz's potential as a theater commander pushed him ahead of Halsey, whose talents were better suited for jobs at the battle front. The brilliant performance of Spruance pushed him to the top over more senior admirals. Merit clearly worked for Mitscher too.

Noyes and Fletcher had carrier commands in the cautious early days of the war and were moved on to other assignments. Fitch left the carriers in 1942 to command in the South Pacific, and then he moved on to Washington. Murray spent much of the war running the aviation training program, and as ComAirPac.

When it came to selecting task force commanders, King made the assignments. He wanted offensive-minded, combat-experienced officers.[47] Pownall was battle-tested in 1943, then kicked upstairs as ComAirPac. By 1944 there were only three flag aviators King and Nimitz trusted to handle large carrier task forces at sea. These were Halsey, Mitscher, and McCain. There were other senior air admirals out there, but Towers was not high in King's esteem, and Sherman probably was too outspoken. But both made it at the end.

The rest were basically too young. They hadn't paid their dues yet, although they had fine careers.

Summing Up

So all of them, including even the bosses, Nimitz and King, had their good times and their bad times. They all made mistakes, but all achieved victories. They were criticized and they were praised.

They all had their roles. Spruance was the strategist. He was in charge of detailed planning when a conservative approach to operations was needed. Halsey and McCain were the cavalry, dashing and hitting hard when a hard hit was needed. Thus Spruance and Mitscher commanded during the invasion of Okinawa. Halsey and McCain came in to smash the airfields that were spawning the kamikazes.

So maybe a lot of the bickering, nitpicking, backbiting, and jealousy about command styles (including McCain's) were just that; bickering, nitpicking, backbiting, and jealousy. After all, if the fighting admirals weren't an assertive and outspoken bunch, they wouldn't have been on the front line of the war.

King and Nimitz, Spruance and Halsey, Mitscher and McCain, and Towers and Sherman were solid commanders and genuine American heroes. They were all at the top of the heap, and not by accident.

And, as Jocko Clark commented, "After all we did win the war."[48]

17

FINALE

McCain didn't particularly want to stay around for the formal surrender ceremony. He was sore about losing his command. It's easy to imagine that he just wanted to just pick up and get out of there, back to Kate and whatever was to come next. McCain had sent a message to Admiral Mick Carney, Halsey's chief of staff, saying he would like to see Carney on board the *Shangri-La*. Once aboard the carrier, Carney found McCain sick in his bunk. McCain said: "I've had it. I fought all the way from the South Pacific up to here. It's all over now, and I want to go home." Carney told him that was a very good reason he *should* stay and witness the surrender. McCain replied, "I don't give a damn about seeing the surrender, I want to get the hell out of here."[1]

When Carney conveyed McCain's request to Halsey, he replied, "Of course I'm not going to let him go home. The old SOB is entitled to witness the surrender, and that's what he's going to do. He was commanding this task force when the war ended, and I'm making sure that history gets it straight. I'll tell you what I'll do: the minute the thing is over, I'll put him on a plane and start him home."[2]

McCain accepted this with good grace and gratitude. Then he scrawled a note to Kate:

All's well that ends well. Bill Halsey is, on his own, holding me in command until the surrender, now scheduled for Sept 2. This will occasion some grief in some quarters. "*Cheers.*"
Further he says will order me to attend on the *Missouri*

which I take very kindly. Jack will be present on a submarine tender so I may see him on that to-be-historic day. Not bad, not bad. "The first shall be last and the last shall be first."

Now plan to stop in San Diego one night, thence on to Washington to investigate. Will put in a strong bid for leave and we will discuss the situation.

No hurry about nothing whatever. Them days is gone. Take it easy.

The tone of his letters was pretty upbeat. He may have not felt physically well during this period, and he was unhappy about the job change. But in these notes he didn't sound downhearted about anything. Maybe he just didn't want Kate to worry.

Change of Command (III)

Inasmuch as the court of inquiry into June's Typhoon Viper recommended a change of assignment for McCain, it's convenient to link cause and effect. But a change had been in the wind for some time.

The plans for the next Halsey/McCain rotation (in May) were not in question in February, when McCain met with King in Washington. McCain's resumption of command occurred on schedule.

About this time, in the spring, John Towers was being considered for a super logistics billet and a promotion to four stars. Nimitz and King had spoken about several other possibilities for Towers, including relief of either Mitscher or McCain. The logistics job for Towers fell through, so during the first weeks of June, King and Nimitz tried several more combinations. They finally settled on Ted Sherman to relieve Mitscher and John Towers to relieve McCain. Nimitz told Towers of this on June 19 just as the Typhoon Viper court was winding up its work.[3] Although King and Nimitz knew about Viper and the court, there were lots of other factors being considered.

After a period of leave and work on building a staff, Towers journeyed to Guam on August 17, and on August 22 was transferred by high-line to *Shangri La*. After conferences with Halsey on the 23rd, Vice Admiral John H. Towers relieved Vice Admiral John Sidney McCain as Commander, Task Force 38, on September 1, 1945.[4]

It must have been a blow to McCain to have been made the sacrificial goat for the typhoon incident, if indeed that was the case. In any event, Halsey noted that the orders made Slew thoroughly sore.[5] But on the other hand, McCain was going out at the top; he had led the world's most powerful naval force at the war's end.

A few days earlier, on August 20, Sidney had written to Kate:

> There is a high justice over and above that of commanders in chief. Am so glad to be in at the finish, and am gratified at great numbers of congrats to that effect.
>
> Make no preparations to move. There may be something that does not meet the eye. When settled will get you to me as quick as may be.
>
> It now looks as tho I may follow closely on the heels of this letter.
>
> To h_ with war and work. Want to sleep half a year.

So, something may have been afoot about McCain's future that has not been recorded. Maybe some alternative to the job at the Veterans' Administration had surfaced. Maybe McCain was considering retirement. He only had a few years left before he would be due to hang up his wings and stars. We can only speculate.

Actually, the Veteran's Administration job would have been a soft landing for a tired warrior. McCain's extensive experience with personnel administration might have served both himself and the country well. Further, with the Navy shrinking after the war, top command opportunities were to shrink too. Marc Mitscher got well-deserved posts. He was commander of the Atlantic Fleet when he died in 1947. John Towers moved up to command the Pacific Fleet. All of the top commanders but Spruance (who got his wish to be president of the Naval War College), were retired by the end of 1947.

Formal Surrender

After McCain had been relieved by Towers on September 1, both admirals and their key staff transferred to a destroyer for overnight passage to Tokyo Bay. Halsey requested that McCain bring Jimmy Thach along.[6] At 6:45 a.m. on September 2, 1945, they received honors and boarded *Missouri* for the surrender ceremony.

McCain's staff presented him with a marvelous remembrance as he left his command. Every morning during the campaigns, the previous night's messages (at least the routine messages that did not require awakening the admiral) were handed to McCain to read. They were bound in a hinged metal dispatch board with three stars and "Admiral" engraved on the cover. The staff converted this binder into a photo album with a signed picture of every officer. Added to the inside of the cover was the inscription "To The Boss of the Fast Carrier Task Force From 'Them Eggs'."

The salutations were stirring: "To the man who licked Japan; Against all enemies whomsoever—I recommend 'Dr. McCain' with his fast carrier treatment; The best damn boss I've ever had; It was never duty—always a special privilege; We knew years ago you would take us to Tokyo!"

Admiral John Sidney McCain stood in the front rank of admirals and generals to witness the signing of the surrender documents. His head is bowed in one of the most famous photos of the surrender signing, that of Nimitz signing for the United States. His posture suggests that he was tired, or maybe he was impatient to get moving, or maybe neither. But in other photos he is erect and smiling. Before and after the ceremony he was at ease, dashing about and greeting his friends, enjoying the moment."[7]

Thach related to the press that after the surrender documents had been signed, Halsey walked over to Slew, placed an arm around his shoulder and told McCain, "Thank God you were in this fight with me!" McCain had a compliment for Halsey too; "Thank God you made me stay, Bill. You had better sense than I did."[8]

When John McCain left his command on September 1, he sent the following message to all hands:

I am glad and proud to have fought through my last year of active service with the renowned fast carriers. War and victory have forged a lasting bond among us. If you are to be as fortunate in peace as you have been victorious in war, I am now talking to one hundred and ten thousand prospective millionaires.

Goodbye, good luck, and may God be with you.

This caught one of McCain's commanders by surprise. Radford replied, "Thought you were returning tomorrow. If not, goodbye and good luck to you."

Bill Halsey bid farewell to John McCain with this message:

I have given you "well done" so many times for individual achievements that this fine traditional Navy expression of approval is inadequate to express my feelings for the sum total of your contribution to victory.

Your resourcefulness, ingenuity, stamina, and fighting spirit have been superb. Inadequate though it may be I give you one more rousing farewell "well done."

Following the surrender ceremony aboard *Missouri*, McCain went aboard *Proteus,* a submarine tender anchored in Tokyo Bay. There he had lunch with his son Jack, who had just brought in a surrendered Japanese submarine. They had a private meeting in one of the state-rooms, and then they parted.[9]

In a letter dated September 2, Kate wrote to their son Gordon: "Just had a message from Captain Crommelin that your Dad has left Tokyo Bay for Pearl Harbor. They stop briefly here then to Washington. They are the first from surrender scene."

The Warrior Comes Home

Bill Halsey kept his word. John McCain left Tokyo Bay in the company of Jimmy Thach, Lieutenant Commander Don Thornburn (his public information officer), Lieutenant Commander A. M. Grafmueller (his logistics officer), and his flag secretary, the affable and well-liked Lieutenant Charles A. Sisson (a fellow Mississippian). The trip via Iwo Jima, Guam, and Johnston Island put them in Pearl Harbor on Tuesday, September 4. There McCain discussed the surrender at a press conference. Reporters remarked about the lines of strain and fatigue that marked McCain's face.

After a strenuous 6,000-mile, 45-hour trip, John Sidney arrived in Coronado on Wednesday, September 5.

The next afternoon, September 6, Kate and Sidney invited neighbors and Navy friends to a homecoming party at their Coronado home. Sidney was the first to return from Japan and his guests wanted to know all about the surrender ceremony and when others, particularly the prisoners of war, might be returning. As expected of John Sidney, he enjoyed the party and being the center of attention. But some noticed that he looked tired and was perhaps a little quieter that usual.[10]

About 4:00 p.m., as Slew chatted with Kate and Charlie Sisson, he remarked that he did not feel well and thought he would go upstairs to rest. Kate was worried about Sidney's health; she summoned Captain John Vann of the Navy Medical Corps, a friend and neighbor. He examined Sidney and reported that he was "worn out" and had a slight cold. McCain's pulse and heart appeared to be normal.

Then, without warning or pain, John Sidney McCain died at 5:10 p.m. At his side were Kate, Captain Vann, and Lieutenant Commander Thornburn. Captain Vann said, "His heart just stopped. He was thoroughly fatigued."

At some point along the way that afternoon, in those last minutes, Sidney was able to take a 3"x 5" card in hand and write, "No last words—I know you are close to me."

Senator John S. McCain III wrote of his grandfather: "He was sixty-one years old. He had fought his war and died. His Navy physician attributed his fatal heart attack to 'complete fatigue resulting from the strain of the last months of combat.' Halsey's chief of staff, Admiral Robert Carney, believed McCain had suffered an earlier heart attack at sea and had managed to keep it hidden. According to Carney, the admiral 'knew his number was up, but he wouldn't lie down and die until he got home.'"[11]

Thach described the day: "We landed back here in North Island after stopping at Pearl Harbor for about a day . . . Admiral McCain didn't act too well then, either. In fact, he looked worse, but he invited me and my wife to come by his house for a little while that afternoon, which we did. While we were there, he said, 'I think I'll go in and get some rest.' We weren't there very long . . . and went over to San Diego. I got over there to my father-in-law's house, and got a telephone call that said that he [McCain] had died of a heart attack. I felt like I'd lost my father for the second time."[12]

In an interview given thirty years later for the Naval Institute's

Oral History Project, Admiral Jack McCain briefly described the last time together with his father on USS *Proteus* in Tokyo Bay. Nothing in Slew's manner gave Jack reason to worry about his father's health. "I knew him as well as anybody in the world, with the possible exception of my mother. He looked in fine health to me, and God knows his conversation was anything but indicative of a man who was sick. And two days later he died of a heart attack."[13]

18

RESPECT AND AFFECTION

John Sidney McCain's death was covered in the press from San Diego to New York City. Messages of respect, affection, and condolence flowed in. President Truman's telegram read, "My Dear Mrs. McCain: I wish to send you the sympathy of the nation and my personal condolences on the death of your husband, Vice Admiral John McCain, USN, a fighting admiral. He must be considered a front line casualty, for although his original orders would have returned him from the Pacific sooner, his devotion to duty caused him to remain in action until the triumphant end. The country knew him as a brilliant daring tactician in naval aviation: his associates knew him as an officer capable of ardent and intense attention to the task at hand. His death deprives the country of his future services, for his ability and devotion would have been utilized to serve the nation in peace as well as in war."

James Forrestal, Secretary of the Navy, sent this message: "Please accept my deepest sympathy on the death of your husband. He was deep in the affections of all who knew him in the Navy, both civilian and professional people. His conduct in war was an inspiration and example to all Americans."

Forrestal later wrote to Kate: "John Sidney was a fighting man to the core of his being—and you know better than I the deep affection in which he was held by his Navy friends."

Ernest King expressed his feelings: "I do not quite know how to tell you how shocked and grieved we all are at the sad news which reached us last night. I know that 'all hands' of the Navy join with me in this expression of deepest sympathy and sincerest condolences. Mrs. King and the rest of my family join with me in this expression. He fought the good fight. The Navy will never be quite the same without him."

Other messages of condolence came from the Royal Navy, British Pacific Fleet, French Naval Mission, and Royal New Zealand Air Force. Assistant Secretary of the Navy John Sullivan told Kate: "I don't know how to express to you my grief on hearing the sad news of the admiral's death. . . . One of the most pleasant memories of my life is the eleven days I spent with him on the *Shangri La*. . . . The Navy lost one of its ablest leaders and I have lost a friend with whom I had hoped to spend many a happy hour in the years to come."

Towers, now commanding Task Force 38, sent condolences from McCain's old command: "We of Task Force 38 who were privileged to serve under Admiral McCain's command know how great a loss the Navy and our country have suffered. The spirit of loyalty and affection created by his deep personal interest in each of us will always remain a proud memory. It is from the bottom of our hearts that we send our sympathy in this hour of sorrow."

Carl Vinson expressed his personal grief: "I have lost an intimate friend and a most valued advisor. The Navy has lost one of its outstanding leaders who had that rare combination of fighting ability and human compassion. I hope that you will find some comfort in this tragic hour in the fact that your grief is shared by so many and in the pride we all have of Johnny."

Matt Gardner, McCain's former chief of staff and a task group commander, telegraphed, "Need not and indeed can not tell the tremendous loss not only to me but to all those who have worked for him which the passing of John Sidney brings us. Thus we share it with you even though your burden is not lightened thereby."

The lead story in the September 17, 1945, issue of *Life* magazine was the surrender ceremony on the *Missouri*. The photo coverage was detailed. Slew was memorialized in one of the captions: "The U.S. signs, Admiral Nimitz officiating. Among the naval officers present was Vice Admiral John McCain, Task Force 38 commander. He died of heart attack four days later in San Diego."[1]

A few days later, on September 18, Admiral Halsey sent a captured Japanese naval officer's sword to Kate:

Dear Katie,
I am sending you a captured Japanese Naval Officer's sword which I would like to have been able to present to my good friend John Sidney. I know you will accept this sword as representing a small but significant tribute in recognition of your husband's superb leadership of our carriers in pressing relentlessly the war against Japan.

His loss is a great personal shock to me and the news of it came at a time when it seemed all the more poignant to me. I am so glad that, having completed his fight and seen it brought so successfully to a finish, he was able to be with you at the end.

In his autobiography Halsey wrote, "It grieves me bitterly to realize that this great friend and fighting man is gone. I will never forget anything about him—his curses, his jumping-jack behavior, the leaky cigarettes he rolled . . ."[2]

Halsey was also quoted, "With the death of John Sidney McCain America has lost a great man—one with the heart of a lion—whose courage and ability stood us in good stead when we needed it most. As a magnificent naval leader, he contributed beyond any measuring to the victory we enjoy today. For myself, I can only say I have lost a good friend."[3]

General MacArthur observed "He was one of our Navy's finest sailors and we will not soon forget his brilliant service in the Pacific."

Marc Mitscher spoke about his colleague, "Naval aviation has lost an outstanding leader. As Commander Fast Carrier Task Force 38, he carried the war to the heart of the enemy's homeland."

Burial

Accompanied by a guard of honor, Vice Admiral John McCain's body was flown to Washington on the evening of September 8, 1945. On Monday afternoon, September 10, funeral services were held at the

Fort Meyer chapel with Rear Admiral William Thomas, chief of chaplains, officiating. Gordon and Catherine were able to be there. Also attending were Secretary of the Navy Forrestal, Admiral King, Admiral Leahy, and General Vandegrift. Then, to the cadence of muffled drums, John McCain was borne by a caisson and six white horses to Arlington National Cemetery. The procession was headed by the Navy Band, two platoons of sailors, two platoons of Marines, and an honor guard bearing his admiral's flag draped in black crepe. Honorary pall bearers were General Vandegrift; Vice Admirals Russell Willson, Leigh Noyes, and Ferdinand Reichmuth; and Rear Admirals George Bryan and Matthias Gardner. McCain lies there today with family members, including his wife Kate, son Jack, and brother, Brigadier General William Alexander McCain.

Sadly, Jack was not able to return from the Pacific in time for the services. But he admitted that it was probably for the best. He was strongly attached to his father and felt that attending the funeral "would have killed me."[4]

Honors

President Harry Truman signed and presented Kate with a formal citation in grateful memory of John McCain's service to his country. On September 10, 1945, John Sidney McCain was honored by speeches from the floor of the House of Representatives.

In December 1945, King George VI appointed McCain an Honorary Knight Commander in the Military Division of the Most Excellent Order of the British Empire. The investiture occurred aboard HMS *Sheffield* in Long Beach harbor in July 1948.

In January 1946 the Veterans of Foreign Wars established a post in Long Beach, California as the "Admiral John S. McCain Ship." Mrs. McCain and Gordon attended the christening ceremony.

In April 1946 McCain was posthumously presented a gold star in lieu of a third Distinguished Service Medal. The award was presented to Kate at the Eleventh Naval District headquarters in San Diego by Rear Admiral Jesse B. Oldendorf, commandant of the Naval District and hero of the Battle of Surigao Strait. The citation reads: "For exceptionally meritorious service to the Government of the United States in a duty of great responsibility as Commander of the Second

Carrier Task Force and Commander Task Force Thirty-eight from May 28 to September 1, 1945. . . . Combining brilliant offensive tactics with effective measures to counter the enemy's fanatic aerial onslaughts, he hurled the might of his aircraft against the remnants of the once-vaunted Japanese Navy to destroy or cripple every remaining major hostile ship by July 28. An inspiring and fearless leader, Vice Admiral McCain maintained a high standard of fighting efficiency in his gallant force while pressing home devastating attacks which shattered the enemy's last vital defensive hope and rendered him unable to protect his shipping even in waters off the mainland of Japan.

In October 7, 1947, the Observatory Building at the University of Mississippi was renamed McCain Hall. The offices and classrooms were used until 1989 by the Naval ROTC unit. Mrs. McCain made the dedication, and Fleet Admiral William F. Halsey made the principal address. He noted that "Just four days after the United States accepted the formal surrender of Japan, a man who had devoted his life's energies to the defense of his country lay down to rest, his mission completed. His reward was deeply satisfying—he had lived to see the offensives he planned so brilliantly and executed so skillfully pay off in final victory. His forces were among the vanguard of those which delivered the final crushing blows on the enemy's homeland, culminating months of grueling offensives on the long road to Tokyo."

The dedication ceremony was followed by a reception and a formal and colorful Navy ball.

By joint resolution of Congress, Vice Admiral John Sidney McCain was posthumously promoted to full admiral. The date of rank was set as September 6, 1945, the day he died. The presentation ceremony was held aboard the USS *Valley Forge* on September 10, 1949, while she was moored at North Island Naval Air Station. Kate McCain received the citation. Fleet Admiral Halsey, in civilian clothes, described his friend as "a very great man and a great sailor. . . . No man deserved more of his country than John Sidney McCain."

Today the main gate to the North Island base opens onto McCain Boulevard, termed the "Champ Elysees" of the Naval Air Station.

The frigate USS *John S. McCain* (DL-3) was launched in July 1952 at the Bath Iron Works in Maine, sponsored by Slew's daughter-in-law, Roberta. The *McCain* was commissioned in Boston in October 1953.

She was later reclassified as DDG-36, a guided missile destroyer, and finally decommissioned in 1978.

On July 14, 1961, the landing field at the Naval Air Station, Meridian, Mississippi, was named "McCain Field." A large plague was dedicated. Attending were Rear Admiral Jack McCain, Jack's wife Roberta, and Jack's son, Navy aviator Lieutenant John S. McCain III.

The second USS *John S. McCain* (DDG-56) was launched in September 1992, sponsored by Mrs. John Sidney McCain III, and commissioned in July 1994. She remains in active service today. This vessel is uniquely named for *both* Admirals John Sidney McCain.

Although the name "McCain Hall" was lost at Ole Miss when the building was refurbished and renamed Barnard Observatory, in April 2003 the ceremonial entrance to the Naval ROTC spaces, now in another building, was named "McCain Quarterdeck." The original 1947 dedication plaque has been mounted alongside a companion plaque celebrating the new honor.

Final Notes

John Sidney "Slew" McCain is often overlooked as one of the great leaders of World War II. Marc Mitscher, McCain's counterpart, spent more time in battle, was a pioneer in naval aviation, and received deserved attention. Bill Halsey, McCain's boss, was a giant figure in the Pacific war, a public favorite. The spotlight naturally fell on Halsey, not on John McCain. It might be concluded that Slew McCain tended to hide his light under the allegorical bushel. He was a show-man—witness the hat—but he was also modest. Further, he did not leave behind much in the way of papers and mementos.

What he did leave behind was a great sadness about his loss. Roberta McCain remembered that "He had the gift of joy in his voice. People always felt good around Sidney. There were no mean words from him."

His friends in the Navy were legion. He was larger than life to his shipmates. His laugh was described as something between a cackle and a giggle. It exploded often. His smile was beautiful.

Slew McCain had brains—but he may have hidden his intellect under his cigarette-smoking, hard-cussing Mississippi farm boy facade. He loved books. He wrote extensively. He thought deeply about today's tactics and tomorrow's strategy. He probably made mistakes that we don't know about, and he probably got too much blame for the mistakes laid on him by history.

He often seemed to be caught in the middle of things—between the aviators and the battleship admirals, between the fleet commander above and the task group commanders below, and between Halsey and the typhoons.

McCain was a bulldog himself. He wouldn't let go of an idea very easily, such as his proposals for small carriers, fast carrier mobility, moving aviators into command positions, and defeating Japan by wiping out its air power. But that tenacity, coupled with his social skills, must have made a dynamite combination in Washington, where he was particularly successful in dealing with Congress.

It must have hurt John McCain deeply to see the steady loss of his pilots and plane crews, both at Guadalcanal and from the fast carrier task force. His job was to send brave men into harm's way, while he could do nothing but sit and wait for their return. For a man who brought joy into life, seeing "his" men lose their lives must have been a great injury. It might have broken his health.

John Sidney "Slew" McCain was a great naval officer and a great American hero. He gave his life for his country.

Kate stayed on in Coronado. Through the years before and after Sidney's passing, she was active with the American Red Cross, Navy Relief, and the Daughters of the American Revolution.

Daughter-in-law Roberta describes Kate as a "Rock of Gibraltar." "You always knew where you stood with Kate. She let you know just how things were going to be, but she was always nice about it."

Kate McCain died on May 29, 1959. In her heritage was her recipe for McCain salad dressing. It is still a family favorite:

McCain Salad Dressing

Place 2 cups oil, 1 cup vinegar, 1 tablespoon salt, 1 tablespoon sugar, 1 teaspoon paprika, 2 teaspoons dry mustard, ? teaspoon pepper, and 1 teaspoon Worcestershire sauce in a jar and shake. Place in refrigerator and let it age . . . it gets better as it gets older.

Jack was the second McCain four-star admiral, one of only two father-son four-star combinations in U.S. naval history.[5] Jack served as Commander-in-Chief, Pacific Command, from 1968 to 1972. During that period his son, John Sidney McCain III, was a prisoner of war in North Vietnam. McCain III subsequently became a United States Senator from Arizona.

Slew's younger son, James Gordon McCain, became a distinguished attorney, specializing in water rights issues. He had a dominant hand in writing water rights legislation in California.

Daughter Catherine (whom McCain called "Bug") lived in her dad's home in Coronado until her death in 2000. During the war she served overseas with the Red Cross, and after the war she worked in Public Works at North Island, McCain's old command. She retained most or all of his personal effects and papers. In 1982 a portion of the papers were sent to the Hoover Institution at Stanford University.

The Hat

Admiral John Sidney McCain's famous combat slouch hat was donated to the San Diego Aerospace Museum where, sadly, it was destroyed in a fire that leveled the entire building in 1978. Although that icon was lost, the memory of this great wartime leader lives on with the USS *John S. McCain* on the high seas, and in the hearts of his family and shipmates.

ACKNOWLEDGMENTS

This book would not have been possible or even started without the encouragement and support of Margaret La Grange, John Sidney McCain's granddaughter. She made available his personal files and mementos, and she opened the door for the first contact with her cousin, Joseph P. McCain. Joe provided some wonderful anecdotes, and in turn paved the way for interviews with his mother, Roberta McCain (Mrs. John S. McCain, Jr.). Joe also set up visits with the admiral's nephew, William A. McCain in Greenwood, Mississippi.

Roberta McCain was an eyewitness to many events in the last ten years of McCain's life. Her memories of Sidney and his contemporaries are phenomenal. For his part, Bill McCain gave us a wonderful tour of Teoc, the McCain farm in Carroll County, Mississippi. Bill and his wife Edwina also hosted a fine party to meet the Teoc neighbors.

A most valuable personal contribution was made by Henry Fluck of Easton, Pennsylvania. Hank was a radioman on McCain's staff in 1944–45. His job was to man the TBS (Talk Between Ships voice radio) in the flag plot compartment where the admiral and his staff did their work. Hank sat behind his typewriter facing McCain from about twelve feet away. Hank (and other veterans of the USS *Shangri La*) provided vivid recollections about the admiral.

A number of other individuals told wonderful stories and rendered their personal opinions. These include Helen Sampson Blanchard (daughter of McCain's aide and pilot, William S. Sampson), Noel Gayler (from McCain's task force staff), Wilder Baker (son of McCain's chief of staff), and Bill Halsey III (Admiral Halsey's son).

Literary advice was provided by Steve Ewing (who chronicled O'Hare, Flatley, and Thach), and Craig Gill of the University Press of Mississippi. A number of friends made most valuable suggestions about the manuscript. My wife Kathrine, a dedicated quilter, set her hobby aside to edit and comment on the draft.

Top billing must also go to Eric Hammel, a very successful author and expert on the war in the Pacific. Eric believed in this project and was an absolute genius in reviewing and editing the story line.

The final editing was done by Steven Smith, the extremely capable senior editor at Casemate Publishers. His words of encouragement were beyond value and came at exactly the right time. He asked all the right questions about the manuscript and his advice was always right on the money.

Many thanks are also due to the Hoover Institution at Stanford University. The war diaries and action reports housed there provided the framework for the World War II chapters. Also thanks are due to the National Personnel Records Center in St. Louis, which provided some key dates from Admiral McCain's service record; the Naval Historical Center; and the library of the San Diego Aerospace Museum.

Finally, the facilities and collections of the military base libraries were invaluable, particularly the library at Marine Corps Air Station, Miramar, and the Emil Buehler Naval Aviation Library in Pensacola.

GLOSSARY

AA	Antiaircraft guns or gunfire
AE	Ammunition ship
AK	Cargo ship
AV	Seaplane tender
B-17	Boeing "Flying Fortress" heavy bomber
B-24	Consolidated "Liberator" heavy bomber
B-26	Martin "Marauder" medium bomber
BB	Battleship
Bogeys	Unidentified contacts, usually enemy planes
Bos'n	Boatswain, a petty officer in charge if the ship's hull and related equipment
BuAer	Bureau of Aeronautics
BuNav	Bureau of Navigation
Cactus	Code name for Guadalcanal
Capt	Captain
Cdr	Commander
CO	Commanding Officer
CominCh	Commander-in-Chief, U.S. Fleet
CinCPac	Commander-in-Chief, Pacific Fleet
Clipper	Boeing Model 314 4-engine flying boat
CNO	Chief of Naval Operations
ComAirPac	Commander, Air Force, Pacific Fleet
ComAirScoFor	Commander, Aircraft, Scouting Force, Pacific Fleet
ComAirSoPac	Commander, Aircraft, South Pacific
ComSoPac	Commander, South Pacific Area, and South Pacific

	Force
CTF	Commander, Task Force
CTG	Commander, Task Group
CV	Fleet aircraft carrier
CVE	Escort aircraft carrier (merchant hull)
CVL	Light aircraft carrier (cruiser hull)
DCNO(Air)	Deputy Chief of Naval Operations for Air
D-day	The date for an invasion
DDG	Guided missile destroyer
DL	Frigate
DSM	Distinguished Service Medal
F4F	Grumman "Wildcat" fighter
F4U	Vought "Corsair" fighter
F6F	Grumman "Hellcat" fighter
F7F	Grumman "Tigercat" fighter
FR-1	Ryan "Fireball" composite jet fighter
High-line	Method of transferring men and materials between ships at sea using heavy ropes and pulleys
Jacob's ladder	A temporary ladder hanging on the side of a ship
JCL	"Johnny-come-lately," referring to officers who became naval aviators late in their careers.
Lcdr	Lieutenant Commander
Lt	Lieutenant
Lt(jg)	Lieutenant (junior grade)
Marston mat	Perforated metal covering for dirt airfields
NASA	National Aeronautics and Space Administration
NAS	Naval Air Station
NC	NC-1, NC-3, and NC-4 flying boats that made the first flight across the Atlantic
OBE	Order of the British Empire
OPNAV	Office of the Chief of Naval Operations
Ordnanceman	Ammunition handler
OTC	Officer in Tactical Command
PatWing	Patrol Wing
P-38	Lockheed "Lightning" fighter
P-39	Bell "Airacobra" fighter
P-400	Export version of the P-39

PB2Y	Consolidated "Coronado" patrol bomber
PB4Y	Consolidated "Privateer" land-based heavy bomber
PBY	Consolidated "Catalina" patrol bomber
Plank-owner	Part of the original crew of a vessel
Pollywog	One who has not crossed the equator, subject of a ritual initiation
PT	Patrol torpedo boat
R4D	Douglas 2-engine DC-3 transport plane
RNZAF	Royal New Zealand Air Force
RDF	Radio direction finder device
RN	Royal Navy
ROTC	Reserve Officers Training Corps
SB2C	Curtis "Helldiver" mono-plane dive bomber
SBC	Curtis "Helldiver" bi-plane dive bomber
SBD	Douglas "Dauntless" dive bomber
Shellback	One who had crossed the equator, and usually the tormentor of pollywogs
Stearman	Navy biplane training plane
TAD	Temporary Additional Duty
TBS	Talk Between Ships
TF	Task Force
TG	Task Group
USNA	United States Naval Academy
U-156	German submarine
VA	Veteran's Administration
VF	Navy fighter squadron (or fighters)
VPB	Patrol bomber squadron
Zero	Japanese Mitsubishi fighter

NOTES

Introduction
[1] Reynolds, Clark G., *The Fast Carriers The Forging of an Air Navy*, New York: McGraw-Hill Book Company, 1968; Kemp, Paul, *A Pictorial History of the Sea War 1939-1945*, Annapolis MD: Naval Institute Press, 1995.
[2] Hoyt, Edwin P., *How They Won The War In The Pacific, Nimitz and His Admirals*, New York: Weybright and Talley, 1970.
[3] Potter, E. B., *Bull Halsey*, Annapolis MD: Naval Institute Press, 1985.
[4] Potter, E. B., *Bull Halsey*, Annapolis MD: Naval Institute Press, 1985.
[5] McCain, John with Mark Salter, *Faith of My Fathers*, New York: Random House, 1999.

Chapter 1
[1] Spencer, Elizabeth, *Landscapes of the Heart, A Memoir*, New York: Random House, 1998.
[2] Comment by Bill McCain, the current proprietor of Teoc.
[3] Letter written by Tillman Richard Foster in 1984.
[4] McCain, John with Mark Salter, *Faith of My Fathers*, New York: Random House, 1999.
[5] United States Naval Institute, *The Class of 1906 United States Naval Academy*, Annapolis MD: 1954; Sweetman, Jack, *The U. S. Naval Academy An Illustrated History*, Annapolis MD: Naval Institute Press, 1979 *and* 1995.
[6] Sweetman, Jack, *The U. S. Naval Academy An Illustrated History*, Annapolis MD: Naval Institute Press, 1979 *and* 1995.
[7] *Ibid.*
[8] United States Naval Institute, *The Class of 1906 United States Naval Academy*, Annapolis MD: 1954.
[9] Sweetman, Jack, *The U. S. Naval Academy An Illustrated History*,

Annapolis MD: Naval Institute Press, 1979 and 1995.
[10] McCain, John with Mark Salter, *Faith of My Fathers*, New York: Random House, 1999.
[11] Cressman, Robert J., *USS Ranger The Navy's First Flattop From Keel to Mast, 1934-46*, Annapolis MD: Naval Institute Press, 2003.
[12] United States Naval Institute, *The Class of 1906 United States Naval Academy*, Annapolis MD: 1954.
[13] Sweetman, Jack, *The U. S. Naval Academy An Illustrated History*, Annapolis MD: Naval Institute Press, 1979 and 1995.
[14] United States Naval Institute, *The Class of 1906 United States Naval Academy*, Annapolis MD: 1954.
[15] Hoyt, Edwin P., *The Lonely ships The Life and Death of the U.S. Asiatic Fleet*, New York: David McKay Company, 1976.
[16] Navy Department, Office of the Chief of Naval Operations, Naval History Division, *Dictionary of American Naval Fighting Ships*, Washington D. C.: U. S. Government Printing Office, 1963-1981.
[17] Reckner, James R., *Teddy Roosevelt's Great White Fleet*, Annapolis MD: Naval Institute Press, 1988.
[18] McCain, John with Mark Salter, *Faith of My Fathers*, New York: Random House, 1999.
[19] Navy Department, Office of the Chief of Naval Operations, Naval History Division, *Dictionary of American Naval Fighting Ships*, Washington D. C.: U. S. Government Printing Office, 1963-1981.

Chapter 2
[1] Navy Department, Office of the Chief of Naval Operations, Naval History Division, *Dictionary of American Naval Fighting Ships*, Washington D. C.: U. S. Government Printing Office, 1963-1981.
[2] *Ibid.*
[3] *Ibid.*

Chapter 3
[1] McCain, J. S., Commander, U. S. Navy, *A Personnel Survey*, Annapolis MD: U. S. Naval Institute *Proceedings*, January 1923.
[2] Wheeler, Gerald E., *Kinkaid of the Seventh Fleet*, Annapolis MD: Naval Institute Press, 1996.
[3] McCain, J. S., Commander, U. S. Navy, *The Staff Equalization Bill*, Annapolis MD: U. S. Naval Institute *Proceedings*, March 1924.
[4] McCain, J. S., Commander, U. S. Navy, *A Personnel Survey*, Annapolis MD: U. S. Naval Institute *Proceedings*, January 1923.
[5] McCain, J. S., Commander, U. S. Navy, *Service Since Graduation vs. Age*

In Grade Retirement, Annapolis MD: U. S. Naval Institute *Proceedings,* May 1925.

[6] Turnbull, Archibald D., Captain, USNR, and Clifford L. Lord, Lieutenant Commander, USNR, *History of United States Aviation,* New Haven CT: Yale University Press, 1949.

Chapter 4

[1] Navy Department, Office of the Chief of Naval Operations, Naval History Division, *Dictionary of American Naval Fighting Ships,* Washington D. C.: U. S. Government Printing Office, 1963-1981.

[2] *Ibid.*

[3] *Ibid.*

[4] Spencer, Elizabeth, *Landscapes of the Heart, A Memoir,* New York: Random House, 1998.

Chapter 5

[1] Porter, Thurston, "100 Aircraft Carriers Can Ruin Japan, Says Admiral McCain", *New York Sunday News,* April 22, 1943.

[2] Buell, Thomas B., *The Quiet Warrior A Biography of Admiral Raymond A. Spruance,* Boston MA: Little Brown & Co., 1974.

[3] Grady, Patricia, "Man of War John Sidney McCain".

[4] Wheeler, Keith, "'Foxy Grampa' Look Disguises Ability of Admiral McCain", *The Sunday Star,* January 14, 1945.

[5] Potter, E. B., *Bull Halsey,* Annapolis MD: Naval Institute Press, 1985.

[6] Taylor, Theodore, *The Magnificent Mitscher,* Annapolis MD: Naval Institute Press, 1991.

[7] McCain, John with Mark Salter, *Faith of My Fathers,* New York: Random House, 1999.

[8] Cressman, Robert J., *USS Ranger The Navy's First Flattop From Keel to Mast, 1934-46,* Annapolis MD: Naval Institute Press, 2003.

[9] Navy Department, Office of the Chief of Naval Operations, Naval History Division, *Dictionary of American Naval Fighting Ships,* Washington D. C.; U. S. Government Printing Office, 1963-1981; Belote, James H. & William M. Belote, *Titans of the Sea,* New York: Harper & Row, 1975; Humble, Richard, *United States Fleet Carriers of World War II 'In Action,'* Poole, Dorset: Blandford Press, 1984.

[10] Humble, Richard, *United States Fleet Carriers of World War II 'In Action,'* Poole, Dorset: Blandford Press, 1984.

[11] Cressman, Robert J., *USS Ranger The Navy's First Flattop From Keel to Mast, 1934-46,* Annapolis MD: Naval Institute Press, 2003.

[12] Reynolds, Clark G., *Admiral John H. Towers The Struggle for Naval Air*

Supremacy, Annapolis MD: Naval Institute Press, 1991.

[13] Cressman, Robert J., *USS Ranger The Navy's First Flattop From Keel to Mast, 1934-46,* Annapolis MD: Naval Institute Press, 2003.

[14] Cressman, Robert J., *USS Ranger The Navy's First Flattop From Keel to Mast, 1934-46,* Annapolis MD: Naval Institute Press, 2003; Department, Office of the Chief of Naval Operations, Naval History Division, *Dictionary of American Naval Fighting Ships,* Washington D. C.: U. S. Government Printing Office, 1963-1981.

[15] Turnbull, Archibald D., Captain, USNR, and Clifford L. Lord, Lieutenant Commander, USNR, *History of United States Aviation,* New Haven CT: Yale University Press, 1949.

[16] Cressman, Robert J., *USS Ranger The Navy's First Flattop From Keel to Mast, 1934-46,* Annapolis MD: Naval Institute Press, 2003.

[17] Wildenberg, Thomas, *All the Factors of Victory Admiral Joseph Mason Reeves and the Origins of Carrier Airpower,* Washington, DC: Brassey's, Inc., 2003.

[18] Turnbull, Archibald D., Captain, USNR, and Clifford L. Lord, Lieutenant Commander, USNR, *History of United States Aviation,* New Haven CT: Yale University Press, 1949.

[19] Sudsbury, Elizabeth, *Jack Rabbits to Jets The History of North Island, San Diego,* Neyenish Printers, 1967.

[20] Related by Mrs. James B. Stockdale.

[21] Forrestal, Vice Admiral E. P., USN (Retired), *Admiral Raymond A. Spruance, USN,* Washington D.C.: Department of the Navy, 1966.

Chapter 6

[1] Reynolds, Clark G., *The Fast Carriers The Forging of an Air Navy,* New York: McGraw-Hill Book Company, 1968.

[2] Prange, Gordon W., *At Dawn We Slept,* New York: Penguin Books, 1981.

[3] *Ibid.*

[4] Report from Commander Task Force NINE (Commander Patrol Wing TWO) to Commander-in-Chief, United States Pacific Fleet, dated 20 December 1941, on the subject "Operations on December 7, 1941."

[5] Miller, Commander Norman M., USN, *I Took The Sky Road,"* New York: Dodd, Mead & Company, 1945.

Chapter 7

[1] Buell, Thomas B., *Master of Sea Power A Biography of Fleet Admiral Ernest J. King,* Boston MA: Little, Brown & Co., 1980 and Annapolis MD: Naval Institute Press, 1995.

[2] Navy Department, Office of the Chief of Naval Operations, Naval

History Division, *Dictionary of American Naval Fighting Ships,* Washington D. C.: U. S. Government Printing Office, 1963-1981.

[3] Crichton, Kyle, "Navy Air Boss", *Colliers,* October 23, 1943.

[4] Griffith, Samuel B. II, *The Battle for Guadalcanal,* New York: J. B. Lippencott Co., 1963.

[5] Hoyt, Edwin P., *Guadalcanal,* New York: Stein and Day, 1982.

[6] Miller, John Jr., *United States Army in World War II The War in the Pacific Guadalcanal: The First Offensive,* Washington D. C.: Center of Military History, United States Army, 1949.

[7] Hammel, Eric, *Guadalcanal Starvation Island,* New York: Crown Publishers Inc., 1987; Miller, Thomas G. Jr., *The Cactus Air Force,* New York: New York: Harper & Row, 1969.

[8] Crichton, Kyle, "Navy Air Boss", *Colliers,* October 23, 1943.

[9] Dyer, Vice Admiral George Carroll, USN (Ret), *The Amphibians Came to Conquer The Story of Admiral Richard Kelly Turner,* Washington D. C.: Department of the Navy, 1972, and U. S. Marine Corps, 1991.

Chapter 8

[1] Hoyt, Edwin P., *How They Won The War in the Pacific Nimitz and His Admirals,* New York: Weybright and Talley, 1970.

[2] Crichton, Kyle, "Navy Air Boss", *Colliers,* October 23, 1943.

[3] Miller, John Jr., *United States Army in World War II The War in the Pacific Guadalcanal: The First Offensive,* Washington D. C.: Center of Military History, United States Army, 1949.

[4] Dyer, Vice Admiral George Carroll, USN (Ret), *The Amphibians Came to Conquer The Story of Admiral Richard Kelly Turner,* Washington D. C.: Department of the Navy, 1972, and U. S. Marine Corps, 1991.

[5] Miller, John Jr., *United States Army in World War II The War in the Pacific Guadalcanal: The First Offensive,* Washington D. C.: Center of Military History, United States Army, 1949.

[6] Lundstrom, John B., *The First Team and the Guadalcanal Campaign Naval Fighter Combat from August to November 1942,* Annapolis MD: Naval Institute Press, 1994.

[7] *Ibid.*

[8] *Ibid.*

[9] Miller, John Jr., *United States Army in World War II The War in the Pacific Guadalcanal: The First Offensive,* Washington D. C.: Center of Military History, United States Army, 1949; Hammel, Eric, *Guadalcanal Starvation Island,* New York: Crown Publishers Inc., 1987; Miller, Thomas G. Jr., *The Cactus Air Force,* New York: New York: Harper & Row, 1969.

[10] Loxton, Bruce with Chris Coulthard-Clark, *The Shame of Savo,*

Annapolis MD: Naval Institute Press, 1994.

[11] Warner, Dennis and Peggy, *Disaster in the Pacific New Light on the Battle of Savo Island,* Annapolis MD: Naval Institute Press, 1992.

[12] Evans, David C., *The Japanese Navy in World War II In the Words of Former Japanese Naval Officers,* Annapolis MD: Naval Institute Press, 1986.

[13] Loxton, Bruce with Chris Coulthard-Clark, *The Shame of Savo,* Annapolis MD: Naval Institute Press, 1994.

[14] Dyer, Vice Admiral George Carroll, USN (Ret), *The Amphibians Came to Conquer The Story of Admiral Richard Kelly Turner,* Washington D. C.: Department of the Navy, 1972, and U. S. Marine Corps, 1991.

[15] Miller, Thomas G. Jr., *The Cactus Air Force,* New York: New York: Harper & Row, 1969.

[16] Warner, Dennis and Peggy, *Disaster in the Pacific New Light on the Battle of Savo Island,* Annapolis MD: Naval Institute Press, 1992.

[17] Dyer, Vice Admiral George Carroll, USN (Ret), *The Amphibians Came to Conquer The Story of Admiral Richard Kelly Turner,* Washington D. C.: Department of the Navy, 1972, and U. S. Marine Corps, 1991.

[18] Letter, 25 October 1943, from Lieutenant Commander J. R. Ogden (acting commanding officer of VP-23 in July 1942) to Vice Admiral John McCain.

[19] Loxton, Bruce with Chris Coulthard-Clark, *The Shame of Savo,* Annapolis MD: Naval Institute Press, 1994; Miller, Thomas G. Jr., *The Cactus Air Force,* New York: New York: Harper & Row, 1969.

[20] Miller, John Jr., *United States Army in World War II The War in the Pacific Guadalcanal: The First Offensive,* Washington D. C.: Center of Military History, United States Army, 1949.

[21] Hammel, Eric, *Guadalcanal Starvation Island,* New York: Crown Publishers Inc., 1987; Miller, Thomas G. Jr., *The Cactus Air Force,* New York: New York: Harper & Row, 1969.

[22] Miller, John Jr., *United States Army in World War II The War in the Pacific Guadalcanal: The First Offensive,* Washington D. C.: Center of Military History, United States Army, 1949.

[23] Hammel, Eric, *Guadalcanal Starvation Island,* New York: Crown Publishers Inc., 1987; Morison, Samuel Eliot, *History of the United States Navy Operations in World War II,* Boston MA: Boston MA: Little, Brown and Company, 1949.

[24] Miller, John Jr., *United States Army in World War II The War in the Pacific Guadalcanal: The First Offensive,* Washington D. C.: Center of Military History, United States Army, 1949.

[25] Hammel, Eric, *Guadalcanal Starvation Island,* New York: Crown

Publishers Inc., 1987; Miller, Thomas G. Jr., *The Cactus Air Force,* New York: New York: Harper & Row, 1969; Sherrod, Robert, *History of Marine Corps Aviaiton in World War II,* Washington D.C.: Combat Forces Press, 1952.

[26] Twining, General Merrill B., USMC (Ret), *No Bended Knee,* Novato CA: Presidio Press, 1996.

[27] Hammel, Eric, *Guadalcanal Starvation Island,* New York: Crown Publishers Inc., 1987; Miller, Thomas G. Jr., *The Cactus Air Force,* New York: New York: Harper & Row, 1969; Miller, John Jr., *United States Army in World War II The War in the Pacific Guadalcanal: The First Offensive,* Washington D. C.: Center of Military History, United States Army, 1949.

[28] Miller, Thomas G. Jr., *The Cactus Air Force,* New York: New York: Harper & Row, 1969.

[29] Hammel, Eric, *Carrier Clash The Invasion of Guadalcanal & The Battle of the Eastern Solomons August 1942,* St. Paul MN: Zenith Press, 2004.

[30] Humble, Richard, *United States Fleet Carriers of World War II 'In Action,'* Poole, Dorset: Blandford Press,1984.

[31] Miller, John Jr., *United States Army in World War II The War in the Pacific Guadalcanal: The First Offensive,* Washington D. C.: Center of Military History, United States Army, 1949.

[32] Vandegrift, General A. A., *Once A Marine,* New York: Ballantine Books, 1984.

[33] Twining, General Merrill B., USMC (Ret), *No Bended Knee,* Novato CA: Presidio Press, 1996.

[34] Vandegrift, General A. A., *Once A Marine,* New York: Ballantine Books, 1984; Miller, Thomas G. Jr., *The Cactus Air Force,* New York: New York: Harper & Row, 1969.

[35] Frank, Richard B., *Guadalcanal The Definitive Account of the Landmark Battle,* New York: Penguin Books, 1990.

[36] Miller, Thomas G. Jr., *The Cactus Air Force,* New York: New York: Harper & Row, 1969.

[37] *Ibid.*

[38] Lundstrom, John B., *The First Team and the Guadalcanal Campaign Naval Fighter Combat from August to November 1942,* Annapolis MD: Naval Institute Press, 1994.

[39] Potter, E. B., *Nimitz,* Annapolis MD: Naval Institute Press, 1976.

[40] Clark, Admiral J. J. "Jocko" with Clark G. Reynolds, *Carrier Admiral,* New York: David McKay Company, Inc., 1967.

[41] Buell, Thomas B., *Master of Sea Power A Biography of Fleet Admiral Ernest J. King,* Boston MA: Little, Brown & Co., 1980 and Annapolis MD:

Naval Institute Press, 1995; Potter, E. B., *Nimitz,* Annapolis MD: Naval Institute Press, 1976.

[42] Buell, Thomas B., *Master of Sea Power A Biography of Fleet Admiral Ernest J. King,* Boston MA: Little, Brown & Co., 1980 and Annapolis MD: Naval Institute Press, 1995.

[43] Potter, E. B., *Nimitz,* Annapolis MD: Naval Institute Press, 1976.

[44] Hoyt, Edwin P., *How They Won The War in the Pacific Nimitz and His Admirals,* New York: Weybright and Talley, 1970.

[45] Reynolds, Clark G., *Admiral John H. Towers The Struggle for Naval Air Supremacy,* Annapolis MD: Naval Institute Press, 1991.

[46] Potter, E. B., *Nimitz,* Annapolis MD: Naval Institute Press, 1976.

[47] Hoyt, Edwin P., *Guadalcanal,* New York: Stein and Day, 1982.

[48] Reynolds, Clark G., *Admiral John H. Towers The Struggle for Naval Air Supremacy,* Annapolis MD: Naval Institute Press, 1991.

[49] Vandegrift, General A. A., *Once A Marine,* New York: Ballantine Books, 1984.

Chapter 9

[1] Potter, E. B., *Nimitz,* Annapolis MD: Naval Institute Press, 1976.

[2] Hoyt, Edwin P., *How They Won The War in the Pacific Nimitz and His Admirals,* New York: Weybright and Talley, 1970.

[3] Miller, Nathan, *War At Sea A Naval History of World War II,* New York: Scribner, 1995.

[4] Potter, E. B., *Nimitz,* Annapolis MD: Naval Institute Press, 1976.

[5] Hoyt, Edwin P., *How They Won The War in the Pacific Nimitz and His Admirals,* New York: Weybright and Talley, 1970.

[6] Buell, Thomas B., *Master of Sea Power A Biography of Fleet Admiral Ernest J. King,* Boston MA: Little, Brown & Co., 1980 and Annapolis MD: Naval Institute Press, 1995.

[7] Furer, Rear Admiral Julius Augustus, USN (Ret.), *Administration of the Navy Department in World War II,* Washington D. C.: U. S. Government Printing Office, 1959.

[8] *Ibid.*

[9] Reynolds, Clark G., *The Fast Carriers The Forging of an Air Navy,* New York: McGraw-Hill Book Company, 1968.

[10] Furer, Rear Admiral Julius Augustus, USN (Ret.), *Administration of the Navy Department in World War II,* Washington D. C.: U. S. Government Printing Office, 1959.

[11] Johnson, Thomas M., "No. 1 Air Sailor Takes Vital Job – Speeding Planes to Guadalcanal", October 31, 1942.

[12] Grady, Patricia, "Man of War John Sidney McCain".

[13] Johnson, Thomas M., "No. 1 Air Sailor Takes Vital Job—Speeding Planes to Guadalcanal", October 31, 1942.

[14] Grady, Patricia, "Man of War John Sidney McCain".

[15] Goodwin, Bernard, "American War Leaders," March 26, 1944.

[16] Potter, E. B., *Bull Halsey*, Annapolis MD: Naval Institute Press, 1985.

[17] Halsey, Fleet Admiral William F., Jr., and Lieutenant Commander J. Bryan III, *Admiral Halsey's Story*, New York: McGraw-Hill Book Company, Inc. 1947; Potter, E. B., *Bull Halsey*, Annapolis MD: Naval Institute Press, 1985.

[18] Goodwin, Bernard, "American War Leaders," March 26, 1944.

[19] Reynolds, Clark G., *The Fast Carriers The Forging of an Air Navy*, New York: McGraw-Hill Book Company, 1968.

[20] Gunston, Bill, *Night Fighters A Development & Combat History*, New York: Charles New York: Scribner's Sons, 1976.

[21] *Ibid*.

[22] Reynolds, Clark G., *The Fast Carriers The Forging of an Air Navy*, New York: McGraw-Hill Book Company, 1968.

[23] *U. S. Air Services* Magazine, October 1945.

[24] Goodwin, Bernard, "American War Leaders," March 26, 1944.

[25] Clark, Admiral J. J. "Jocko" with Clark G. Reynolds, *Carrier Admiral*, New York: David McKay and Company, Inc., 1967.

[26] *U. S. Air Services* Magazine, October 1945.

[27] *U. S. Air Services* Magazine, October 1945; Tillman, Barrett, *Hellcat: The F6F in World War II*, Annapolis MD: Naval Institute Press, 1979.

[28] Buell, Thomas B., *Master of Sea Power A Biography of Fleet Admiral Ernest J. King*, Boston MA: Little, Brown & Co., 1980 and Annapolis MD: Naval Institute Press, 1995.

[29] Woolridge, E. T., ed. *Carrier Warfare in the Pacific, An Oral History Collection*, Washington D.C.: Smithsonian Institution Press, 1993

Chapter 10
[1] Reynolds, Clark G., *The Fast Carriers The Forging of an Air Navy*, New York: McGraw-Hill Book Company, 1968.

[2] Furer, Rear Admiral Julius Augustus, USN (Ret.), *Administration of the Navy Department in World War II*, Washington D. C.: U. S. Government Printing Office, 1959.

[3] Buell, Thomas B., *Master of Sea Power A Biography of Fleet Admiral Ernest J. King*, Boston MA: Little, Brown & Co., 1980 and Annapolis MD: Naval Institute Press, 1995; Furer, Rear Admiral Julius Augustus, USN (Ret.), *Administration of the Navy Department in World War II*, Washington D. C.: U. S. Government Printing Office, 1959.

[4] Buell, Thomas B., *Master of Sea Power A Biography of Fleet Admiral Ernest J. King*, Boston MA: Little, Brown & Co., 1980 and Annapolis MD: Naval Institute Press, 1995.

[5] Reynolds, Clark G., *The Fast Carriers The Forging of an Air Navy*, New York: McGraw-Hill Book Company, 1968.

[6] Buell, Thomas B., *The Quiet Warrior A Biography of Admiral Raymond A. Spruance*, Boston MA: Little Brown & Co., 1974; Reynolds, Clark G., *Admiral John H. Towers The Struggle for Naval Air Supremacy*, Annapolis MD: Naval Institute Press, 1991.

[7] Reynolds, Clark G., *Admiral John H. Towers The Struggle for Naval Air Supremacy*, Annapolis MD: Naval Institute Press, 1991.

[8] Reynolds, Clark G., *The Fast Carriers The Forging of an Air Navy*, New York: McGraw-Hill Book Company, 1968.

[9] Buell, Thomas B., *Master of Sea Power A Biography of Fleet Admiral Ernest J. King*, Boston MA: Little, Brown & Co., 1980 and Annapolis MD: Naval Institute Press, 1995; Reynolds, Clark G., *The Fast Carriers The Forging of an Air Navy*, New York: McGraw-Hill Book Company, 1968.

[10] Buell, Thomas B., *Master of Sea Power A Biography of Fleet Admiral Ernest J. King*, Boston MA: Little, Brown & Co., 1980 and Annapolis MD: Naval Institute Press, 1995.

[11] Reynolds, Clark G., *The Fast Carriers The Forging of an Air Navy*, New York: McGraw-Hill Book Company, 1968.

[12] Reynolds, Clark G., *Admiral John H. Towers The Struggle for Naval Air Supremacy*, Annapolis MD: Naval Institute Press, 1991.

[13] Reynolds, Clark G., *The Fast Carriers The Forging of an Air Navy*, New York: McGraw-Hill Book Company, 1968.

[14] Buell, Thomas B., *Master of Sea Power A Biography of Fleet Admiral Ernest J. King*, Boston MA: Little, Brown & Co., 1980 and Annapolis MD: Naval Institute Press, 1995; Morrison, Wilbur H., *Above and Beyond 1941-1945*, New York: St. Martin's Press, 1983.

[15] Furer, Rear Admiral Julius Augustus, USN (Ret.), *Administration of the Navy Department in World War II*, Washington D. C.: U. S. Government Printing Office, 1959; Jurika, Stephen, Jr. (Ed.), *From Pearl Harbor to Vietnam The Memoirs of Admiral Arthur W. Radford*, Stanford University, CA: Hoover Institution Press, 1980.

[16] Furer, Rear Admiral Julius Augustus, USN (Ret.), *Administration of the Navy Department in World War II*, Washington D. C.: U. S. Government Printing Office, 1959.

[17] Porter, Thurston, "100 Aircraft Carriers Can Ruin Japan, Says Admiral McCain", *New York Sunday News*, April 22, 1944.

[18] Crichton, Kyle, "Navy Air Boss", *Colliers*, October 23, 1943.

[19] Thach, John S., *The Reminiscences of Admiral John S. Thach, USN (Retired)*, Volumes 1 and 2, Annapolis MD, Naval Institute Press, 1977.

[20] Potter, E. B., *Nimitz*, Annapolis MD: Naval Institute Press, 1976; Reynolds, Clark G., *The Fast Carriers The Forging of an Air Navy*, New York: McGraw-Hill Book Company, 1968.

[21] Potter, E. B., *Bull Halsey*, Annapolis MD: Naval Institute Press, 1985.

[22] Hoyt, Edwin P., *How They Won The War in the Pacific Nimitz and His Admirals*, New York: Weybright and Talley, 1970.

[23] Reynolds, Clark G., *Admiral John H. Towers The Struggle for Naval Air Supremacy*, Annapolis MD: Naval Institute Press, 1991.

[24] Hoyt, Edwin P., *How They Won The War in the Pacific Nimitz and His Admirals*, New York: Weybright and Talley, 1970.

[25] Reynolds, Clark G., *The Fast Carriers The Forging of an Air Navy*, New York: McGraw-Hill Book Company, 1968.

[26] Hoyt, Edwin P., *How They Won The War in the Pacific Nimitz and His Admirals*, New York: Weybright and Talley, 1970.

[27] Thach, John S., *The Reminiscences of Admiral John S. Thach, USN (Retired)*, Volumes 1 and 2, Annapolis MD, Naval Institute Press, 1977.

[28] Hoyt, Edwin P., *Closing The Circle War In The Pacific: 1945*, New York: Van Nostrand Reinhold Company, 1982.

[29] Reynolds, Clark G., *Admiral John H. Towers The Struggle for Naval Air Supremacy*, Annapolis MD: Naval Institute Press, 1991.

[30] Hoyt, Edwin P., *McCampbell's Heroes The Story of the U. S. Navy's Most Celebrated Carrier Fighters of the Pacific War*, New York: Van Nostrand Reinhold Company, 1983; Buell, Thomas B., *The Quiet Warrior A Biography of Admiral Raymond A. Spruance*, Boston MA: Little Brown & Co., 1974.

[31] Hoyt, Edwin P., *McCampbell's Heroes The Story of the U.S. Navy's Most Celebrated Carrier Fighters of the Pacific War*, New York: Van Nostrand Reinhold Company, 1983.

[32] Buell, Thomas B., *The Quiet Warrior A Biography of Admiral Raymond A. Spruance*, Boston MA: Little Brown & Co., 1974.

[33] Potter, E. B., *Admiral Arleigh Burke*, New York: Random House, 1990.

[34] Morrison, Wilbur H., *Above and Beyond 1941-1945*, New York: St. Martin's Press, 1983.

[35] Woolridge, E. T., ed. *Carrier Warfare in the Pacific, An Oral History Collection*, Washington D.C.: Smithsonian Institution Press, 1993.

Chapter 11
[1] Potter, E. B., *Bull Halsey*, Annapolis MD: Naval Institute Press, 1985.

[2] Potter, E. B., *Bull Halsey*, Annapolis MD: Naval Institute Press, 1985;

Buell, Thomas B., *The Quiet Warrior A Biography of Admiral Raymond A. Spruance,* Boston MA: Little Brown & Co., 1974.

[3] Potter, E. B., *Bull Halsey,* Annapolis MD: Naval Institute Press, 1985; Taylor, Theodore, *The Magnificent Mitscher,* Annapolis MD: Naval Institute Press, 1991; Merrill, James, *A Sailor's Admiral A Biography of William F. Halsey,* New York: Thomas Y. Crowell Company, 1976.

[4] Taylor, Theodore, *The Magnificent Mitscher,* Annapolis MD: Naval Institute Press, 1991.

[5] Potter, E. B., *Bull Halsey,* Annapolis MD: Naval Institute Press, 1985; McCain, John with Mark Salter, *Faith of My Fathers,* New York: Random House, 1999.

[6] Sweetman, Jack, *The U. S. Naval Academy An Illustrated History,* Annapolis MD: Naval Institute Press, 1979 and 1995.

[7] Reynolds, Clark G., *The Fast Carriers The Forging of an Air Navy,* New York: McGraw-Hill Book Company, 1968; Taylor, Theodore, *The Magnificent Mitscher,* Annapolis MD: Naval Institute Press, 1991.

[8] Taylor, Theodore, *The Magnificent Mitscher,* Annapolis MD: Naval Institute Press, 1991.

[9] Clark, Admiral J. J. "Jocko" with Clark G. Reynolds, *Carrier Admiral,* New York: David McKay Company, Inc., 1967.

[10] Taylor, Theodore, *The Magnificent Mitscher,* Annapolis MD: Naval Institute Press, 1991.

[11] Thach, John S., *The Reminiscences of Admiral John S. Thach, USN (Retired),* Volumes 1 and 2, Annapolis MD, Naval Institute Press, 1977.

[12] Reynolds, Clark G., *The Fast Carriers The Forging of an Air Navy,* New York: McGraw-Hill Book Company, 1968.

[13] Buell, Thomas B., *The Quiet Warrior A Biography of Admiral Raymond A. Spruance,* Boston MA: Little Brown & Co., 1974.

[14] Hoyt, Edwin P., *How They Won The War in the Pacific Nimitz and His Admirals,* New York: Weybright and Talley, 1970.

[15] *Time,* January 14, 1945.

[16] Reynolds, Clark G., *The Fast Carriers The Forging of an Air Navy,* New York: McGraw-Hill Book Company, 1968.

[17] Newcomb, Richard F., *Abandon Ship Saga of the USS Indianapolis the Navy's Greatest Sea Disaster,* New York: HarperCollins, 1958, 2001.

[18] Reynolds, Clark G., *The Fast Carriers The Forging of an Air Navy,* New York: McGraw-Hill Book Company, 1968.

[19] Clark, Admiral J. J. "Jocko" with Clark G. Reynolds, *Carrier Admiral,* New York: David McKay Company, Inc., 1967; Reynolds, Clark G., *The Fast Carriers The Forging of an Air Navy,* New York: McGraw-Hill Book Company, 1968.

[20] McCain, John with Mark Salter, *Faith of My Fathers,* New York: Random House, 1999.

[21] Thach, John S., *The Reminiscences of Admiral John S. Thach, USN (Retired),* Volumes 1 and 2, Annapolis MD, Naval Institute Press, 1977.

[22] Reynolds, Clark G., *The Fast Carriers The Forging of an Air Navy,* New York: McGraw-Hill Book Company, 1968.

[23] Buell, Harold L., *Dauntless Helldivers,* Orion Books, 1991.

[24] Taylor, Theodore, *The Magnificent Mitscher,* Annapolis MD: Naval Institute Press, 1991.

[25] Merrill, James, *A Sailor's Admiral A Biography of William F. Halsey,* New York: Thomas Y. Crowell Company, 1976.

[26] Clark, Admiral J. J. "Jocko" with Clark G. Reynolds, *Carrier Admiral,* New York: David McKay Company, Inc., 1967; Potter, E. B., *Bull Halsey,* Annapolis MD: Naval Institute Press, 1985.

[27] Karig, Captain Walter, USNR, Lieutenant Commander Russell L. Harris, USNR, and Lieutenant Frank A. Manson, USN, *Battle Report The End of an Empire,* Reinhart and Company, 1948.

[28] Ewing, Steve, *Thach Weave The Life of Jimmie Thach,* Annapolis MD: Naval Institute Press, 2004.

[29] Clark, Admiral J. J. "Jocko" with Clark G. Reynolds, *Carrier Admiral,* New York: David McKay Company, Inc., 1967.

Chapter 12

[1] Potter, E. B., *Bull Halsey,* Annapolis MD: Naval Institute Press, 1985.

[2] *Ibid.*

[3] Thach, John S., *The Reminiscences of Admiral John S. Thach, USN (Retired),* Volumes 1 and 2, Annapolis MD, Naval Institute Press, 1977.

[4] Evans, David C., *The Japanese Navy in World War II In the Words of Former Japanese Naval Officers,* Annapolis MD: Naval Institute Press, 1986.

[5] Cutler, Thomas J., *The Battle of Leyte Gulf 23-26 October 1944,* New York: HarperCollins, 1994; Taylor, Theodore, *The Magnificent Mitscher,* Annapolis MD: Naval Institute Press, 1991.

[6] Cutler, Thomas J., *The Battle of Leyte Gulf 23-26 October 1944,* New York: HarperCollins, 1994.

[7] "Bull's Run," *Life* magazine, November 24, 1947

[8] McCain, John, with Mark Salter, *Faith of My Fathers,* New York: Random House, 1999; Spector, Ronald H., *Eagle Against The Sun,* The Free Press, 1985.

[9] Cutler, Thomas J., *The Battle of Leyte Gulf 23-26 October 1944,* New York: HarperCollins, 1994.

[10] *Ibid.*
[11] Potter, E. B., *Bull Halsey,* Annapolis MD: Naval Institute Press, 1985.
[12] Tillman, Barrett, *Hellcat: The F6F in World War II,* Annapolis MD: Naval Institute Press, 1979.
[13] Buell, Thomas B., *Master of Sea Power A Biography of Fleet Admiral Ernest J. King,* Boston MA: Little, Brown & Co., 1980 and Annapolis MD: Naval Institute Press, 1995.

Chapter 13
[1] Taylor, Theodore, *The Magnificent Mitscher,* Annapolis MD: Naval Institute Press, 1991; Hoyt, Edwin P., *Carrier Wars Naval Aviation from World War II to the Persian Gulf,* New York: McGraw Hill 1989 and Paragon House, 1992.
[2] Thach, John S., *The Reminiscences of Admiral John S. Thach, USN (Retired),* Volumes 1 and 2, Annapolis MD, Naval Institute Press, 1977.
[3] *Saturday Evening Post,* July 14, 1945.
[4] Thach, John S., *The Reminiscences of Admiral John S. Thach, USN (Retired),* Volumes 1 and 2, Annapolis MD, Naval Institute Press, 1977.
[5] Lawson, Robert and Barrett Tillman, *Carrier Air War in Original WW II Color,* New York: Barnes & Noble Books, 1999.
[6] Potter, E. B., *Bull Halsey,* Annapolis MD: Naval Institute Press, 1985.
[7] Thach, John S., *The Reminiscences of Admiral John S. Thach, USN (Retired),* Volumes 1 and 2, Annapolis MD, Naval Institute Press, 1977.
[8] Potter, E. B., *Bull Halsey,* Annapolis MD: Naval Institute Press, 1985.
[9] Thach, John S., *The Reminiscences of Admiral John S. Thach, USN (Retired),* Volumes 1 and 2, Annapolis MD, Naval Institute Press, 1977.
[10] Woolridge, E. T., ed. *Carrier Warfare in the Pacific, An Oral History Collection,* Washington D.C.: Smithsonian Institution Press, 1993.
[11] Clark, Admiral J. J. "Jocko" with Clark G. Reynolds, *Carrier Admiral,* New York: David McKay Company, Inc., 1967; Ewing, Steve, *Thach Weave The Life of Jimmie Thach,* Annapolis MD: Naval Institute Press, 2004.
[12] Potter, E. B., *Bull Halsey,* Annapolis MD: Naval Institute Press, 1985.
[13] Potter, E. B., *Bull Halsey,* Annapolis MD: Naval Institute Press, 1985; Woolridge, E. T., ed. *Carrier Warfare in the Pacific, An Oral History Collection,* Washington D.C.: Smithsonian Institution Press, 1993.
[14] Clark, Admiral J. J. "Jocko" with Clark G. Reynolds, *Carrier Admiral,* New York: David McKay Company, Inc., 1967.
[15] Woolridge, E. T., ed. *Carrier Warfare in the Pacific, An Oral History Collection,* Washington D.C.: Smithsonian Institution Press, 1993.
[16] Merrill, James, *A Sailor's Admiral A Biography of William F. Halsey,*

New York: Thomas Y. Crowell, 1976; Adamson, Hans Christian, and George Francis Kosko, *Halsey's Typhoons*, New York: Crown, 1967.

[17] Potter, E. B., *Bull Halsey*, Annapolis MD: Naval Institute Press, 1985.

[18] Taylor, Theodore, *The Magnificent Mitscher*, Annapolis MD: Naval Institute Press, 1991.

[19] Johnson, Richard W., "Death of 'Desk Admiral' Robs Bull Halsey of His Right Arm," September 7, 1945.

[20] Adamson, Hans Christian and George Francis Kosko, *Halsey's Typhoons*, New York: Crown Publishers, 1967.

[21] Longstreth, W. Thacher, *Main Line Wasp, the Education of Thacher Longstreth*, New York: W. W. Norton & Company, 1990.

Chapter 14

[1] Potter, E. B., *Bull Halsey*, Annapolis MD: Naval Institute Press, 1985.

[2] Calhoun, Captain C. Raymond, USN (Retired), *Typhoon: The Other Enemy*, Annapolis MD: Naval Institute Press, 1981.

[3] Potter, E. B., *Bull Halsey*, Annapolis MD: Naval Institute Press, 1985.

[4] Merrill, James, *A Sailor's Admiral A Biography of William F. Halsey*, New York: Thomas Y. Crowell Company, 1976.

[5] Condon, John Pomeroy, *Corsairs and Flattops*, Annapolis MD: Naval Institute Press, 1998.

[6] Potter, E. B., *Bull Halsey*, Annapolis MD: Naval Institute Press, 1985.

Chapter 15

[1] Hastings, Robert P., *Privateer in the Coconut Navy*, VPB-106 cruise book, 1946.

[2] Thach, John S., *The Reminiscences of Admiral John S. Thach, USN (Retired)*, Volumes 1 and 2, Annapolis MD, Naval Institute Press, 1977.

[3] *Time*, July 30, 1945.

[4] Thach, John S., *The Reminiscences of Admiral John S. Thach, USN (Retired)*, Volumes 1 and 2, Annapolis MD, Naval Institute Press, 1977.

[5] Potter, E. B., *Bull Halsey*, Annapolis MD: Naval Institute Press, 1985.

[6] Adamson, Hans Christian, and George Francis Kosko, *Halsey's Typhoons*, New York: Crown Publishers, 1967; Merrill, James, *A Sailor's Admiral A Biography of William F. Halsey*, New York: Thomas Y. Crowell Company, 1976.

[7] Potter, E. B., *Bull Halsey*, Annapolis MD: Naval Institute Press, 1985.

[8] Merrill, James, *A Sailor's Admiral A Biography of William F. Halsey*, New York: Thomas Y. Crowell Company, 1976.

[9] Adamson, Hans Christian and George Francis Kosko, *Halsey's Typhoons*, New York: Crown Publishers, 1967.

[10] Merrill, James, *A Sailor's Admiral A Biography of William F. Halsey,* New York: Thomas Y. Crowell Company, 1976; Clark, Admiral J. J. "Jocko" with Clark G. Reynolds, *Carrier Admiral,* New York: David McKay Company, Inc., 1967; Potter, E. B., *Bull Halsey,* Annapolis MD: Naval Institute Press, 1985.

[11] Merrill, James, *A Sailor's Admiral A Biography of William F. Halsey,* New York: Thomas Y. Crowell Company, 1976.

[12] Woolridge, E. T., ed. *Carrier Warfare in the Pacific, An Oral History Collection,* Washington D.C.: Smithsonian Institution Press, 1993.

[13] Potter, E. B., *Bull Halsey,* Annapolis MD: Naval Institute Press, 1985.

[14] Merrill, James, *A Sailor's Admiral A Biography of William F. Halsey,* New York: Thomas Y. Crowell Company, 1976.

[15] Merrill, James, *A Sailor's Admiral A Biography of William F. Halsey,* New York: Thomas Y. Crowell Company, 1976; Potter, E. B., *Bull Halsey,* Annapolis MD: Naval Institute Press, 1985.

[16] Merrill, James, *A Sailor's Admiral A Biography of William F. Halsey,* New York: Thomas Y. Crowell Company, 1976; Potter, E. B., *Bull Halsey,* Annapolis MD: Naval Institute Press, 1985; Reynolds, Clark G., *The Fast Carriers The Forging of an Air Navy,* New York: McGraw-Hill Book Company, 1968.

[17] Stillwell, Paul, *Battleship Missouri An Illustrated History,* Annapolis MD: Naval Institute Press, 1996.

[18] Lawson, Robert and Barrett Tillman, *Carrier Air War in Original WW II Color,* New York: Barnes & Noble Books, 1999.

[19] Potter, E. B., *Bull Halsey,* Annapolis MD: Naval Institute Press, 1985.

[20] *Ibid.*

[21] Hoyt, Edwin P., *Closing The Circle War In The Pacific: 1945,* New York: Van Nostrand Reinhold Company, 1982; Reynolds, Clark G., *The Fast Carriers The Forging of an Air Navy,* New York: McGraw-Hill Book Company, 1968; Halsey, Fleet Admiral William F., Jr., and Lieutenant Commander J. Bryan III, *Admiral Halsey's Story,* New York: McGraw-Hill Book Company, Inc. 1947.

[22] Morrison, Wilbur H., *Wings Over The Seven Seas,* A. S. Barnes and Co., 1975.

[23] Merrill, James, *A Sailor's Admiral A Biography of William F. Halsey,* New York: Thomas Y. Crowell Company, 1976.

[24] Thach, John S., *The Reminiscences of Admiral John S. Thach, USN (Retired),* Volumes 1 and 2, Annapolis MD, Naval Institute Press, 1977.

[25] "A Fighting Man," Peoria *Morning Star,* September 8, 1945.

[26] Morrison, Wilbur H., *Wings Over The Seven Seas,* A. S. Barnes and Co., 1975.

[27] Morison, Samuel Eliot, *History of United States Naval operations in World War II,* Brown and Company, 1960.

[28] Halsey, Fleet Admiral William F., Jr., and Lieutenant Commander J. Bryan III, *Admiral Halsey's Story,* New York: McGraw-Hill Book Company, Inc. 1947.

[29] Halsey, Fleet Admiral William F., Jr., and Lieutenant Commander J. Bryan III, *Admiral Halsey's Story,* New York: McGraw-Hill Book Company, Inc. 1947; Potter, E. B., *Bull Halsey,* Annapolis MD: Naval Institute Press, 1985.

[30] Potter, E. B., *Bull Halsey,* Annapolis MD: Naval Institute Press, 1985; Reynolds, Clark G., *The Fast Carriers The Forging of an Air Navy,* New York: McGraw-Hill Book Company, 1968.

[31] Morrison, Wilbur H., *Wings Over The Seven Seas,* A. S. Barnes and Co., 1975; Potter, E. B., *Bull Halsey,* Annapolis MD: Naval Institute Press, 1985.

[32] Reynolds, Clark G., *The Fast Carriers The Forging of an Air Navy,* New York: McGraw-Hill Book Company, 1968.

[33] Thach, John S., *The Reminiscences of Admiral John S. Thach, USN (Retired),* Volumes 1 and 2, Annapolis MD, Naval Institute Press, 1977.

[34] Hoyt, Edwin P., *Closing The Circle War In The Pacific: 1945,* New York: Van Nostrand Reinhold Company, 1982.

Chapter 16

[1] Buell, Thomas B., *The Quiet Warrior A Biography of Admiral Raymond A. Spruance,* Boston MA: Little Brown & Co., 1974.

[2] Potter, E. B., *Bull Halsey,* Annapolis MD: Naval Institute Press, 1985; Merrill, James, *A Sailor's Admiral A Biography of William F. Halsey,* New York: Thomas Y. Crowell Company, 1976.

[3] Buell, Thomas B., *Master of Sea Power A Biography of Fleet Admiral Ernest J. King,* Boston MA: Little, Brown & Co., 1980 and Annapolis MD: Naval Institute Press, 1995.

[4] Hoyt, Edwin P., *Closing The Circle War In The Pacific: 1945,* New York: Van Nostrand Reinhold Company, 1982.

[5] Potter, E. B., *Bull Halsey,* Annapolis MD: Naval Institute Press, 1985.

[6] *Ibid.*

[7] Potter, E. B., *Bull Halsey,* Annapolis MD: Naval Institute Press, 1985; Merrill, James, *A Sailor's Admiral A Biography of William F. Halsey,* New York: Thomas Y. Crowell Company, 1976

[8] Reynolds, Clark G., *The Fast Carriers The Forging of an Air Navy,* New York: McGraw-Hill Book Company, 1968.

[9] Potter, E. B., *Nimitz,* Annapolis MD: Naval Institute Press, 1976.

[10] Potter, E. B., *Bull Halsey,* Annapolis MD: Naval Institute Press, 1985.

[11] Merrill, James, *A Sailor's Admiral A Biography of William F. Halsey*, New York: Thomas Y. Crowell Company, 1976.

[12] Thach, John S., *The Reminiscences of Admiral John S. Thach, USN (Retired)*, Volumes 1 and 2, Annapolis MD, Naval Institute Press, 1977.

[13] Hoyt, Edwin P., *Battle of Leyte Gulf The Death Knell of the Japanese Fleet*. New York: Weybright and Talley, 1972.

[14] James, D. Clayton, *A Time For Giants Politics of the American High Command in World War II*, Franklin Watts, 1987.

[15] Merrill, James, *A Sailor's Admiral A Biography of William F. Halsey*, New York: Thomas Y. Crowell Company, 1976.

[16] Buell, Thomas B., *The Quiet Warrior A Biography of Admiral Raymond A. Spruance*, Boston MA: Little Brown & Co., 1974.

[17] Woolridge, E. T., ed. *Carrier Warfare in the Pacific, An Oral History Collection*, Washington D.C.: Smithsonian Institution Press, 1993.

[18] Thach, John S., *The Reminiscences of Admiral John S. Thach, USN (Retired)*, Volumes 1 and 2, Annapolis MD, Naval Institute Press, 1977.

[19] *Ibid.*

[20] Reynolds, Clark G., *The Fast Carriers The Forging of an Air Navy*, New York: McGraw-Hill Book Company, 1968.

[21] Thach, John S., *The Reminiscences of Admiral John S. Thach, USN (Retired)*, Volumes 1 and 2, Annapolis MD, Naval Institute Press, 1977.

[22] Buell, Thomas B., *The Quiet Warrior A Biography of Admiral Raymond A. Spruance*, Boston MA: Little Brown & Co., 1974.

[23] Woolridge, E. T., ed. *Carrier Warfare in the Pacific, An Oral History Collection*, Washington D.C.: Smithsonian Institution Press, 1993.

[24] Belote, James H. & William M. Belote, *Titans of the Sea*, New York: Harper & Row, 1975.

[25] Merrill, James, *A Sailor's Admiral A Biography of William F. Halsey*, New York: Thomas Y. Crowell Company, 1976; Taylor, Theodore, *The Magnificent Mitscher*, Annapolis MD: Naval Institute Press, 1991.

[26] Hoyt, Edwin P., *Battle of Leyte Gulf The Death Knell of the Japanese Fleet*. New York: Weybright and Talley, 1972.

[27] Woolridge, E. T., ed. *Carrier Warfare in the Pacific, An Oral History Collection*, Washington D.C.: Smithsonian Institution Press, 1993.

[28] Belote, James H. & William M. Belote, *Titans of the Sea*, New York: Harper & Row, 1975.

[29] *Saturday Evening Post*, July 14, 1945.

[30] Hoyt, Edwin P., *How They Won The War in the Pacific Nimitz and His Admirals*, New York: Weybright and Talley, 1970.

[31] Reynolds, Clark G., *Admiral John H. Towers The Struggle for Naval Air Supremacy*, Annapolis MD: Naval Institute Press, 1991.

[32] Hoyt, Edwin P., *How They Won The War in the Pacific Nimitz and His Admirals,* New York: Weybright and Talley, 1970.

[33] Buell, Thomas B., *Master of Sea Power A Biography of Fleet Admiral Ernest J. King,* Boston MA: Little, Brown & Co., 1980 and Annapolis MD: Naval Institute Press, 1995.

[34] Buell, Thomas B., *The Quiet Warrior A Biography of Admiral Raymond A. Spruance,* Boston MA: Little Brown & Co., 1974.

[35] Reynolds, Clark G., *Admiral John H. Towers The Struggle for Naval Air Supremacy,* Annapolis MD: Naval Institute Press, 1991.

[36] Hoyt, Edwin P., *How They Won The War in the Pacific Nimitz and His Admirals,* New York: Weybright and Talley, 1970.

[37] Buell, Thomas B., *Master of Sea Power A Biography of Fleet Admiral Ernest J. King,* Boston MA: Little, Brown & Co., 1980 and Annapolis MD: Naval Institute Press, 1995.

[38] *Ibid.*

[39] *Ibid.*

[40] Buell, Thomas B., *Master of Sea Power A Biography of Fleet Admiral Ernest J. King,* Boston MA: Little, Brown & Co., 1980 and Annapolis MD: Naval Institute Press, 1995.

[41] James, D. Clayton, *A Time For Giants Politics of the American High Command in World War II,* Franklin Watts, 1987.

[42] Reynolds, Clark G., *The Fast Carriers The Forging of an Air Navy,* New York: McGraw-Hill Book Company, 1968.

[43] Grossnick, Roy A., *United States Naval Aviation 1910-1995,* Naval Historical Washington D. C.: Center, Department of the Navy.

[44] Reynolds, Clark G., *The Fast Carriers The Forging of an Air Navy,* New York: McGraw-Hill Book Company, 1968.

[45] Reynolds, Clark G., *Admiral John H. Towers The Struggle for Naval Air Supremacy,* Annapolis MD: Naval Institute Press, 1991.

[46] Hoyt, Edwin P., *How They Won The War in the Pacific Nimitz and His Admirals,* New York: Weybright and Talley, 1970.

[47] Wheeler, Gerald E., *Kinkaid of the Seventh Fleet,* Annapolis MD: Naval Institute Press, 1996.

[48] Clark, Admiral J. J. "Jocko" with Clark G. Reynolds, *Carrier Admiral,* New York: David McKay Company, Inc., 1967.

Chapter 17

[1] Potter, E. B., *Bull Halsey,* Annapolis MD: Naval Institute Press, 1985.

[2] *Ibid.*

[3] Reynolds, Clark G., *Admiral John H. Towers The Struggle for Naval Air Supremacy,* Annapolis MD: Naval Institute Press, 1991.

[4] *Ibid.*

[5] Halsey, Fleet Admiral William F., Jr., and Lieutenant Commander J. Bryan III, *Admiral Halsey's Story,* New York: McGraw-Hill Book Company, Inc. 1947.

[6] Ewing, Steve, *Thach Weave The Life of Jimmie Thach,* Annapolis MD: Naval Institute Press, 2004.

[7] McCain, John with Mark Salter, *Faith of My Fathers,* New York: Random House, 1999.

[8] Potter, E. B., *Bull Halsey,* Annapolis MD: Naval Institute Press, 1985.

[9] McCain, John with Mark Salter, *Faith of My Fathers,* New York: Random House, 1999.

[10] McCain, John, with Mark Salter, *Faith of My Fathers,* New York: Random House, 1999.

[11] Ibid.

[12] Thach, John S., *The Reminiscences of Admiral John S. Thach, USN (Retired),* Volumes 1 and 2, Annapolis MD, Naval Institute Press, 1977.

[13] McCain, John with Mark Salter, *Faith of My Fathers,* New York: Random House, 1999.

Chapter 18

[1] *Life* magazine, September 17, 1945.

[2] Halsey, Fleet Admiral William F., Jr., and Lieutenant Commander J. Bryan III, *Admiral Halsey's Story,* New York: McGraw-Hill Book Company, Inc. 1947.

[3] Johnson, Richard W., "Death of 'Desk Admiral' Robs Bull Halsey of His Right Arm," September 7, 1945.

[4] McCain, John, with Mark Salter, *Faith of My Fathers,* New York: Random House, 1999.

BIBLIOGRAPHY

Files
A major source is the collection of Admiral McCain's personal files of correspondence, orders, photographs, and reports of physical examinations in the custody of Margaret McCain La Grange. Also key are Admiral McCain's letters, war diaries, and photographs in the archives of the Hoover Institution at Stanford University, donated by James Gordon McCain and Catherine Vaulx McCain in 1982.

War Diaries, Action Reports and Narrative Reports
The following documents can be found in the McCain collection at the Hoover Institution at Stanford University. They provide the chronological framework and substantial content for the chapters about the fast carriers:

Task Group 38.1 War Diary	18 August – 31 August 1944
Task Group 38.1 Narrative Report	29 August – 24 September 1944
Task Group 38.1 War Diary	1 October – 31 October 1944
Task Group 38.1 Action Report	2 October – 29 October 1944
Task Force 38 War Diary	1 November – 30 Nov. 1944
Task Force 38 War Diary	1 December – 31 Dec. 1944
Task Force 38 War Diary	1 January – 31 January 1945
Task Force 38 Action Report	30 October 1944 – 26 Jan. 1945
Task Force 38 War Diary	1 February – 28 February 1945
Task Force 38 War Diary	1 March – 31 March 1945
Task Force 38 War Diary	1 April – 30 April 1945
Task Force 38 War Diary	1 May – 31 May 1945
Task Force 38 War Diary	1 June – 30 June 1945
Task Force 38 Action Report	28 May – 1 July 1945

Task Force 38 War Diary   1 July – 31 July 1945
Task Force 38 Action Report   2 July – 15 August 1945

Conversations

Margaret McCain La Grange: Conversations with the author in 2001, 2002, and 2003.

Joseph Pinckney McCain: Conversations with the author in 2002 and 2003.

William Alexander McCain: Conversations with the author in 2002 and 2003.

Mrs. John S. McCain, Jr.: Conversations with the author 2002 and 2003.

Henry Fluck: Conversations with the author in 2001, 2002, and 2003.

Admiral Noel Gayler: Conversation with the author in 2003.

Wilder Baker, Jr.: Conversations with the author in 2003.

Helen Sampson Blanchard: Conversations with the author in 2004.

Articles

"A Fighting Man," *Peoria Morning Star*, September 8, 1945.

"Bull's Run," *Life*, November 24, 1947.

Crichton, Kyle "Navy Air Boss," *Collier's*, October 23, 1943.

Goodwin, Bernard, "America's War Leaders–15," March 26, 1944.

Grady, Patricia, "Man of War John Sidney McCain."

Johnson, Richard W., "Death of a 'Desk Admiral' Robs Bull Halsey of His Right Arm," September 7, 1945.

Johnson, Thomas M., "No. 1 Air Sailor Takes Vital Job—Speeding Planes to Guadalcanal," October 31, 1942.

Life, September 17, 1945.

McCain, Joseph, "Namesakes of the USS *John McCain*," 1994.

McCain, J. S., Commander, U.S. Navy, "A Personnel Survey," U.S. Naval Institute *Proceedings,* January 1923.

McCain, J. S., Commander, U.S. Navy, "The Staff Equalization Bill," U.S. Naval Institute *Proceedings,* March 1924.

McCain, J. S., Commander, U.S. Navy, "Service Since Graduation vs. Age In Grade Retirement," U.S. Naval Institute *Proceedings,* May 1925.

McCain, J. S., in collaboration with John Bishop, manuscript of an article for the Curtis Publishing Company, "So We Hit 'Em In The Belly," July 1945.

Porter, Thurston, "100 Aircraft Carriers Can Ruin Japan, Says Admiral McCain," *New York Sunday News*, April 22, 1943.

Saturday Evening Post, July 14, 1945.
Time, September 28, October 12, and October 17, 1942.
Time, January 14, 1945.
Time, July 30, 1945.
U.S. Air Services, October 1945.

Books (Cited)
Adamson, Hans Christianson and George Francis Kosko, *Halsey's Typhoons,* New York: Crown Publishers, 1967.
Belote, James H. & William M Belote, *Titans of the Seas,* New York: Harper and Row, 1975.
Buell, Harold L., *Dauntless Helldivers,* New York: Orion Books, 1991.
Buell, Thomas B., *The Quiet Warrior A Biography of Admiral Raymond A. Spruance,* Boston MA: Little Brown & Co., 1974, and Annapolis, MD: Naval Institute Press, 1988.
Buell, Thomas B., *Master of Sea Power A Biography of Fleet Admiral Ernest J. King,* Boston MA: Little, Brown & Co., 1980, and Annapolis, MD: Naval Institute Press, 1995.
Calhoun, Captain C. Raymond, USN (Retired), *Typhoon: The Other Enemy,* Annapolis, MD: Naval Institute Press, 1981.
Clark, Admiral J. J. "Jocko" with Clark G. Reynolds, *Carrier Admiral,* New York: David McKay Company, Inc., 1967.
Condon, John Pomeroy, *Corsairs and Flattops,* Annapolis, MD: Naval Institute Press, 1998.
Cressman, Robert J., *USS Ranger The Navy's First Flattop From Keel to Mast,* Annapolis, MD: Naval Institute Press, 2003.
Cutler, Thomas J., *The Battle of Leyte Gulf 23-26 October 1944,* New York: HarperCollins, 1994 and Annapolis, MD: Naval Institute Press, 2001.
Dyer, Vice Admiral George Carroll USN (Ret), *The Amphibians Came to Conquer The Story of Admiral Richmond Kelly Turner,* Washington, DC: Department of the Navy, 1972, and U.S. Marine Corps, 1991.
Evans, David C. ed., *The Japanese Navy in World War II In the Words of Former Japanese Naval Officers,* Annapolis, MD: Naval Institute Press, 1986.
Ewing Steve, *Thach Weave The Life of Jimmie Thach,* Annapolis, MD: Naval Institute Press, 2004.
Forrestal, Vice Admiral E. P., USN (Retired), *Admiral Raymond A. Spruance, USN,* Washington, DC: Department of the Navy, 1966.

Frank, Richard B., *Guadalcanal The Definitive Account of the Landmark Battle,* New York: Penguin Books, 1990.

Furer, Rear Admiral Julius Augustus, USN (Retired), *Administration of the Navy Department in World War II*, Washington, DC: U.S. Government Printing Office, 1959.

Griffith II, Samuel B., *The Battle for Guadalcanal*, New York: J. B. Lippincott Co., 1963 and Annapolis, MD: Nautical and Aviation Publishing Company of America, 1979.

Grossnick, Roy A . *United States Naval Aviation 1910–1995*, Washington, DC: Naval Historical Center, Department of the Navy, U.S. Government Printing Office, 1997.

Gunston, Bill, *Night Fighters A Development & Combat History,* New York: Charles Scribner's Sons. 1976.

Halsey, Fleet Admiral William F., Jr., and Lieutenant Commander J. Bryan III, *Admiral Halsey's Story*, New York: McGraw-Hill Book Company, Inc., 1947.

Hammel, Eric, *Carrier Clash The Invasion of Guadalcanal & The Battle of the Eastern Solomons August 1942,* St. Paul, MN: Zenith Press, 2004.

Hammel, Eric, *Guadalcanal Starvation Island*, New York: Crown Publishers, Inc., 1987.

Hastings, Robert P., *Privateer in the Coconut Navy,* VPB-106 cruise book, 1946.

Hoyt, Edwin P., *How They Won The War In The Pacific, Nimitz and His Admirals*, New York: Weybright and Talley, 1970, and New York: Lyons Press 2000.

Hoyt, Edwin P., *Battle of Leyte Gulf The Death Knell of the Japanese Fleet,* New York: Weybright and Talley, 1972.

Hoyt, Edwin P., *The Lonely Ships, The Life and Death of the U.S. Asiatic Fleet*, New York: David McKay Company, 1976.

Hoyt, Edwin P., *Guadalcanal*, New York: Stein and Day, 1982.

Hoyt, Edwin P., *Closing The Circle War In The Pacific: 1945*, New York: Van Nostrand Reinhold Company, 1982.

Hoyt, Edwin P., *McCampbells' Heroes The Story of the U.S. Navy's Most Celebrated Carrier Fighters of the Pacific War*, New York: Van Nostrand Reinhold Company, 1983.

Hoyt, Edwin P., *Carrier Wars Naval Aviation from World War II to the Persian Gulf,* New York: McGraw Hill 1989 and Paragon House, 1992.

Humble, Richard, *United States Fleet Carriers of World War II "In Action,"* Poole-Dorset, UK: Blandford Press, 1984.

James, D. Clayton with Anne Sharp Wells, *A Time For Giants Politics of the American High Command in World War II,* New York: Franklin Watts, 1987.

Karig, Captain Walter, USNR, Lieutenant Commander Russell L. Harris, USNR, and, Lieutenant Frank A. Manson, USN, *Battle Report The End of an Empire,* New York: Reinhart and Company, 1948.

Kemp, Paul, *A Pictorial History of The Sea War,* Annapolis, MD: Naval Institute Press, 1995.

Lawson, Robert & Barrett Tillman, *Carrier Air War In Original WWII Color,* Osceola, WS: Barnes & Noble Books, 1996, and New York: Barnes & Noble Books, 1999.

Loxton, Bruce with Chris Coulthard-Clark, *The Shame of Savo,* Annapolis, MD: Naval Institute Press, 1994.

Lundstrom, John B., *The First Team and the Guadalcanal Campaign: Naval Fighter Combat from August to November 1942,* Annapolis, MD: Naval Institute Press, 1994.

McCain, John with, Mark Salter, *Faith of My Fathers,* New York: Random House, 1999.

Merrill, James, *A Sailor's Admiral A Biography of William F. Halsey,* New York: Thomas Y. Crowell Company, 1976.

Miller, John W. Jr., *United States Army in World War II The War in the Pacific Guadalcanal: The First Offensive,* Washington, DC: Center of Military History, United States Army, 1949.

Miller, Nathan, *War At Sea A Naval History of World War II,* New York: Scribner, 1995.

Miller, Commander Norman M., USN, *I Took the Sky Road,* New York: Dodd, Mead & Co., 1945.

Miller, Jr., Thomas G., *The Cactus Air Force,* New York: Harper & Row, 1969.

Morison, Samuel Eliot, *History of United States Naval Operations in World War II,* Volumes V, XIII and XIV, Boston: Little, Brown and Company, 1959 and 1960.

Morrison, Wilbur H., *Wings Over The Seven Seas,* South Brunswick, NJ: A. S. Barnes and Co., 1975.

Morrison, Wilbur H., *Above* and *Beyond 1941-1945,* New York: St. Martin's Press, 1983, and Bantam Books, 1986.

Navy Department, Office of the Chief of Naval Operations, Naval

History Division, *Dictionary of American Naval Fighting Ships*, Volumes II, V, VI, and VIII, Washington, DC: U.S. Government Printing Office, 1963–1981.

Newcomb, Richard F., *Abandon Ship Saga of the USS Indianapolis the Navy's Greatest Sea Disaster,* New York: HarperCollins, 1958, and HarperTorch, 2001.

Potter, E. B., *Nimitz*, Annapolis, MD: Naval Institute Press, 1976.

Potter, E. B., *Bull Halsey*, Annapolis, MD: Naval Institute Press, 1985.

Potter, E. B., *Admiral Arleigh Burke*, New York: Random House, 1990.

Prange, Gordon W., *At Dawn We Slept,* New York: Penguin Books, 1981.

Reckner, James R., *Teddy Roosevelt's Great White Fleet,* Annapolis, MD: Naval Institute Press, 1988.

Reynolds, Clark G., *The Fast Carriers The Forging of an Air Navy*, New York: McGraw-Hill Book Company, 1968 and Annapolis, MD: Naval Institute Press, 1992.

Reynolds, Clark G., *Admiral John H. Towers The Struggle for Naval Air Supremacy,* Annapolis, MD: Naval Institute Press, 1991.

Spencer, Elizabeth, *Landscapes of the Heart, A Memoir*, New York: Random House, 1998.

Spector, Ronald H., *Eagle Against The Sun*, New York: The Free Press, 1985.

Stillwell, Paul, *Battleship* Missouri *An Illustrated History,* Annapolis, MD: Naval Institute Press, 1996.

Sudsbury, Elretta, *Jackrabbits to Jets: the History of North Island*, San Diego, CA: Neyenesh Printers, Inc., 1967.

Sweetman Jack, *The U.S. Naval Academy An Illustrated History,* Annapolis, MD: Naval Institute Press, 1979, rev. 1995.

Taylor, Theodore, *The Magnificent Mitscher*, Annapolis, MD: New York: W. W. Norton Co., 1954, and Annapolis, MD: Naval Institute Press, 1991.

Tillman, Barrett, *Hellcat: The F6F in World War II,* Annapolis, MD: Naval Institute Press, 1979.

Turnbull, Archibald D. & Clifford L. Lord, *History of United States Naval Aviation,* New Haven, CT: Yale University Press, 1949.

Twining, General Merrill B. USMC (Ret.), *No Bended Knee*, Novato, CA: Presidio Press, 1996.

United States Naval Institute, *The Class of 1906 United States Naval Academy*, Annapolis, MD: 1954.

Vandegrift, General A. A., *Once a Marine*, New York: Ballantine, 1964.

Warner, Denis and Peggy, *Disaster in the Pacific New Light on the Battle of Savo Island,* Annapolis, MD: Naval Institute Press, 1992.

Wheeler, Gerald E., *Kinkaid of the Seventh Fleet A Biography of Admiral Thomas C. Kinkaid, U.S. Navy,* Washington, DC: Naval Historical Center, Department of the Navy, 1995.

Woolridge, E. T, ed. *Carrier Warfare in the Pacific, An Oral History Collection,* Washington, DC: Smithsonian Institution Press, 1993.

Other

Congressional Record–House, September 10, 1945

Oral History

Thach, John S., *The Reminiscences of Admiral John S. Thach, USN (Retired),* Volumes 1 and 2, Annapolis, MD, Naval Institute Press, 1977.

Books (Not Cited)

Baer, George w., *One Hundred Years of Sea Power The U.S. Navy, 1890-1990,* Stanford, CA: Stanford University Press, 1994.

Bruce, LCDR Roy W., USNR (Ret.), & LCDR Charles R. Leonard, USN (Ret.), *Crommelin's Thunderbirds Air Group 12 Strikes at the Heart of Japan,* Annapolis, MD: Naval Institute Press, 1994.

Doolittle, General James H. "Jimmy," with Carroll V. Grimes, *I Could Never Be So Lucky Again,* New York: Bantam Books, 1991.

Ewing, Steve, *Reaper Leader The Life of Jimmy Flatley,* Annapolis, MD: Naval Institute Press, 2002.

Forrestel, Vice Admiral E. P., USN (Retired), *Admiral Raymond A. Spruance, USN A Study in Command,* Washington, DC: Department of the Navy, 1966.

Ienaga, Saburo, *The Pacific World War II and the Japanese 1931-1945,* New York: Pantheon Books, 1978.

Leckie, Robert, *Challenge in the Pacific, Guadalcanal, the turning point of the war,* Garden City, NY: Doubleday, 1965.

Love, Richard W., Jr., *History of the U.S. Navy 1775-1941,* Harrisburg PA: Stackpole Books, 1992.

Lundstrom, John B., *The First South Pacific Campaign: December 1941-June 1942,* Annapolis, MD: Naval Institute Press, 1976.

Lundstrom, John B., *The First Team: Naval Fighter Combat from Pearl harbor to Midway,* Annapolis, MD: Naval Institute Press, 1990.

Merillot, Herbert Christian, *Guadalcanal Remembered*, New York: Dodd, Mead & Co., 1982.

Mingos, Howard, ed., *The Aircraft Year Book For 1944*, New York: Lancair Publishers.

Potter, E. B., *Sea Power A Naval History* (Second Ed.), Annapolis, MD: Naval Institute Press, 1981.

Reynolds, Clark G., *Famous American Admirals*, New York: Van Nostrand Reinhold Company, 1978.

Smith, Jim B. & McConnell, Malcolm, *The Last Mission The Secret Story of World War II's Final Battle*, New York: Broadway Books, 2002.

Spector, Roland H., *At War At Sea Sailors and Naval Combat in the Twentieth Century*, New York: Viking, 2001.

Sweetman, Jack, *American Naval History* (Second Ed.), Annapolis, MD: Naval Institute Press, 1984, 1991.

Thruelsen, Richard, *The Grumman Story*, New York: Praeger Publishers, 1976.

Werrell, Kenneth P., *Blankets of Fire: U.S. Bombers Over Japan During World War II*, Washington, DC: Smithsonian Institution Press, 1996.

INDEX